Framing narratives of the Second World War
and Occupation in France, 1939–2009

Manchester University Press

Durham Modern Languages Series
Series editor: Michael Thompson

Framing narratives
of the Second World War and
Occupation in France, 1939–2009

New readings

Edited by Margaret Atack and
Christopher Lloyd

Manchester University Press
Manchester and New York
distributed in the United States exclusively by Palgrave Macmillan

Published by Manchester University Press
Oxford Road, Manchester M13 9NR, UK
and Room 400, 175 Fifth Avenue, New York, NY 10010, USA
www.manchesteruniversitypress.co.uk

Distributed in the United States exclusively by
Palgrave Macmillan, 175 Fifth Avenue, New York,
NY 10010, USA

Distributed in Canada exclusively by
UBC Press, University of British Columbia, 2029 West Mall,
Vancouver, BC, Canada V6T 1Z2

British Library Cataloguing-in-Publication Data
A catalogue record for this book is available from the British Library

Library of Congress Cataloging-in-Publication Data applied for

ISBN 978 0 7190 8755 4 hardback

First published 2012

The publisher has no responsibility for the persistence or accuracy of URLs for any external or third-party internet websites referred to in this book, and does not guarantee that any content on such websites is, or will remain, accurate or appropriate.

Typeset in 10/12pt Minion Pro
by Graphicraft Limited, Hong Kong
Printed in Great Britain
by MPG Books Group, UK

List of contents

Notes on contributors

Margaret Atack is Professor of French at the University of Leeds, author of *Literature and the French Resistance: Cultural Politics and Narrative Forms 1940–1950* (1989) and *May 68 in French Fiction and Film* (1999), co-editor of *Contemporary French Fiction by Women: Feminist Perspectives* (1990), and editor of *War and Occupation 1940–1944: Other Stories/Stories of Otherness* (*French Cultural Studies* 2011). She was Principal Investigator on the AHRC-funded project: *Narratives of the Second World War and Occupation in France 1939 to the Present*.

Nathalie Aubert is Professor of French at Oxford Brookes University. She has published two monographs on Proust (2001 and 2003) and is currently editing a volume on *Proust and the Visual* (forthcoming). She co-edited *La Belgique entre deux siècles laboratoire de la modernité* (2007) and *From Art Nouveau to Surrealism: Belgian Modernity in the Making* (2007). Her latest monograph is dedicated to the Belgian poet and painter Christian Dotremont: *Christian Dotremont la conquête du monde par l'image* (2011).

Penny Brown is an Honorary Senior Lecturer in Comparative Literature, recently retired from the Department of French Studies, University of Manchester. She has published on French and English women writers and, more recently, children's literature. Her two-volume *Critical History of French Children's Literature* was published in 2007.

Katherine Cardin is a graduate of the PhD programme in the Department of Romance Languages at the University of Pennsylvania. She is currently preparing a book about literature by descendants of French Second World War collaborators.

William Cloonan is the Richard Chapple Professor of Modern Languages at Florida State University. His interests include modern and contemporary literature, and the visual arts. He writes an annual essay on the contemporary novel for *The French Review*, and is currently working on a monograph entitled *Americans in Paris, Paris in Americans: Franco-American Culture Wars*.

Béatrice Damamme-Gilbert is Senior Lecturer in the Department of French Studies, University of Birmingham. She has published widely on literary stylistics and twentieth-century literature, particularly Julien Gracq, Patrick Modiano and J.M.G. Le Clézio, and is currently working on the interface between individual and collective memory of the two world wars and the literary forms of representation associated with it.

Hilary Footitt is Professor and Senior Research Fellow in the Department of Languages and European Studies, University of Reading. She has written widely on the liberation of France (*War and Liberation in France: Living with the Liberators*, 2004), is currently Principal Investigator for the AHRC project, *Languages at War: Policies and Practices of Language Contacts in Conflict*, and is a participant in the Reading Leverhulme project 'The Liberal Way of War'.

Richard J. Golsan is Distinguished Professor of French and Head of the Department of European and Classical Languages at Texas A&M University, author of *French Writers and the Politics of Complicity* (2006), and *Vichy's Afterlife: History and Counterhistory in Postwar France* (2000), and editor of *Fascism's Return: Scandal, Revision and Ideology since 1980 (1998) and Gender and Fascism in Modern France* (1997).

Leah D. Hewitt is Professor of French at Amherst College. She is the author of *Autobiographical Tightropes* (1990); her newest book, *Remembering the Occupation in French Film: National Identity in Postwar Europe*, was published in 2008 by Palgrave Macmillan. Her current research explores representations of Jewish identity in French films on the Occupation.

Debra Kelly is Professor of French and Francophone Studies, University of Westminster; Director of the Group for War and Culture Studies; editor of *Journal of War and Culture Studies*; and editor/co-editor of *France at War in the Twentieth Century: Propaganda, Myth and Metaphor* and *Remembering and Representing the Experience of War in Twentieth Century France*. She is currently coordinating a project on the London French from the Huguenots to the present.

Angela Kershaw is Senior Lecturer in French Studies at the University of Birmingham. Her research focuses on French literature and culture of the inter-war and Second World War periods. She is the author of

Forgotten Engagements: Women, Literature and the Left in 1930s France (2007) and *Before Auschwitz: Irène Némirovsky and the Cultural Landscape of Inter-war France* (2010).

Christopher Lloyd is Professor of French at the University of Durham, author of *Henri-Georges Clouzot* (2007), of *Collaboration and Resistance in Occupied France: Representing Treason and Sacrifice* (2003), and *Marcel Aymé: Uranus and La tête des autres* (1994). He was Co-Investigator on the major AHRC-funded project: *Narratives of the Second World War and Occupation in France 1939 to the Present.*

Alan Morris is Senior Lecturer in French at the University of Strathclyde. He has published widely on the Occupation, the *œuvre* of Patrick Modiano and the French *polar*. He is the author of *Collaboration and Resistance Reviewed* (1992) and two separate monographs entitled *Patrick Modiano* (1996; 2000). He also co-edited *Words and Things: Essays in Memory of Keith Foley* (2009).

Colin Nettelbeck is Emeritus Professor at the University of Melbourne, where he was A.R. Chisholm Professor of French and Head of the School of Languages. He has published widely on modern and contemporary French cultural history. His most recent book is *Dancing with de Beauvoir: Jazz and the French* (2004).

Thomas Newman is currently Teaching Fellow at the University of Rouen in translation studies and British cultural history. He obtained his doctorate, examining the literary and philosophical neighbourhood of Jean Genet and Emmanuel Levinas, at UCL, and has authored articles on Genet's later political writings viewed in relation to Dostoevsky and Paul Valéry.

Angela O'Flaherty is a Teaching Assistant in French Studies at Nottingham University. Having completed a thesis on 'Feminine Practices of Writing War in Works by Charlotte Delbo, Marguerite Duras and Anna Langfus' in 2010, she is currently continuing her research into Langfus's work, and in particular her theatrical writing.

Luc Rasson is Professor of French Literature at the University of Antwerp. He has published on war testimonies and novels, as well as on the relationship between literature and totalitarianism. His latest book is *L'Écrivain et le dictateur* (2008). His current research focuses on *Les Bienveillantes* and, more generally, on the question of the Nazi narrator in fiction.

Danièle Sabbah is Maître de conférences de langue et littérature françaises at the Université Michel de Montaigne Bordeaux III. Her research focuses on the writing of trauma (the war and the Shoah), poetics of exile, memory and witnessing (Edmond Jabès, *Le Livre des Questions*). She has co-edited *L'Origine des textes* (2003) and *Mémoire et exil* (2007), and edited *Ecritures de l'exil* (2009), and *L'Exil et la différence* (2011).

Virginie Sansico is a Post-doctoral Researcher at the CNRS-CRHQ (Centre for Historical Quantitative Research), and author of *La Justice du pire: les cours martiales sous Vichy* (2003).

Gisèle Sapiro is Research Director at the CNRS and Director of Studies at the Ecole des hautes études en sciences sociales. She is also head of the Centre européen de sociologie et de science politique, Paris. She is the author of *La Guerre des écrivains, 1940–1953* (1999; forthcoming in English translation), *La Responsabilité de l'Écrivain: Littérature, droit et morale en France (19e–20e siècles)* (2011) and of numerous articles.

Peter Tame is Reader in French Studies at Queen's University Belfast. His publications include *La Mystique du fascisme dans l'œuvre de Robert Brasillach* (1986); *The Ideological Hero in the Novels of Robert Brasillach, Roger Vailland, and André Malraux* (1998); an edited translation of Robert Brasillach's *Notre avant-guerre – Before the War* (2003); and *André Chamson: a Critical Biography* (2006).

David Uhrig is currently Teaching Fellow in French at the University of Leicester. His recent articles include: 'Huxley et Woolf lus par Blanchot en 1937', in *The War in the Inter-War*, Synergies Royaume-Uni, December 2010; and 'La philosophie de l'action: compagne clandestine?', in *Blanchot et la philosophie*, 2010.

Acknowledgements

We acknowledge with gratitude the support of the Arts and Humanities Research Council in its funding for the activities of the FRAME research group, including the conference which was the basis for the papers published here. We would particularly like to thank Veena Prajapati and Dr Nina Sutherland for their outstanding organizational work for the conference.

We would like to thank David Macey for the translations of the essays by Nathalie Aubert, Béatrice Damamme-Gilbert, Luc Rasson, Danièle Sabbah, Virginie Sansico and Gisèle Sapiro; Mike Thompson, editor of the Durham Modern Languages Series, for all his advice and support; and the universities of Durham and Leeds for financial support.

Introduction

Margaret Atack and Christopher Lloyd

It is hardly possible to overestimate the importance of the Second World War and Occupation in French cultural history. In each decade since the 1940s, hundreds of novels, films, essays and memoirs have appeared, weaving the history, memory and representation of the period into the narrative of national identity. During the Occupation and its aftermath, cultural production continued apace and was both weapon and battleground. In the post-war years, it is difficult to think of a major writer who has not addressed the issues of war and Occupation in some way; the evolution of the figure of the public intellectual is indissociable from the understanding of commitment generated in the war years, the philosophy of existentialism, broadly understood, articulated the mood of the times in its analysis of experience, choice and responsibility, and there was widespread reflection on humanism, rendered singularly acute by the experiences of Hiroshima and the Holocaust. Intensive scrutiny of behaviour and ethics, particularly in relation to collaboration and French complicity in the deportation of Jews, and the challenges thus constituted to Resistance narratives, has been the distinguishing feature of more recent decades, but it must be said that all aspects of the Occupation have been exhaustively investigated and reinvestigated over these years as the period continues to generate much public interest and enjoy a high media profile. The *rentrée littéraire* of September 2010 was no exception: the presence of the 'récit de guerre' in the large volume of novels published was important enough to be singled out yet again,[1] with significant numbers devoted to the war in Germany and Eastern Europe revealing the continuing influence of the spectacular success of *Les Bienveillantes* in 2006.[2]

---

[1] See *Le Monde des livres* of 17 September 2010.
[2] And discussed here in the chapters by Cloonan, Golsan, Rasson and Tame.

Many reasons have been put forward to explain what has appeared to be an increasingly obsessional focus on the war years. First, that it is motivated by the post-war attempt to eliminate any narratives that did not conform to a master narrative of national unity embodied in the national Resistance, and which collapsed in spectacular fashion in the late 1960s and early 1970s. This argument is indebted to Henry Rousso's *Le Syndrome de Vichy*, which we discuss below. Secondly, that it is motivated by trauma: the continuing outpouring of writings and films is seen as being in direct proportion with, indeed a direct proof of, the traumatic nature of these years with a compulsion to repeat and return to painful emotions long repressed. The violence of the divisions within France, the bloody war waged by the Milice and by the Resistance, the bitter denunciations and betrayals, the bitterness of the division between collaboration and resistance with so many executions, tortures and deportations, the harrowingly shameful deportations of 76,000 Jews, form a strong basis for arguing that attempts to reconstruct a unified country in the post-war period were always doomed to failure and emotional backlash, and that the truth of the wartime years resides in these dark and bloody narratives of suffering.

The role of subsequent conflicts has been underlined: the Occupation provided a language, a framework, a set of references within which other wars, notably the colonial wars, and particularly Algeria, could be discussed. Collaboration, Occupation, resistance, defence of France, defence of humanist values in the name of national identity and integrity – all these were kept alive in the cold war in communist writing,[3] and in the Algerian war where there were Resisters on either side of the barricades. Conversely, avoidance of other more painful histories has been a factor too. Returning to the conflicts and traumas of the Occupation years from the 1970s onwards provided a means of not talking about the more recent traumas and conflicts of the Algerian war, which involved over a million Frenchmen being sent to fight and which disappeared from view with the signing of the Evian agreements in 1962, only formally recognized as a war by the French state in 1999. Finally, the avoidance of current political and military engagements has been identified, suggesting that the constant stream of popular, historical and imaginative works on the war, offering a perpetual rediscovery of material that has in fact in most cases already been extensively aired, directs attention away from

---

[3] See for example Hilary Footitt, 'Women and the (Cold) War: the Cold War Creation of the Myth of "La Française résistante"', *French Cultural Studies*, 8 (1997), 41–51.

France's engagements in the present. This was the burden of Conan and Rousso's well-known intervention: *Vichy, un passé qui ne passe pas*, where France's role in Bosnia was singled out as a case in point.[4]

Across the twenty essays collected here, these important interdisciplinary perspectives on literary and cultural historical studies, memory and trauma studies, and historiography are very apparent. This volume has developed out of the international conference *Framing Narratives of the Second World War and the Occupation* held at the University of Leeds in 2009, which brought together over seventy participants, including many leading specialists in the field. The dual perspective of a 'narrative frame' and 'narrative as frame' places to the fore the complex mediations of the cultural realm and the imaginary in the experiences of the 1940–44 years, not as a reflective and hierarchical relationship – culture reflecting on experience, for example – but a multiple, multi-faceted set of interacting relationships that are profoundly historical and historicized. The conference was itself generated by the FRAME project, a four-year investigation into fictional narratives of and about the war and Occupation in France which has identified large numbers of novels that have disappeared from literary historical knowledge, and which significantly alter conventional views of the trajectory and evolution of representations of the Occupation in subsequent decades.[5] The contributions selected for this volume[6] include analysis of recent and historical narratives, of fiction, historiography, film, biography and poetic narratives iterating the panoramic nature of the original conference and testifying to the richness in depth and breadth of the material under discussion.

Framing critical narratives

An occupied country will have a much more complicated story to tell in terms of the history of the nation than one that is unequivocally at war with another external power, for history has shown the role that wars play in generating powerful overarching narratives for the nation, even if these are often flattening the much more complex and potentially

---

[4] Paris: Fayard, 1994.

[5] See the database at www.frame.leeds.ac.uk.

[6] Others have appeared in a special issue of *French Cultural Studies* in August 2011; the empirical and theoretical findings of the project of which the conference formed a part will be published in M. Atack and C. Lloyd, *Narratives of the Second World War in France: Remapping the Landscape*, in preparation for Liverpool University Press.

divisive stories that could also be told. The point is that the extraordinarily complex experience of war and Occupation was not only mediated at the time by competing narratives about the ways these experiences should be understood and interpreted, but has since been the subject, as has often been noted, of a continuing battleground between conflicting meanings and often incompatible versions presented as the truth.

Henry Rousso's analysis of *Le Syndrome de Vichy* has been the single most influential overview of public discourse about Vichy and the Occupation. Published in 1987, well into a period of intense reinvestigation of the Occupation, Rousso presents France's post-war effort to come to terms with a bitterly humiliating and divisive past as a national psychodrama, as an ongoing conflict between different interest groups attempting to impose their separate and selective memories by dominating the various media, spaces and processes of memorialization (such as school textbooks, films, commemorative ceremonies, museums, show trials). Rousso's phases of the Vichy syndrome (mourning, repression, return of the repressed, obsession) are mapped on to changing political regimes and generational attitudes. Thus the repressive phase overlaps with de Gaulle's return to power from 1958 to 1968 and the return of the repressed with the more critical stance adopted by post-Gaullist generations after 1968.

Writing in 1995, Rousso asserted that 'l'obsession culmine dans l'opinion sous la forme d'une dénonciation inlassable et réitérée de la génération de la guerre',[7] although he argued that historians should reconstruct events from the recent past in their complexity without anachronistic judgements or militant posturing. What Rousso calls 'opinion' might more accurately be described as opinion formers, in effect what he calls the 'gardiens d'une mémoire officielle',[8] namely government and state agencies and most of the printed and broadcast media.

In a recent article, the historian Philippe Buton[9] reduces and readjusts Rousso's phases, discerning three main shifts in post-war attitudes. While the period from the Liberation to May 1968 'offers a reassuring, but rose-tinted, memory of the Second World War', the post-Gaullist and

[7] Henry Rousso, 'Le Syndrome de l'historien', *French Historical Studies*, 19:2 (1995), 495–518, 525.

[8] *Le Syndrome de Vichy* (Paris: Seuil, 1990), p. 130.

[9] Philippe Buton, 'Occupation, Liberation, Purges: the Changing Landscape of French Memory', in Andrew Knapp (ed.), *The Uncertain Foundation: France at the Liberation* (Basingstoke/New York: Palgrave Macmillan, 2007), pp. 234–249.

Mitterrand decades were a time of uncertainty and fragmentation; after Mitterrand's departure and death (1995–96), along with the demise of the wartime generation, a more balanced and convergent attitude has emerged. Buton notes how, in the immediate post-war decades, quasi-official memory (enshrined for example in school textbooks or commemorative ceremonies stressing the more heroic aspects of France's wartime experience) excluded certain groups, such as Jews, prisoners of war and labour conscripts. But one could criticize his own periodization for being over-reliant on official discourse and overlooking evidence that subverts it, such as the protracted saga of the investigation, prosecution and eventual conviction for complicity in crimes against humanity of Maurice Papon, which dragged on painfully from 1981 into the early twenty-first century.

Both Buton and Rousso rightly see the 1970s as a crucial period when official memory was challenged and forced to adopt a less Manichean posture by more nuanced and less consoling reconstructions of the Occupation years and their aftermath undertaken by writers, film-makers and historians.[10] But neither Buton's assertion that the immediate post-war decade is a period of reassuring, rose-tinted memories, nor Rousso's that this is a time of reverential 'mourning', actually corresponds to the attitudes and judgements evinced by many post-war novels. While Rousso deliberately leaves the novel out of his discussion, unlike film, to which he does give detailed consideration, the literary historian Michael L. Berkvam has shown that novels taking a critical or cynical stance towards French behaviour and spurious myths of mass resistance during the Occupation were not only published in the late 1940s and early 1950s, but were well received, widely read and sometimes awarded prestigious literary awards (thus the *prix Goncourt* was awarded to Triolet in 1944, Bory in 1945, Curtis in 1947 and Merle in 1949, though none of them adopt a consensual, Gaullist perspective).[11]

Novels and other forms of literary testimony about the war can thus be used as a counter-cultural outlet which contradicts the consensual myths of official discourse, whose omissions and distortions are usually justified by a dubious claim to be defending national unity. When Henry Rousso states that 'les historiens sont des "vecteurs de mémoire" parmi

---

[10] For a cultural overview, see Alan Morris, *Collaboration and Resistance Reviewed: Writing the Mode rétro in Post-Gaullist France* (New York: Berg, 1992).

[11] Michael L. Berkvam, *Writing the Story of France in World War II: Literature and Memory 1942–1958* (New Orleans: University Press of the South, 2000).

d'autres, dépositaires et concepteurs d'une dimension savante de la mémoire collective',[12] one might add that novelists constitute another vector. However, although there are innumerable monographs and articles devoted to individual writers, relatively few commentators have attempted the more ambitious task of reviewing and analysing fictional narratives about the Occupation as a mass phenomenon.[13] In an article on four less well known women novelists (Beck, Arban, Maurel, Pagniez), Denis Boak observes that the recognized canon of French Second World War narratives is small and somewhat arbitrary, perhaps because 'until recently works dealing with the War were not placed on the same aesthetic level as "imaginative" literature, whether written by men or women'.[14] By his choice of authors and insistence on the 'referential imperative' to bear witness, coupled with the blurring of fiction and memoir (Beck and Arban changed their names but recount genuine experiences), Boak is effectively challenging often unstated presuppositions about genre, gender and the intrinsic value of neglected books.

Literary historians who prefer to ignore such outlying material may sometimes assert in justification that only masterpieces are worthy of attention, and there are very few about the Second World War (the literature of which is contrasted unfavourably with classic works written about the First World War). This position is adopted, for example, by Samuel Hynes, who states (provocatively, no doubt): 'The canon of the Second War does not exist'.[15] On the other hand, his argument that the experience of the Second World War was too vast and too diverse to create a 'single tale' (unlike that of the Western Front), or that the Second War was a sort of literary footnote to the horrors of the First, has more merit. Damon Marcel Decoste takes a similar line,[16] arguing that whereas the Great War was memorialized as tragedy (the destruction

---

[12] Henry Rousso, *Vichy: l'événement, la mémoire, l'histoire* (Paris: Gallimard Folio, 2001), p. 12.

[13] For an example of a survey that precedes Rousso, see Colin Nettelbeck, 'Getting the Story Right: Narratives of World War II in Post-1968 France', *Journal of European Studies*, 15 (1985), 77–116.

[14] Denis Boak, 'Four Frenchwomen's Narratives of World War II', *Journal of European Studies*, 25 (1995), 381–397, p. 381.

[15] Samuel Hynes, *The Soldier's Tale: Bearing Witness to Modern War* (London: Allen Lane, The Penguin Press, 1997), p. 173.

[16] Damon Marcel Decoste, 'The Literary Response to the Second World War', in Brian W. Shaffer (ed.), *A Companion to the British and Irish Novel 1945–2000*, Blackwell Reference Online, 2005 (accessed 4 February 2009).

of patriotic and manly ideals as witnessed at the Front), the Second War induces terror and guilt in the face of mass killings and destruction, as the boundaries between combatants and civilians, legitimate retribution and crimes against humanity break down. Can literature deal adequately with the 'death of tragedy'? Paul Fussell (best known for his masterly book *The Great War and Modern Memory*, 1979), when writing of the Second World War from first-hand experience asserts that 'the Allied war has been sanitized and romanticized almost beyond recognition', for in reality it was 'a savage, insensate affair, barely conceivable to the well-conducted imagination (the main reason there's so little good writing about it)'.[17] At its most extreme, such a position would self-denyingly assert the futility of any cultural expression in the face of massively destructive events like war; the very existence of thousands of literary works about warfare seems to refute its validity and to suggest their value and utility as personal or collective testimony may be distinct from their aesthetic or philosophic weaknesses.

A more typical critical posture, when selecting and delineating a corpus from a vast range of material, is to seek the familiar, an understandable tactic, but likely to appear unduly cautious or restricting. Books sometimes betray the promises of their titles; a venial sin perhaps. For example, David Boal's *Journaux intimes sous l'Occupation* actually covers works by nine writers, all of them very well known, all of them male, eight of them French and one of them German (Ernst Jünger, inevitably). Léon Werth is the only representative chosen to offer the viewpoint of a marginalized minority, as a Jewish intellectual trapped in the Jura, although Boal asserts (unfairly) that Werth 'n'a rien à observer' other than 'la situation d'impuissance des petites gens en temps de guerre'.[18] The many diaries written by women about the private sphere, perhaps unsurprisingly, gain no attention. Françoise Calin's promisingly titled *Les Marques de l'Histoire dans le roman français (1939–1944)* proves on closer investigation to comprise five well-honed essays on single works by Beauvoir, Gracq, Simon, Vercors and Camus. She argues initially that 'Les récits de fiction sont des archives où nous pouvons puiser à notre gré', citing Claude Prévost's claim that the novel 'met au jour le non-dit de l'Histoire', but is ultimately more interested in the aesthetic

---

[17] Paul Fussell, *Wartime: Understanding and Behavior in the Second World War* (New York: Oxford University Press, 1989), pp. ix, 132.
[18] David Boal, *Journaux intimes sous l'Occupation* (Paris: Armand Colin, 1993), pp. 162–163.

transformation of experience: the markers of highbrow literature rather than of history, one might say. Hence her conclusion that in the works examined, 'Les techniques narratives utilisées rompent avec les codes traditionnels de maintes façons'.[19] What distinguishes these works is thus their singularity, rather than their 'archival' potential or typicality.

Some commentators have cast their net far more widely, it is true. The most ambitious is probably Gisèle Sapiro, whose 800-page *La Guerre des écrivains 1940–1953* encompasses 185 French writers who were active in 1940. But her interest is essentially the socio-political positioning and function of the writer and intellectual within key institutions (such as academies, the press, resistance bodies) during the war and its aftermath; the study of literary texts or other types of narrative as aesthetic representations of history and experience plays little part in this investigation.[20] In fact, it is quite frequently researchers based outside France who have attempted to offer a broader perspective on the literary output inspired by the war and Occupation.[21] As the historian Norman Davies observes, scholarly history-writing can account for only part of the record, is inconclusive and slow by nature, and does not command mass audiences, whereas fictional narratives may not only offer 'a valid point of entry into a knowledge of events that really happened' but also can convey otherwise inaccessible realms of human experience.[22]

Critics who have published panoramic studies of Occupation narratives since the beginning of the twenty-first century tend to stress either their testimonial function or how they problematize memory.[23] Other recent commentators have further validated the study of fiction as a means of

[19] Françoise Calin, *Les Marques de l'histoire dans le roman français (1939–1944)* (Paris: Lettres modernes Minard, 2004), pp. 5–6, 7, 166.

[20] Gisèle Sapiro, *La Guerre des écrivains 1940–1953* (Paris: Fayard, 1999). Her contribution to this volume is however focused on the active role of literature as producer of knowledge. For a more concise overview of literary production during the Occupation, see Francine de Martinoir, *La Littérature occupée: les années de guerre 1939–1945* (Paris: Hatier, 1995).

[21] Cf. Margaret Atack, *Literature and the French Resistance: Cultural Politics and Narrative Forms, 1940–1950* (Manchester: Manchester University Press, 1989).

[22] Norman Davies, *Europe at War 1939–1945: No Simple Victory* (London: Macmillan, 2006), p. 430. Richard Vinen's *The Unfree French: Life under the Occupation* (London: Allen Lane, 2006) likewise cites novels and autobiographies as informative sources.

[23] For example, Margaret-Anne Hutton, *Testimony from the Nazi Camps: French Women's Voices* (London: Routledge, 2005); Richard J. Golsan, *Vichy's Afterlife: History and Counter-history in Postwar France* (Lincoln/London: University of Nebraska Press, 2000); Susan Rubin Suleiman, *Crises of Memory and the Second World War* (Cambridge/London: Harvard University Press, 2006); Philippe Carrard, *The French Who Fought for Hitler: Memories from the Outcasts* (New York: Cambridge University Press, 2010).

understanding the past, and interrogated the taxonomy of available texts. William Cloonan contends that since 'all sources of information remain deeply suspect, the novel continues to function as a valued repository of insight and intelligence', focusing on a small group of 'serious' but accessible novels.[24] Catharine Savage Brosman[25] identifies seven types of Second World War fiction in French, related to: defeat and occupation; resistance; aerial warfare; prisoners of war; combat; collaboration; and liberation and its aftermath. Yan Hamel adopts a different taxonomic approach, judiciously combining sensitive analysis of sixteen key novels with reference to a broader corpus of about 100 texts and acknowledging the existence of a still vaster corpus of popular fiction aimed at a wide public (citing the examples of Régine Deforges and Max Gallo).[26] In *Une Occupation très romanesque*, Michel Jacquet invests French novels written about the Occupation between 1945 and 1969 with a purpose that is both demystifying and cathartic. Whereas most post-war film-makers validate the bland, patriotic consensus of universal resistance and national unity, novelists establish:

> Un îlot de liberté insolemment exempt des contraintes morales et politiques accablant une société refermée sur ses blessures intimes et sur d'inavouables secrets.
> ... si la perception du passé restituée par l'Histoire se fonde sur un savoir critique et objectif, celle du roman tend à esthétiser un vécu purement émotionnel, la mémoire individuelle bouleversant le plus souvent les hiérarchies et les restrictions mentales que la mémoire collective impose.[27]

Conventional genre boundaries (between fiction, autobiography and history) are increasingly seen as permeable, as are those between elite and more popular forms (with increasing attention being paid to films, thrillers and BDs as well as more literary texts).[28] This continuing

[24] William Cloonan, *The Writing of War: French and German Fiction and World War Two* (Gainesville: University Press of Florida, 1999), p. 161.
[25] Catharine Savage Brosman, *Visions of War in French Fiction, Art, Ideology* (Baton Rouge: Louisiana State University Press, 1999).
[26] Yan Hamel, *La Bataille des mémoires: La Seconde Guerre mondiale et le roman français* (Montréal: Presses de l'Université de Montréal, 2006).
[27] Michel Jacquet, *Une Occupation très romanesque: ironie et dérision dans le roman français de 1945 à nos jours* (Paris: Les Éditions La Bruyère, 2000), pp. 7, 16.
[28] See, for example, Leah D. Hewitt, *Remembering the Occupation in French Film* (New York: Palgrave Macmillan, 2008); Michel Jacquet, *Travelling sur les années noires: l'Occupation vue par le cinéma français depuis 1945* (Paris: Alvik Éditions, 2004); Christopher Lloyd, *Collaboration and Resistance in Occupied France: Representing Treason and Sacrifice* (Basingstoke: Palgrave Macmillan, 2005).

fascination with the French cultural legacy of the Second World War, both inside and outside France, indicates not the narcissistic obsession of a traumatized nation, but rather a legitimate desire for knowledge about a period of history whose impact on present times remains undeniable.[29]

New readings

Starting from the premiss that the work of the imaginary, broadly conceived, plays a structural role in the understanding of the experiences of war and their representations, this volume has been structured around some of the key constituent elements involved in the multi-layered processes of narrative and historiography fundamental to stories of the war and Occupation. Narratives of the war years are a vital part of contemporary French cultural, social and political life, and the essays here are clustered around questions which give us a firm platform from which to elucidate their workings: how, theoretically and methodologically, do we approach the role of narrative and other cultural forms in constructing attitudes and approaches to the war; how do narratives interact with the expectations of their public, how do they shape them and how in their turn are they shaped by them; how is this historical subject matter itself historicized in relation to its moment of enunciation?

By way of detailed introduction to these questions, Roger Boussinot's novel of 1960, *Les Guichets du Louvre*,[30] offers a good point of departure, for the image of 'le miroir brisé', a key metaphor for Henry Rousso and discussed in some detail in Leah Hewitt's chapter below, plays an important role here. A consideration of the importance of this image in the novel will not only serve as an interesting contrast to the widespread use of the broken mirror as symbol of the destruction of a false if comforting reflection to the French nation, but the novel itself is also an excellent example of the narrative and historical complexity of literary and cultural production which is the focus of this volume and encapsulated in the title of 'framing narratives'.

Les Guichets du Louvre is devoted to the mass round-up of Jews in Paris on 16 July 1942 and gives a vivid account of the day, the arrival in the early hours of large numbers of policemen accompanied by militants

---

[29] For a German perspective, see Wolfgang Geiger, *L'Image de la France dans l'Allemagne nazie (1933–45)* (Rennes: Presses Universitaires de Rennes, 1999).

[30] Paris: Denoël, 1960. Subsequent page references here to Folio, 1980 edition. Michel Mitrani directed the film adaptation in 1974.

of the Parti Populaire Français, and the buses lined up to take all those arrested to the Vélodrome d'Hiver from where they would be taken to camps, primarily Drancy, and then transported to Auschwitz. It records a range of reactions from the non-Jewish French inhabitants of the affected areas. However, its subject is not only the account of the herding of Jews into buses by the French police, and the rather pitiful attempts of the 'jeune homme seul', the narrator's younger self, to convince one of them to leave the area with him, but the complexity of individual memory, story-telling and history:

> Pendant vingt ans presque, j'ai porté cette journée du 16 juillet dans la poche arrière de ma besace aux souvenirs, comme nous disait Gaston Bachelard. Elle fut pour moi une sorte de miroir qui se brisa le soir même entre mes doigts, après que j'eus franchi de nouveau les guichets du Louvre et que j'eus regagné la rive gauche. Un à un, avec obstination, j'en avais jeté les débris par-dessus mon épaule, espérant les perdre à jamais. Ce n'est point tant qu'ils se laissaient oublier, que ma volonté de les oublier. (p. 52)

The mirror here is not the 'myth' that Rousso describes as 'résistancial-isme', and that the series of events of 1971–74, the years of the breaking of the mirror, destroyed; here, it is the record of the day that is deliberately smashed and discarded, by a twenty-year-old who needs to put it behind him and behave as if it never happened. The spur to putting the pieces back together again, in an anticipation of the double historical structure typical of many novels of the 1980s, is the sight nearly twenty years later, that is, in the late 1950s, of a young man in the metro daubing 'Mort aux juifs' on a poster (p. 52). This is the broken shard that draws blood and prompts the narrator to reconstitute his memory mirror in order to see, relive and record the events of that day.[31]

The narrator's experiences on 16 July 1942 are profoundly disturbing for him, partly because he fails to save anyone in a series of encounters,

[31] Boussinot is drawing on Bachelard's presentation in *L'Air et les songes* (Paris: José Corti, 1950) of the psychoanalyst Robert Desoille whose work on the 'directed daydream' was influential. Its therapeutic role was to work on what was troubling or difficult for the analysand, to substitute other associations and produce an effective sublimation of the anxiety, working like a broom, in Bachelard's words, to 'déblayer', 'débloquer', 'balayer vos soucis' (pp. 131–133). For a specific anxiety, Desoille's technique is the one mobilized in the novel: 'Au sujet préoccupé par un souci défini, Desoille conseille de le mettre avec tous les autres, dans la besace du chiffonnier, dans la poche *derrière le dos*, d'accord en somme avec le geste, si expressif et si efficace, d'une main qui rejette derrière le dos ce qu'on se décide à mépriser' (p. 133, original emphasis).

and particularly for the role that his own inhibitions, stemming from his emotional and sexual immaturity, played in the most important encounter with Jeanne, like him on the threshold of adulthood and sexual maturity. The technique of the daydream allows the young man to eliminate the emotional impact of this appalling day, erasing the events themselves:

> Comme si j'abandonnais à une vie antérieure désormais mal connue les ombres . . . de tous ces visages, de toutes les expressions que mon regard avait saisies . . . J'avais déjà fait toute la place, dans mon esprit, aux journées insouciantes, ensoleillées qui m'attendaient. Il me sembla que mon coin de verdure et de fraîcheur, au bord de l'eau, en face de l'île, méritait seul d'occuper ma rêverie. (p. 154)

When asked, having walked away from the station, 'qu'est-ce qui se passe à Paris?', he replies with the words that powerfully close the novel: 'Rien . . . , dis-je. Et j'étais sincère' (p. 155).[32] He has brushed away his memories, just as Paris has been cleansed, in the classic military metaphor.[33]

But however haunting its coincidence with the theses of the 'Resistance myth' aimed at smothering uncomfortable memories, this would surely be an anachronistic reading. It could not be clearer that this is the deliberate decision of an individual, at the end of the day itself in 1942, and who, seeing 'mort aux juifs', would not have forgotten the appalling events eighteen years earlier in the same Paris métro. But if, in 1960, there is no thesis of collective amnesia on which the narrative might draw, this is not the case in 1980, the year of the Folio edition, whose synopsis on the back cover starts precisely by interpellating the reader/ purchaser as collective (forgetful) subject: 'Vous souvenez-vous de ce 16 juillet 1942?', the only reply to which has to be 'surely not', as the text then succinctly explains what it was. The historiographical 'knowledge' unavailable to the fictional narrative can be traced in the text inscribed on the book itself, and a fortiori in a more recent edition of 1999, where

---

[32] Cf. Bachelard on the reason why one cannot use this technique deceitfully: 'Il n'en sera pas de même si le sujet imagine sincèrement – ce qui est un pléonasme, car que serait une imagination sans sincérité?' (*L'Air*, p. 134).

[33] And the reference to *nettoyage* of the area (p. 120) is also pointing to the possibility of an 'interstitial' narrative of contemporary *rafles* due to the Algerian war shadowing the historical account. This, and the various models underlying the 'obsession' with the Vichy years described above, tend now to be read in the light of Michael Rothberg's *Multidirectional Memory* (Stanford: Stanford University Press, 2009).

the author's postscript identifies various points of 'censorship' within himself, against his publisher and against possible film producers,[34] all combating the 'silence' about the events, reiterating the theses of collective amnesia and repression: 'La deuxième censure fut celle qui régna au cours des deux décennies après la Libération. On ne devait plus parler de tout cela.'[35] But this is writing out of history the fact that Drancy and deportations of the Jews were indeed present in post-war novels of the Occupation,[36] and prominently so if one considers the public success of André Schwartz-Bart's *Le Dernier des justes* (Prix Goncourt 1960) and Anna Langfus's *Les Bagages de sable* (Prix Goncourt 1962).[37]

Les Guichets du Louvre is also interesting because, in addition to the historiographical paradigms operating in the text and its subsequent editions, it integrates reflection on the writing process and the paradigms of fiction and life-writing it deploys. A quotation from Aragon's *Le Roman inachevé*, a poetic autobiography which, as the title indicates, is a narrative of incompleteness and process, is placed as epigraph to the novel; having reconstituted his mirror, the narrator ponders on the various formal options open to him, such as the 'nouveau roman' approach or a stream of consciousness novel, before, not very surprisingly, deciding on the 'degree zero' of the filmic eye. The metaphors of the mirror and the film used to suggest a faithful, undistorted record of the experience are indeed classic tropes of realist fiction disavowing its own substance, as the process of construction in language is rhetorically set aside as 'literature', but can also be read as the identification of the mask of artifice in a text where the conscious manipulation of representation is

[34] Roger Boussinot, 'Post-scriptum', *Les Guichets du Louvre* (Paris, éditions Gaïa). In fact the film of 1974 was particularly controversial because of depiction of the passivity of the Jews and of the Union Générale des Israélites de France, which Boussinot does not explicitly mention though he obliquely defends his view of UGIF.

[35] 'Post-scriptum', p. 153.

[36] See, for example, Brice Parain, *La Mort de Socrate* (Paris: Gallimard, 1950); Beauvoir, *Les Mandarins* (Paris: Gallimard, 1954), analysed in Susan Suleiman's paper at the Leeds conference and published in 'Memory Troubles: Remembering the Occupation in Simone de Beauvoir's *Les Mandarins*', *French Politics, Culture and Society*, 28:2 (2010), 4–17; Michel Breitman, *Fortunat ou l'enfant adopté* (Paris: Denoël, 1955); and G. Morris, *Du Rébecca rue des Rosiers* (Paris: Laffont, 1957), analysed in Claire Gorrara's paper at the conference, published in 'Forgotten Crimes? Representing Jewish Experience of the Second World War in French Crime Fiction', *South Central Review*, 27:1–2 (2010), 3–20.

[37] Analysed in detail in this volume in Angela O'Flaherty's essay, where she draws attention to the increasing public awareness of the figure of the survivor and the portrayal of denial in the text.

central to the plot. Furthermore, his stated inability to give an account
of what happens to the Jews that he leaves on the buses, 'aux portes de
l'enfer' (p. 53) is countered by a series of disparate but, in the circumstances, extremely charged incidents pointing almost impersonally to the
brutal destruction of individual lives that awaits.

Reading *Les Guichets du Louvre* opens multiple avenues of enquiry
which are of fundamental importance to the critical metanarrative of
this volume. It demonstrates the benefit of retrieving texts outside the
'canon' of post-war Occupation literature. Taking as its subject a day which
has come to be seen as one of the defining events of the Occupation,
and re-creating the range of reactions it provoked in the despair, puzzle-
ment, fear, misplaced trust, of the arrested families and the onlookers,
it invites reflection on the politics and ethics of the behaviour of all
those involved, on the adequacy or otherwise of the classic humanist
frames of reference in accounting for it, on cultural representation, its
modalities and limits, the nature of its relation to society and history,
and on the permeability of genre (autobiography, life-writing, poetry and
fiction). It raises questions about the 'silence' of the first post-war decades
about subjects which have been later constituted as 'taboo' subjects, and
in a way that leads us to be more historically aware of how these questions may or may not be posed. In the layering of memory and history,
and the layering of different histories over time, the complexity of
the narrative process can be seen to be an essential part of the story to
be told.

Framing Narratives discusses a wide range of texts across seven
decades, grouped in three main sections. It includes analysis of canonical
writing and films on Occupation and war (Modiano, Resistance poetry,
Aragon, Genet, Chaix, Tournier, *Le Vieil Homme et l'enfant*, *Les Violons
du bal*), of texts that have recently made a real impact (Berr, Humbert,
Némirovsky, Bauchau, Sansal, Suzin, *Un Héros très discret*), at times
a very controversial one (*Les Bienveillantes*, *Jan Karski*), or that have
been neglected (Rachline, *Mademoiselle Swing*), and from diverse fields:
fiction, poetry, film, historiography, diary, personal testimony, the
popular cultural best-seller and children's literature. The themes that cross
the volume are many and varied: the representation and understanding of heroism; the interactions, convergence and inseparability of the
individual and the collective; the strength and vitality of literature; the
ever complex issues of memory and its relation to history, individual
and collective; the continuing importance of *Le Syndrome de Vichy* and
its historiographical map of the post-war years, together with a range

of indications of other readings emerging; and the power and interest of the novels and films that have appeared in recent decades. Far from some eternal rehashing or obsessional repetition, the work of the critics assembled here shows how contemporary literature re-sets the issues for its contemporary audience, as new novels and films themselves serve as frames for the past, setting new agendas, causing established work to be reconsidered and bringing neglected texts out of the cold. *Les Bienveillantes* is no doubt the most prominent example of this phenomenon, provoking new critical work as we see here,[38] on perpetrators, violence and victims as well as bringing forth imitators.

Framing Narratives also bears witness to the liveliness of current work in the field, the quality of the interrogation of historical and literary critical paradigms, the breadth of methodologies deployed and the extraordinary richness of the material under investigation. The endless fascination of an apparently inexhaustible creative domain, combined with the ethical imperatives of the issues it raises for writers and critics alike, makes for compellingly important work.

---

[38] See also Margaret-Anne Hutton's paper delivered at the conference and published in: 'Jonathan Littell's *Les Bienveillantes*: Ethics, Aesthetics and the Subject of Judgment', *Modern and Contemporary France*, 18:1 (2010), 1–15.

Part 1

Constructing the war in narrative

Introduction

'Constructing the war in narrative' addresses the dynamic role of narrative and other cultural forms in representations of the Second World War. From the critical and aesthetic narratives underpinning Resistance poetry to controversial texts of the twenty-first century such as *Les Bienveillantes* and *Jan Karski*, these chapters raise theoretical and methodological issues of the relationship between literature and experience: how do we conceptualize the role of the literary, what are the consequences of different aesthetics of literature and narrative, how is narrative exploited to enact complex dramas of memory and identity?

To explore the ways literature has framed experiences of defeat and occupation, rendering them 'knowable', Gisèle Sapiro mobilizes Bourdieu's work on schemes of perception structuring a field, and takes as a case study Aragon's poetic work and its relation to the events of the time. She shows how the aesthetic of 'art for art's sake', appropriated by the occupying authorities as a basis for literary collaboration, is reappropriated by Aragon in the name of patriotism and the defence of France. William Cloonan reviews a variety of fictional modes, from the more formal *nouveau roman* to realism, evaluating the relation between narrative aesthetic and representation of experience. Through analysis of Tournier's *Le Roi des aulnes* and Haenel's *Jan Karsky*, he raises major issues about the nature and function of war literature in society, particularly how far and how successfully it avoids the stock clichés of popular representations of the war, and how far serious war literature engages with the stylistic and structural development of post-war fiction.

Colin Nettelbeck demonstrates the importance of the relationship between the critical metanarrative and nature of the primary material under scrutiny. Looking at the issues involved in tackling individual testimony, the recollections of the personal secretary of Philippe Henriot and the popular film of 1942 *Mademoiselle Swing*, he underlines the multiplicity and heterogeneity of much primary narrative material, and its problematic relation to historical 'truth'. In a detailed reading of the

work of the surrealist group of poets in *La Main à plume*, Nathalie
Aubert considers both the strengths and the perceived limitations of
the waging of resistance in committed poetry under the Occupation.
The rejection of the realist narrative in the surrealist vision of the role
of literature produces a poetic stance articulating a collective aesthetic.

Both Thomas Newman and Peter Tame explore the interface of literature and the reality of external events, or historically attested accounts
of the facts of the narrative. Newman provides a reading of Genet's texts
that demonstrates the intricate complexity of his writing, arguing against
reductive readings framed by a realistic aesthetic of referentiality in favour
of the process of stylization, if misleading interpretations of texts which
cannot be taken at face value are to be avoided, and proposing a reading
informed by literary awareness revealing obsessional French responsibility.
Peter Tame's essay on *Les Bienveillantes* studies the role of the literary
structuration of space in the novel, and reveals the importance of the
construction of the manifold public and private spaces – utopian and
dystopian locations, literary spaces of fantasy, erotics and death, inner
and outer worlds – to the thematic architecture of the novel.

Béatrice Damamme-Gilbert's study of Henry Bauchau's great success
of 2008, *Le Boulevard périphérique*, draws out the psychoanalytical and
poetic material generating the text and its reflection on the nature of
heroism. She stresses the importance of historiography and memorialization in this very personal text that deploys the double historical
structure – here the interweaving of the 1940s and the 1980s – typical
of so many literary re-creations that explore the impact of the past upon
the present.

Perhaps it is because the experiences of the Occupation years and
their subsequent retellings in narratives of memory were so very complex
and diverse that the nature of their representation cannot be taken for
granted, and this is underlined by the importance of considering formal
and structural possibilities and constraints of genre and mode in creating experience as recognized and recognizable. In all these essays, then,
considerations of form and structure are shown to involve ethical material,
and the ethical questions raised by representations of war cannot be
separated from the aesthetic issues of representation itself.

Chapter 1

The role of literature in framing perceptions of reality: the example of the Second World War

Gisèle Sapiro

Far from being a passive activity, as the empiricists assume it to be, there is, as the rationalist and especially the neo-Kantian traditions insist, an active dimension to the perception of reality. Durkheim and Mauss were the first to emphasize the socialized nature of 'forms of classification' and the extra-logical origins of logical notions.[1] The idea that modes of categorization are historical and not universal, and that they vary from one society to another, can also be found in Cassirer's notion that an era's 'world-view' (*Weltanschauung*) is underpinned by 'symbolic forms'.[2] Panofsky demonstrates, for example, that the same symbolic forms can, in a given era, underpin activities as different as gothic art and scholasticism.[3] In Pierre Bourdieu's sociological theory, 'schemes' of perception, action and evaluation constitute the 'habitus', or the structured structures that are internalized by individuals in the course of their socialization, and these become structuring structures at both the cognitive and behavioural levels.[4] The idea that cognition is an active process is also present in the interactionist sociology of Goffman who,

[1] Emile Durkheim and Marcel Mauss, 'De Quelques Formes primitives de classification (contribution à l'étude des représentations collectives)', *L'Année sociologique*, no. 6 (1903), in Marcel Mauss, *Œuvres*, Tome 2 (Paris: Minuit, Coll. 'Le Sens commun', 1974), pp. 13–89.

[2] Ernst Cassirer, *The Philosophy of Symbolic Forms, Vol 1. Language* [1923] (New Haven: Yale University Press, 1953).

[3] Erwin Panofsky, *Gothic Architecture and Scholasticism* [1951] (New York: Penguin, 1985).

[4] Pierre Bourdieu, *Le Sens pratique* (Paris: Minuit, Coll. 'Le Sens commun', 1980).

referring to Bateson, speaks of 'frames of experience'.[5] Literature is part
of this cognitive activity, and helps to shape an era's world-view: it produces and reproduces representations of the world, expresses shared
feelings, symbolizes, and so on.

As the division of labour becomes more pronounced, what Durkheim
calls the 'collective consciousness' – which might more pertinently be
called the collective 'unconscious' or, to avoid any confusion with the
psychoanalytic understanding of the notion of the unconscious, the
collective 'pre-conscious' – no longer has the unity that it had in classless
societies. The schemes that frame the perception and interpretation of
the world are one of the things that are at stake in struggles between
different social groups. This is even more so in the times of crisis that
lead to 'frame-breaks'. As Goffman writes, 'When, for whatever reason,
the individual breaks frame and perceives he has done so, the nature
of his engrossment and belief suddenly changes . . . Reality anomically
floats.'[6]

The defeat of 1940 and the German Occupation of France destroyed
the frames of experience on a grand scale, as they forced individuals
to reorganize their day-to-day lives. They also resulted in a loss of points
of reference: 'Je flotte comme un bouchon', Roger Martin du Gard wrote
to Maria van Rysselberghe on 22 July 1940.[7] This loss of points of
reference, which can be traced back to the ideological confusion of the
pre-war period (right-wing neo-pacifism, the split between pacifists and
anti-fascists, the Soviet–German Pact), was exacerbated by the suicide
of the Republic, the coming of the Vichy regime and the *appel du 18
juin*. How the defeat was to be interpreted was one of the issues at stake
in the struggle between the various factions, even though they shared
the same national framework, which structured the world-view of almost
all the parties involved.

Literature played an active part in this ideological warfare. The context
of censorship and repression saw the flourishing of a literature that rejected
the dominant ideology and which had no right to free expression.
As Margaret Atack and James Steel have demonstrated with reference
to fiction, this resistance literature helped to produce and legitimize

---

[5] Erving Goffman, *Frame Analysis. An Essay on the Organization of Experience*
(Harmondsworth: Penguin, 1975).

[6] Goffman, *Frame Analysis*, pp. 378, 379.

[7] Roger Martin du Gard, *Journal, tome III, 1937–1949* (Paris: Gallimard, 1993),
p. 347.

a different perception of the reality of the Occupation.[8] I will be looking here, on a more limited scale, at the case of poetry and, more specifically, at the poetry of Aragon, who played a leading role at this time and who also reflected upon the social role of poetry. The choice of poetry makes it possible to place the emphasis on the formal dimension, which is the dimension most specific to literature. This example allows me to try to raise some more general questions about the role played by literature in framing perceptions of reality.

Between representation and symbolization

If we wish to theorize literature's contribution to the framing of perceptions, we must get away from the simplistic schema that discusses representation in terms of the degree to which the fictional world is true to the real world. It is not that the question is not in itself pertinent, but there is a danger that it might distract us from the essential issue of how literature helps to shape an era's 'world-view', or even its 'knowledge'. In a recent book, the philosopher Jacques Bouveresse suggests that literature should be seen as a mode of 'practical knowledge'.[9] This approach raises the question of the relationship between literature and other forms of knowledge.[10] It is, for instance, almost a cliché to say that naturalism drew heavily upon medicine, not only at the level of representations but also at the level of language and of the causal schemata that organize the narrative. The same could be said of the surrealists and psychoanalysis. But whereas naturalism used medical knowledge without really calling it into question, surrealism turns literature into an original way of exploring the unconscious (and turns the unconscious into a source for literature). The degree to which literary representational schemes are (or are not) independent of existing frames of perception and analysis – be they media-based, political or scientific – might therefore provide a way of classifying works on the basis of their ability to change 'world-views'.

[8] Margaret Atack, *Literature and the French Resistance: Cultural Politics and Narrative Forms 1940–1950* (Manchester: Manchester University Press, 1989); James Steel, *Littératures de l'ombre. Récits et nouvelles de la Résistance 1940–1944* (Paris: PFNSP, 1991).
[9] Jacques Bouveresse, *La Connaissance de l'écrivain. Sur la littérature, la vérité et la vie* (Paris: Agone, 2008), pp. 63–64.
[10] See, for example, the special 'Savoirs de la littérature' issue of *Annales HSS*, no. 2, March–April (2010).

In a period of crisis such as that inaugurated by the defeat of 1940, science, which had gained a near-monopoly on knowledge under the Third Republic, was not able to give an answer to the questions that arose. The press was quickly gagged, controlled and pressed into service by the authorities. It was used to spread a new dominant ideology, and the news, which was strictly 'framed', was subordinated to that ideology. While the press was divided by struggles between different tendencies, opposition to the Vichy regime and its collaborationist policy could not be freely expressed.[11]

The failure of both science and the press to provide an answer opened up a space for other ways of experiencing or understanding the world. The defeat and the Occupation gave birth to competing narratives, some in fictional form and others (Rebatet's pamphlet, *Les Décombres*) in non-fictional form. In a tradition going back to the narratives of the First World War,[12] a large number of war novels were published during the first year of the Occupation: examples include Paul Mousset, *Quand le temps travaillait pour nous*; Jean de Baroncelli, *Vingt-six hommes*; Pierre Béarn, *De Dunkerque à Liverpool*; Georges Blond, *L'Angleterre en guerre*; Yves Dautun, *La Batterie errante*; Roland Tessier, *Le Bar de l'escadrille*; Benoist-Méchin, *La Moisson de quarante*; and Maurice Betz, *Dialogue des prisonniers*.

In addition to these narratives about the experience of war, which relate to an immediate past, history was mobilized primarily as a way of understanding the event of the defeat. Because it could evoke significant experiences, history was spontaneously evoked at the level of both individual and collective memory.[13] That is why the comparisons vary from one generation to another: the generation of men aged over sixty evokes 1870 (a recurrent point of reference for the

---

[11] See particularly Philippe Amaury, *Les Deux Premières Expériences d'un 'ministre de l'information' en France* (Paris: Librairie générale de Droit et de Jurisprudence, 1969); Laurent Gervereau and Denis Peschanski (eds), *La Propagande sous Vichy* (Paris: Bibliothèque de Documentation Internationale Contemporaine, 1990); Rita Thalmann, *La Mise au pas. Idéologie et stratégie sécuritaire dans la France occupée* (Paris: Fayard, coll. 'Pour une histoire du XXe siècles', 1991).

[12] Maurice Rieuneau, *Guerre et révolution dans le roman français 1919–1939* (Paris: Klincksieck, 1974); see also Léon Riegel, *Guerre et littérature. Le Bouleversement des consciences dans la littérature romanesque inspirée par la Grande Guerre (littératures française, anglo-saxonne, allemande (1910–1939)* (Paris: Klincksieck, 1978).

[13] Maurice Halbwachs, *Les Cadres sociaux de la mémoire* [1925] (Paris: Albin Michel, 1994).

Vichyistes),[14] while men aged forty, like Aragon, evoke the First World War (see his poems 'Vingt ans et après' and 'La Valse des vingt ans' in *Le Crève-coeur* and 'Les Larmes se Ressemblent'). Other historical periods are also evoked, and especially the Middle Ages, which had been in vogue since the mid-1930s. Under the Occupation, the function of the uses made of history is in fact ideological rather than cognitive. The history of the nation was a major issue in the struggles between political forces. The Resistance fought to reappropriate it (in Aragon's 'Les Croisés' Eleanor of Aquitaine becomes a symbol of freedom).[15] As under the Restored Monarchy, history is also used as a code that makes it possible to talk about the present while outwitting the censors.[16] It is not used as causal explanation for the present and has a purely allegorical function. This therefore raises the question of how knowledge is used, and of how shared historical references are used to 'read' the present.

The 'world-view' issue therefore goes beyond the issue of 'knowledge', as it also involves axiological principles. Durkheim and Mauss contend that 'toute classification implique un ordre hiérarchique',[17] while Bourdieu argues that classificatory schemes cannot be divorced from evaluative schemes (positive/negative, top/bottom, noble/ignoble, etc.).[18] If we look in historical terms at the process whereby science and literature become autonomous from public morality and ideological cadres (the principles of neutrality and objectivity, which were transposed into literature by Flaubert thanks to his impassive narrators and the theory of *l'art pour l'art*),[19] it is obvious that this divorce can never be complete because no representation of the world can be neutral and is always inscribed in relational fashion within a broader space of representations. The interpretation of a book is never independent of the socio-historical context

[14] See, for example, Daniel Halévy, *Trois Épreuves 1814, 1871, 1940* (Paris: Plon, 1941); Michel Mohrt, *Les Intellectuels face à la défaite de 1870* (Paris: Corrêa, 1941). Cf. the analysis put forward in Francine Muel-Dreyfus, *Vichy et l'éternel féminin. Contribution à la sociologie politique de l'ordre des corps* (Paris: Seuil, Coll. XXe siècle, 1996), p. 27f.

[15] Aragon, 'Les Croisés', *Le Crève-coeur* [1940], in *L'Œuvre poétique*, t. IX (Paris: Livre Club Diderot, 1975), pp. 153–154 (future references will be given as *L'Op*).

[16] On the use of coded language in what Aragon calls 'littérature de contrebande' under the Occupation, see Sapiro, *La Guerre des écrivains (1940–1953)* p. 432f. On the Restoration period, see Chapter 1 of Gisèle Sapiro, *La Responsabilité de l'écrivain. Littérature, droit et morale en France (XIXe–XXIe siècle)* (Paris: Seuil, 2011).

[17] Durkheim and Mauss, 'De Quelques Formes de classification'.

[18] Bourdieu, *Le Sens pratique*.

[19] See Sapiro, *La Responsabilité de l'écrivain*.

in which it is read. Despite Flaubert's insistence on adopting a neutral and objective point of view, *Madame Bovary* caused a scandal.

This is why, thanks to a seeming paradox, the principle of *l'art pour l'art* could be used for heteronomous purposes. To be more specific, the discourse of *l'art pour l'art* was used to justify continued literary activity under the Occupation: it was used as bait to attract prestigious writers to the *Nouvelle Revue Française*, which had resumed publication under the editorship of Pierre Drieu La Rochelle.[20] This ideal, which had served the struggle for the autonomy of literature,[21] was now subverted by the German authorities in order to normalize the Occupation situation by concealing the heteronomous conditions that had been forced upon literature by censorship, repression and the exclusion of Jews and anti-Nazis for reasons that had nothing to do with literature. This is the context in which we have to understand the politicization of the literary opposition, which Aragon explains in his poem 'Contre la poésie pure', which challenged Paul Valéry.[22] In the case of Aragon, the principle was obviously grounded in his communist loyalties, but he succeeded in rallying those opposed to the Vichy regime – and not just communists – around little magazines such as *Poésie 40, 41* and *Confluences* in the southern zone and the journal *Fontaine* in Algiers, and then around the clandestine Comité national des écrivains. How are we to explain this politicization of literature? It should be recalled, first of all, that the issue of committed literature pre-dates the war: the *roman à these* flourished during the inter-war period, and even poetry has its revolutionary aspirations for the surrealist avant-garde.[23] But it is the heteronomous conditions that were imposed on literature during 'les années noires' that explain why Aragon was able to win over so many prestigious writers. Under the Occupation, writers actually mobilized in the name of the autonomy of literature, which was, as I have demonstrated elsewhere,[24] articulated with a defence of 'l'esprit français': the independence of France is the only thing that can restore literature's lost autonomy.

[20] On the *NRF* during the Occupation, see Pierre Hebey, *La NRF des années sombres (juin 1940–juin 1941). Des intellectuels à la derive* (Paris: Gallimard, 1992); Sapiro, *La Guerre des écrivains*, chapter 6.

[21] Pierre Bourdieu, *Les Règles de l'art. Genèse et structure du champ littéraire* (Paris, Seuil, coll. «libre examen», 1992).

[22] See Wolfgang Babilas, '"Contre la poésie pure". Lecture d'un poème poétologique d'Aragon', *Recherches Croisées Aragon/Triolet*, 2 (1989), 233–252.

[23] Susan Suleiman, *Authoritarian Fictions. The Ideological Novel as a Literary Genre* (New York: Columbia University Press, 1983).

[24] Sapiro, *La Guerre des écrivains*.

If there was one framework that unified the world-view of the day, it was indeed the national framework. How to define the nation in terms of its history and make-up was, of course, one of the things at stake in the bitter and bloody struggle between Vichyists, collaborators and *résistants*, but the national interest functioned as a positive 'axiological operator'[25] within a set of oppositions that made it possible to frame the enemy's activities by using the negatively connoted concepts of 'treason' and 'terrorism' (a term designating violence on which the authorities did not have a legitimate monopoly).[26] The foreign Occupation had the paradoxical effect of 'renationalizing' French intellectuals' world-view. This was even true of those who had, in the inter-war period, taken the most anti-nationalist positions (the internationalists, pacifists and communists), though a small minority (consisting mainly of Trotskyists and surrealists, but also including those who, like Lucien Combelle, promoted a fascist socialism) continued to defend those positions. Even intellectuals on the far left who had been won over to internationalism were convinced by the situation of the Occupation and the way the Resistance constructed a new frame of reference that there had to be a new emphasis on 'the national'. This reawakened a 'national feeling' that had been inculcated into them by their education, but from which they had distanced themselves or which they had even rejected by adopting an ideological system that was critical of national frameworks. Jean Lescure recalls:

> Il y avait un mot que nous avions, bizarrement, du mal à prononcer. Et pourtant c'était lui qui désignait le mieux ce sentiment d'appartenance que nous avions si fort éprouvé en juin 1940.... C'était ce sentiment, sans doute, qui nous avait dressés contre l'invasion, qui nous révulsait quand on rencontrait un Allemand sur les quais, devant Notre-Dame [. . .] Nous n'avions pas été formés à en prononcer le nom. Nous avions biberonné *l'Internationale*. Nous n'avions jamais parlé de patriotisme. La liberté nous paraissait plus universellement avouable. A notre insu, pourtant, notre rébellion était celle de *patriotes*. Simplement, notre culture était décontenancée par quelque chose qu'elle n'avait pas appris à nommer, au contraire.[27]

---

[25] I forged this concept to describe notions that make it possible to unify heterogeneous systems of oppositions and to move from one classificatory system to another, as illustrated by the 'disinterestedness/utilitarianism' opposition. See Gisèle Sapiro, 'Défense et illustration de "l'honnête homme": les hommes de lettres contre la sociologie', *Actes de la recherche en science sociales*, 153 (June 2004), 11–27.

[26] I refer of course, but reversing it, to Weber's definition of the state as having a monopoly on legitimate violence.

[27] Lescure, *Poésie et liberté: histoire des "Messages" 1939–1946* (Paris: Editions de L'IMEC, 1998), pp. 82–83 (emphasis in original).

The Parti communiste also contributed to the national reframing. Although it initially defined the war as 'imperialist' at the time of the Soviet–German pact, the Parti communiste adopted a national line in May 1941, which saw the launch of the Front national pour l'indépendance de la France.[28] This reframing was in keeping with the spirit of the 1937 Congrès d'Arles, when Maurice Thorez announced there was a national road to communism. This is the 'vent d'Arles' evoked by Aragon in 'Plus belles que les larmes'; this is the wind that allowed him to 'retrouver les couleurs de la France'.[29]

If we wish to understand the role of literature in this ideological war, we must extend the discussion beyond the representations it conveys. Literature in fact oscillates between representation and symbolization. 'Representation' assumes that language is transparent and that the signified has priority, and tends to use metonymy, while the 'symbolization' function contends that language is opaque, language signifies. This is the realm of metaphor, and form becomes the focus of attention. This first opposition must be articulated with a second describing the tension between narration and expression (which is not reducible to the novel/poetry dichotomy, as it can also be found in the epic poetry/lyric poetry dichotomy, for example).

Narration

Realism	[Allegory]	Myth

Represent   **Symbolize**
(transparency)   (opacity)

Lyricism	Symbolism

Expression

---

[28] Daniel Virieux, *Le Front national de lutte pour la liberté et l'indépendance de la France. Un mouvement de Résistance - période clandestine (mai 1941–août 1944)*. Doctoral thesis written under the supervision of Claude Willard, Paris VIII, 1995; Atelier de reproduction des thèses de Lille, 5 vols.

[29] Aragon, 'Le Vent d'Arles', *L'Op*, t VII, p. 460. See also Aragon, 'Maurice Thorez et la France', *L'Homme communiste* (Paris: Gallimard, 1946), p. 228.

Deconstructing the dominant narrative of the defeat: poetic 'contraband'

As under the Restored Monarchy and after the Commune, the Vichyist and collaborationist interpretation of the defeat of 1940 fell back on the schema of *mea culpa* and repentance. Given the way the dominant narrative explained the defeat as an atonement for the Republic's sins and exploited events in order to justify the policy of collaboration, opposition writers could not openly offer a different interpretation. They either took a vow of silence (like Martin du Gard) or were forced to resort to symbolism by using allusions, metaphors or allegories. It is this, rather than the conditions of production that are so often mentioned, that provides a partial explanation for the revival of poetry at this time: the debacle, the displacement of the population and the volatile situation did not prevent Aragon from buckling down to *Aurélien*, the long novel he would not publish until after the war.

It was Aragon who developed the technique of what he called 'contrebande littéraire'. He had been thinking about this problem for a long time: how can one speak while being censored and what 'trick' can one use to unmask lies and tell the truth? This was the task that Bertold Brecht had assigned to writers who were opposed to Nazism, and Spanish poets such as Antonio Machado and Federico Garcia Lorca used 'tricks' when confronted with Francoism.[30] Like Barbusse during the First World War, when *Le Feu* conveyed a pacifist message, Aragon initially tried to find the device he was looking for in the novel, but then found it in a technique borrowed from medieval poetry. He rediscovered, that is, the 'trobar clus', or the hermetic art form that 'permettait aux poètes de chanter leurs Dames en présence même de leur Seigneur'.[31] He tried out his technique when the Parti communiste was banned in 1939. The fact that he was once more in contact with Jean Paulhan and had published poems in the *NRF* gave the poet the legitimacy and visibility that the novelist had already won when *Les Cloches de Bâle* won the Prix Renaudot in 1937.

The analogy with the First World War dominates the poems of 1939, collected in *Le Crève-Cœur*, which were written when Aragon was in the

---

[30] The beginning of Brecht's text, which was published in *Commune*, no. 32 (April 1936), is cited by Aragon in 'Rolland et Brecht. Pour ne pas quitter avril . . .', *L'Op*, t VII, p. 95.

[31] Aragon, 'La Lecon de Ribérac ou l'Europe française', *Fontaine* (June 1941), *L'Op*, t IX, p. 308.

army. They criticize war propaganda: 'L'ère des phrases mécaniques recommence' ('Vingt ans après', *L'Op*, t XI, p. 104). The pacifist message had a very concrete political meaning in the context of the Soviet–German pact, but it is concealed by the theme – being both more universalist and more individualist – of the experience of war, and especially by the lived experience of lovers who have been separated by war and who, in the tradition of lyric poetry, speak in the first person of their melancholy, nostalgia, and so on. While this tone deliberately rejects Apollinaire's 'beautés de la guerre' (Aragon attacked Apollinaire for concealing the horrors of war), it does very little to evoke the war itself, mentioning only the fate of the 'enfants-soldats roulés vivants sans autre lit/Que la fosse qu'on fit d'avance à votre taille' ('La Valse des vingts ans', p. 120). It is rumour that surreptitiously introduces the event of the defeat in 'Les lilas et les roses' in 1940 (p. 137): 'Tout se tait. L'ennemi dans l'ombre se repose/On nous a dit ce soir que Paris s'est rendu.' 'Tapisseries de la grande peur' (pp. 140–141) describes the debacle:

> Reconnais-tu les champs la ville et les rapaces
> Le clocher qui plus jamais ne sonnera l'heure
> Les chariots bariolés de literies
> Un ours Un châle Un mort comme un soulier perdu
> Les deux mains prises dans son ventre. Une pendule
> Les troupeaux échappés les charognes les cris
> Des bronzes d'art à terre Où dormez-vous ce soir

From this point onwards, the predominant theme is that of love for *la patrie*, which is identified with the beloved. Aragon becomes a national poet. Let me cite the famous strophe that opens the poem 'Richard II Quarante' (p. 146):

> Ma patrie est comme une barque
> Qu'abandonnèrent ses haleurs
> Et je ressemble à ce monarque
> Plus malheureux que le malheur
> Qui restait roi de ses douleurs

The national reframing takes place at the formal as well as the thematic level. Aragon resorts to rhyme, and to popular forms, including the song and ballad forms ('Complainte pour l'orgue de la nouvelle barbarie', p. 142). In his view, it was rhyme that really made French poetry and the French language autonomous from Latin and the grip of Rome when they first emerged in the twelfth century:

Si le problème de la rime est tout d'abord celui sur lequel j'ai voulu
m'exprimer en 1940, c'est parce que l'histoire du vers français débute où
apparaît la rime, c'est que la rime est l'élément caractéristique qui libère
notre poésie de l'emprise romaine, et en fait la poésie française.[32]

The lyrical ('lived') 'je' is used in turn by the soldier separated from
the woman he loves and the French citizen who has lost his country.
It sometimes becomes a 'nous', as in 'Complainte pour l'orgue de la
nouvelle barbarie' and in 'Ombres': 'Nos vignes nos enfants nos rêves
nos troupeaux' (p. 151). But the 'je' is also the clear-sighted witness
who takes a stand against 'them', meaning the false prophets and 'oiseaux
querelleurs', those who divide the nation rather than coming together
in their misery, and the Vichy regime, which tries to find an explanation
for the defeat in the spirit of hedonism that had prevailed over the
spirit of sacrifice: 'Avons-nous attiré la foudre par nos rires' ('Ombres',
p. 150).

At the level of the 'message' – and this eminently occasional poetry
('poésie de circonstance') does have a message – Aragon's strategy is to
offer an alternative vision of European history to biological racism,
Nazi myths and the plan to create a German-dominated Europe: the
French nation was born of the fusion of North and South and of the
intermingling of 'races'. France 'a envahi poétiquement l'Europe à la
fin du Moyen-Age' thanks to the reception of Chrétien de Troyes' work.
This peaceful poetic invasion is obviously contrasted with the armed
invasion. Courtly morality is contrasted with chivalric morality, seen
as the expression of a warrior civilization based upon a virile order.
Nazism claimed to be the heir to that civilization. In France, it was
promoted by Montherlant. According to Montherlant, this chivalric
morality was perverted by women when gallantry replaced it with the
'morale de midinette' or the 'morale courtoise' that is, in his view,
responsible for France's decadence. Opposing Montherlant, Aragon
puts forward the virtues of the 'morale courtoise' that served as a vector
for the diffusion of the 'passion de justice, [du] goût de la chevalerie,
de la défense des faibles, de l'exaltation des hautes pensées'. The 'culte
de la femme' reflects women's elevation to a recognized social status.
Aragon points out that this theme 'pren[d] de nos jours un sens de
protestation' at a time when women were forbidden access to jobs in

---

[32] Aragon, 'Arma virumque canto', L'Op, t XI, p. 180.

the state sector and when there was an attempt to force them back into the home.[33]

Aragon gives shape to his project in his poems, not only by introducing more and more references to the history of France, and especially the Middle Ages, but also by transgressing the classical rules or prosody, and especially the masculine/feminine rhyme distinction and the rules on enjambment and rhyme. These departures, which draw upon the medieval tradition of the troubadours, are also inspired by modern poetry, and especially Apollinaire and Mayakovsky.

Aragon explains what he is doing in the prose text he published outside France ('La Leçon de Riberac ou l'Europe française', which appeared in *Fontaine* in June 1941, and 'Arma virumque canto', the preface to *Les Yeux d'Elsa*, which appeared in 1942 in the 'Cahiers du Rhône' collection published by Edition de la Baconnière in Neuchâtel).

This 'littérature de contrebande' did not follow the Parti communiste's line of the day: the Party did not support open publication. Aragon succeeded in influencing the Party's line during this period of uncertainty, not least because his strategy had succeeded in uniting the opposition writers in the Southern zone. But he had to justify the way he was using the national traditions' myths to the Party, and to the rationalist philosopher Georges Politzer. After the Liberation, he explained the poetic use he had made of history and its legends. He had used them metaphorically to invoke the collective memory of the nation as a way of talking about the present, while emphasizing their mobilizing power: the purpose of the myths he claimed to have 'remis sur leurs pieds' was to reawaken an epic sense that could express the national feelings and the heroic tradition.[34] If we translate this into (somewhat unorthodox) Marxist terms we can say that these myths bring to life past national struggles against the oppressor which counter the mystifications of Vichy's discourse of repentance. Acting on Politzer's advice, Aragon now placed more emphasis on the hero theme, which is no more than outlined in 'La Leçon de Riberac', in his *Brocéliande* collection (1942).

---

[33] Aragon, 'La Leçon de Ribérac. . . .', *L'Op*, t IX, pp. 298, 306n 1. For what the ideologues of the Révolution nationale had to say about women, see Muel-Dreyfus, *Vichy et l'éternel féminin*.

[34] Aragon, 'De l'exactitude historique en poésie', *L'Op*, t X, p. 67. On 'le sens épique' and 'sens national', see especially 'Les Poissons noirs ou de la réalité en poésie' (which is the introduction to the new edition of *Le Musée Grévin*, Paris: Minuit, 1946), *L'Op*, t X, pp. 152 ff.

From allegory to act of witness: clandestine literature

This development corresponds to the transition from a literature that centres on the theme of a pacifist refusal to cooperate (*Le Silence de la mer*) to a militant literature that is designed to support the armed struggle.[35] In more general terms, it also corresponds to the decision to go underground (which did not, of course, come about automatically),[36] though the two things did not occur simultaneously in either chronological or spatial terms. 'Littérature de contrebande' proved to have its limitations. It could be deciphered by initiates like Drieu La Rochelle, who denounced it in the *NRF* in September 1941. The practice was too dangerous to be developed any further in the Northern zone and soon ran foul of the censors in the Southern zone. In August 1942, *Confluences* was forced to halt publication for two months because Aragon's poem 'Nymphée' made reference to Mithridates, 'vieux roi malheureux contre qui tout conspire': the censors did not find it difficult to decode the accents of revolt. Its suspension was meant to serve as an example, as was clear from the warning letter from the Ministry for Information to *Poésie 42* and *Fontaine* threatening that further use of the poetic 'contraband' device would not go unpunished.[37] From this point onwards, Aragon published under a variety of pseudonyms. The extension of Nazi jurisdiction to the Southern zone in November made conditions of production even more difficult and hastened the decision to go underground.

Oppositional literature now moved closer to the representative function. Symbolization gave way to the representation of the reality of the Occupation, while the subjective representation of experience gave way to acts of witness. One text signals the transition from allegory and myth to the act of witness: signed 'le témoin des martyrs', it is based upon the documents about the execution of the Chateaubriant hostages sent to Aragon by the Party in January 1942 with a message from Jacques Duclos: 'Fais de cela un monument'. After Gide, Martin du Gard and a third writer declined to do anything with these documents; Aragon himself shaped them in February. The text was copied and distributed all over France and outside the country, where it was read on the radio in London and Boston.

---

[35] On this point, see Steel, *Littératures de l'ombre*.
[36] See Anne Simonin, *Les Editions de Minuit 1942–1955. Le Devoir d'insoumission* (Paris: IMEC, 1994).
[37] The letter is reproduced in Seghers, *La Résistance et ses poètes*, p. 201.

'Bearing witness' means first of all 'making known' the occupant's crimes and abuses, which were committed with the active help of the Vichy regime, as in the poem 'Le Médecin de Villeneuve', which describes a round-up of Jews in Nice in the summer of 1942 (*L'Op*, t X, p. 124):

> Qui frappe à la porte au noir du silence
> Il se lève un vent de la violence
> Sur la ville un vol de coquecigrues
> Traque des fuyards à travers les rues
> Qui frappe à la porte au noir du silence

It also means laying a wreath on the graves of the martyrs who died in the fight for national liberation: Guy Moquet, Gabriel Péri and those who were shot in May (the communist intellectuals arrested in January 1942, including Jacques Decour, the founder of the Front national des écrivains), and making them part of the nation's memory: 'Je n'oublierai jamais/Les morts du mois du Mai' ('Plainte pour le grand escort de France', *L'Op*, t IX, p. 235). Here, the poet is no longer dealing with myths but with an unvarnished reality: the dead are the only *résistants* who can be named, and elegiac poetry gives back their name and identity to the dead. Poetry extracted them from the red posters that described them as terrorists and allows a humiliated nation to pay tribute to them. It re-presents them, shows them in a new light, reveals them to be martyrs and sets them up as an example, as we can see from the title of the text Aragon dedicates to Jacques Decour, *alias* Daniel Decourdemanche: 'Jacques Decour ou "Comme je vous en donne l'exemple".' Clandestine poetry also gives a voice to those who died under torture without talking in the 'Ballade de celui qui chanta dans les supplices' (*L'Op*, t X, p. 324):

> Et s'il était à refaire
> Je referais ce chemin
> Une voix monte des fers
> Et parle des lendemains

In a period when the legal press abdicated its responsibilities, failed to print any news and was reduced to publishing propaganda, literature once more took on the task of bearing witness, which has been well analysed by Margaret Atack.[38] It bore witness in the quasi-juridical sense of the term: this is evidence to be used against Nazism and its

---

[38] Atack, *Literature and the French Resistance*.

collaborators. Although literature was not used as documentary evidence during the trials of the *épuration*, it did feed into the collective imaginary and helped to create the 'épuration' state of mind. It is obviously not restricted to that function, as it is a committed act of witness designed not only to make known what has happened but also to instruct. Whereas the dominant narrative describes a France under terrorist attack, the Resistance recites the epic of the martyrs who died in the fight to liberate France, who thus become symbols of the nation's history, and constructs the figure of the traitor or collaborator who will be put on trial for treason after Liberation.[39]

Most descriptions of the figure of the traitor are in prose, and they also analyse the dilemmas with which the heroes are faced. But poetry also plays a part in constructing this great narrative. Yet, when it goes underground, it loses something of this national function and takes on more prophetic accents as it denounces Nazi barbarism and murders that cannot be talked about legally, or defends great universal principles such as freedom. Poetry becomes a scream, as Eluard puts it in the preface to the clandestine collection *L'Honneur de poètes*, which was published by Minuit in 1943: 'Une fois de plus la poésie mise au défi se regroupe, retrouve un sens précis à sa violence latente, crie, accuse, espère.' Aragon said the same in verse: 'Mots mariés mots meurtris/ Rime où le crime crie' ('Art poétique', *L'Op*, t X, p. 7). Aragon describes this return to the original function of metrics and rhyme, namely the mnemotechnical function, in his preface to Jean Cassou's *33 sonnets composés au secret*, which was also published by Minuit. What is more important, he explains that 'Désormais il sera impossible de ne pas voir dans le sonnet l'expression de la liberté contrainte, la forme même de la pensée prisonnière.' The poetic form itself symbolizes the experience of captivity. The national dimension is there just beneath the surface, as the French spirit is identified with the defence of freedom in the tradition of the French Revolution.

As we have seen, literature had its part to play in the struggle to reframe the perception and interpretation of social and political reality during this period of national crisis. We can, *grosso modo*, identify two main phases in the history of oppositional literature and, more specifically, poetry, and they relate to the two modalities of the relationship between literature and reality. In the first, reality is symbolized by myths and legends,

---

[39] See Anne Simonin, *Le Déshonneur dans la République. Une histoire de l'indignité 1791–1958* (Paris: Grasset, 2008); Sapiro, *La Responsabilité de l'écrivain*, 4e partie.

most of them drawn from the history of the nation. In the second, real examples become symbols of a people's resistance to oppression, as when the *fusillés* are turned into heroes and martyrs. The effect of this second phase is to frame later perceptions. As we know, it was a very long time before the moral dichotomy between hero and traitor could be called into question,[40] except on the far right.

Both forms of framing – representation and symbolization – can take either a narrative or an expressive form. I have emphasized the formal dimension, which is more obvious in the case of poetry though it is also present in prose, because the history of representations often tends to overlook it. And it is the formal dimension that differentiates literature from other forms of writing – much more so than the fictional dimension, as it can also include poetry and non-fiction. This formal dimension is obviously more dominant in some works than in others. It is of course dominant in poetry, but it can also be dominant in prose. In, for instance, Claude Simon's *La Route des Flandres* (1960), the historical event is filtered through memory: the narration is dominated by memory, which muddles the chronology of the narrative and the plot, but these chaotic memories also symbolize the breakdown of the military, social and spatio-temporal order during the debacle. It therefore reconstructs one of the ways in which the debacle was experienced, and the 'frame break' described in the introduction.

---

[40] See especially Rousso, *Le Syndrome de Vichy.*

Chapter 2

Representing the war: contemporary narratives of the Second World War

William Cloonan

Towards the end of *Jan Karski*, a 2009 novel by Yannick Haenel which provides a fictionalized account of the life of the Polish diplomat who was among the first to provide eye-witness accounts of the Warsaw Ghetto and other Nazi atrocities, the elderly Karski thinks back on the filming of *Shoah*. He recalls that 'Claude Lanzmann m'avait dit que la question du sauvetage des Juifs serait l'un des thèmes du film; mais sans doute a-t-il modifié son projet en cours de route afin de se concentrer sur l'extermination elle-même. C'était historiquement nécessaire, car ainsi *Shoah* constitue une réponse aux négationnistes.'[1] The fictional Karski is generous in his judgement in explaining Lanzmann's decision to focus on extermination rather than rescue, on a subject brutally dramatic, rather than one more nuanced, more complicated and ultimately perhaps more difficult to bring to the screen. Yet Lanzmann's choice, a good one in 1985, raises the question which might be at the heart of today's fiction about the war: what are the current issues to examine, what are the paths of inquiry which merely lead us to places we have already been, and what are the byways to follow which will take us into poorly mapped areas which we nevertheless need to explore? To put the matter most simply: do we look to novelists to tell us the too-well-known tales about the past, or do we expect from them narratives about the war which challenge our sense of the past and impact upon the present?

Possible responses to these sorts of questions entail an examination of the development of French fiction from 1945 until today with specific

---

[1] Yannick Haenel, *Jan Karski* (Paris: Gallimard, 2009), p. 180. For an account of the controversy aroused by this book, see Adrian Tahourdin, 'Mr Karski: a Hero and his Myths', *Times Literary Supplement*, 8 October 2010, pp. 14–15. Subsequent references to this title are given in text.

regard to the degree to which the contemporary novel can engage with complicated moral and social issues. I would like to look at several very recent literary treatments of the war, and in doing so set the war novel in the larger context of the evolution of French fiction from the end of the Second World War to the present.

The changes in French fiction dealing with the Second World War are linked with the development of the post-war novel in ways which may initially appear somewhat surprising. When speaking of post-war French fiction it seems mandatory to invoke the *nouveau roman* and its myriad challenges to the traditional novel. While the best French writing about the war does indeed question many of the hoarier assumptions about the nature of the novel, the work I believe marks a break with both earlier texts about the war and with traditional French fiction in general, is at antipodes to the literary theory and practice associated with the *École de Minuit*. I am referring to Michel Tournier's *Le Roi des aulnes*.

Now it is true that Tournier is no stranger to exaggeration and we may be well within our rights should we wonder whether he would have been, as he claimed, the greatest philosopher of his generation had he passed the *agrégation*. Yet when he asserts in *Le Vent paraclet* that he aspires in his books to express in a traditional, safe and reassuring form a content that possesses none of these qualities, we may wish to pay attention.

Certainly *Le Roi des aulnes* has all the trappings of traditional fiction: a mysterious hero who claims to have emerged from 'the night of time', whose name, Abel Tiffauges, is a treasure chest of symbolism, as is the whole novel. The story is rife with sexual innuendo, featuring as it does a man taking a seemingly illicit delight in the portage of little boys. The themes are of the putatively profound variety: the meaning of time, the possibility of predestination, the 'significance' of the Second World War. The novel constantly hints at the proximity of vast truths just beyond the reach of the average person's understanding. What I have described is a formula for a best-seller, a work potentially on a par with *Les Bienveillantes*, and in fact *Le Roi des aulnes* was a best-seller and a prize-winner as well.

However, except for its success with the general public, and winning le Prix Goncourt, everything I have said about *Le Roi des aulnes* is false. The symbolism turns out to be empty because it is without consistency, Abel's sexuality is more confused than ominous, what purports to be profound is more properly described as opaque, and the vast truths, while they may exist, are beyond the human understanding on display in this novel.

Le Roi des aulnes illustrates the arbitrary, artificial nature of literary symbolism. To cite a single example: Abel's friend, Nestor, may be the reincarnation of the wise old soldier in *The Odyssey*, or perhaps he is the invocation of the centaur-pederast in Greek mythology. Or maybe he is neither, just an oversized, self-deluded misfit, exactly like Abel, who dies in a stupid accident. Symbolism, omnipresent in *Le Roi des aulnes*, tends to point the reader in opposite, conflicting directions, and by doing so cancels it own value. The symbolism in this novel reveals its own nature as a creation of the human imagination, a decoration which purports to provide meaning but without any necessary relationship to objective truth.

In terms of Abel's sexuality, his precise orientation is never clear, and to focus on what *may* be Abel's erotic inclinations towards children and the harm he *might* do, is to obscure the fact that his very concrete actions get many of these young people killed. The sexual ambiguity only distracts attention from Abel's truly immoral acts.

With regard to the great questions Abel poses, his musings about life's deepest significance are never clearly articulated. In his frequent interior monologues, he conflates obscurity with profundity, since from his perspective, the more obtuse the rumination, the more potentially profound the thought.

This is not to say that the novel is devoid of serious intellectual content. One such example occurs in the scene where Dr Essig, the moronic Nazi researcher, fires a rifle and kills, quite by chance, Candélabre, the greatest deer in Göring's preserve. The operative term here is 'chance'. In a novel seemingly obsessed by structure, coherence and hidden meaning, chance emerges as one of the truly dominant themes. Freak circumstances got Abel to Germany, only by an accident of birth and nationality is Abel any different from Stefan Raufeisen, the Nazi commandant whose background so resembles his own. Abel's discovery of Ephraim, the deranged Jewish boy who reveals to him the reality of Nazism, has nothing foreordained about it, and if he sinks into the mud in the novel's final scene, the most coherent explanation is that he stepped in the wrong place.

Le Roi des aulnes, so radically different from *le nouveau roman* in so many ways, nevertheless embodies many elements theorized by Alain Robbe-Grillet and Nathalie Sarraute. Symbolism is deconstructed, the possibility of the psychological novel called into question, the primary narrative voice is unreliable in the extreme, and fiction's ability to venture into metaphysical realms is roundly derided.

With *Le Roi des aulnes* French writing about the Second World War begins to find a new orientation. Subsequent authors will generally avoid Tournier's vast canvas and the degree of irony which accompanies it, yet they will abandon too cosmic, insoluble questions to address issues of importance whose dimensions are more circumscribed. Most importantly, the best contemporary writing about the Second World War tends to focus on how the events of the past continue to make themselves felt in the present.

This would appear to be the appropriate place to explain what I mean by 'contemporary writing about the Second World War'. As we all know, writing about the war, both by novelists and scholars, has become something of an industry, and hardly of the cottage variety, producing as it does on a regular basis books of varying degrees of intelligence, hysteria and self-righteousness. For the purposes of my discussion I am not interested in works that do little except deplore the Final Solution, concentrate primarily on the physical/sexual abuse foisted on the victims of Nazism, or explain away the SS and the Gestapo as a bunch of degenerates. My focus is on novels which seek to avoid the clichés and stock situations which have become integral parts of writing about the Second World War, and reflect instead a concern with more complicated issues and display aspects of the stylistic and structural development of fiction in France today. I am interested in novels which consciously address the past from the perspective of the present.

The reorientation of fictional themes in the contemporary novel corresponds to another change in the French literary landscape. Michel Winock in *Le Siècle des intellectuels* talks of a tradition in French letters which concerns a sort of Gallic writer/intellectual whom Dominique Noguez refers to somewhat ironically as the *grantécrivain*. Winock and Noguez are alluding to male authors over the last three centuries whom literary success has turned into self-appointed spokesmen on all major French cultural and social issues. The list of *granzécrivains* would include Voltaire, Hugo, Gide, Sartre and Foucault. Yet this sort of oracular presence has disappeared from the contemporary intellectual scene, as writers today display a healthy distrust in their own omniscience. If ours is an era of suspicion, what is doubted are not simply intellectual methodologies, or vast ideological syntheses, but the simple capacity of the human mind to grasp the complexity of the world around it. Contemporary literature reflects this unease in its choice of themes and limited parameters, yet this state of affairs should not be perceived as a crisis. Rather, it is a simple attestation of the heightened sense of what is within the ability of the human intellect to absorb and describe.

The implicit assumption that literature has limits is a principal characteristic of the novel today. Contemporary French literature has thus become a more modest affair with authors more circumscribed in their purview, a situation which often gives the misleading impression that today's novelists are less inclined to confront the social and moral issues of the day than were their great predecessors. This hesitancy has in turn created a rift between novelists and their readers, and helps explain to a great extent the success of *Les Bienveillantes*.

I do not propose rehashing all the faults critics have found with this work. I simply want to point out that *Les Bienveillantes* has succeeded so well because it has given readers what they want: a big narrative, with lots of symbols from that most sanctified of literary regions, classical Greek theatre and mythology. It raises a seemingly profound issue: the nature of the Nazi mentality, and provides a neat answer. What might be the novel's greatest appeal to many people is the reassuring fashion in which the Nazi personality is described. Max Aue, the SS officer, has grandiose character flaws and perverse tendencies. Yet his thoughts and acts do provide a bizarre form of comfort to the reader. The very enormity of his personal misdeeds distances him, the 'Nazi', from the ordinary citizen, the high-minded reader. Max is a closet homosexual who pines for the halcyon days when he enjoyed incest with his sister; he is an axe-murderer who strangled his French mother and later killed his best friend moments after the man saved his life. A villain worthy of Hollywood, a personage like Max Aue places the 'typical Nazi' safely in the category of the Other. Thus, in a rather ugly way, the reader's horror at Max is also a form of reassurance. *Les Bienveillantes* may shock, but it does not challenge, and readers can eventually put the novel down reassured of their moral superiority.

If *Les Bienveillantes* is an anomaly both in terms of serious war novels and contemporary French fiction as a whole, its failure to move beyond the convenient stereotype is instructive. In appearing to explain so much about the war, the novel really clarifies nothing. This is why contemporary French literature's tendency to circumscribe its parameters, to limit its scope, is not a sign of exhaustion, but a very healthy movement towards confronting society in terms of what can be said in a meaningful fashion and without necessarily depending upon traditional literary techniques to justify its claim to being serious art.

What is true generally about contemporary French fiction is particularly germane to works dealing with the Second World War. If today's writers are eschewing the 'big themes', they are not shying away from difficult, often perplexing issues associated with the war. The results of the efforts of younger novelists who write about the Second World War are uneven, but they have the merit of often providing disquieting and challenging scenarios, of exploring uncharted areas of inquiry. Thus, much of today's fiction on the subject is more concerned with the ramifications rather than the events of the Second World War. Current novels about the war quite often examine the ways the contemporary self has become its victim.

Marie Suzin's *La Femme de l'Allemand* (2007) is a case in point. The story deals with an adolescent girl, Marion, whose mother, Fanny, was guilty of 'horizontal collaboration' during the war. This is a familiar enough motif, and in initially reading the text one expects the usual account of social ostracism and contempt. None of this occurs. Fanny comes from a wealthy family that remains willing to help her after the war. She, however, prefers to live with Marion in a small apartment in the Marais where she battles depression and nurses the myth of the German soldier's great love for her. Towards the novel's end Marion gleans information about the officer which indicates that her mother was for him nothing more than a dalliance. As Marion gets older, her mother sinks into deeper depression. Eventually Marion comes to the painful decision that she must leave her mother unless she too wishes to become a prisoner of the past.

In this novel there really is no villain. What happened in Paris during the war was so long ago that the author does not dwell on it. The focus instead is upon Fanny today, a victim to be sure, but also someone who has learned to luxuriate in her victimhood, and by doing so make miserable the lives of those who try to help her. Fanny was done an injustice in the past, but in the present she is the victimizer.

The excellence of Marie Suzin's novel is due in large measure to its ability to create a situation which elicits concrete reactions which are not always very assuring while at the same time exploring from a new perspective a well-known phenomenon: the situation of French women linked romantically with Germans during the war. The results challenge and disturb the reader since the image of a young woman abandoning her deranged mother in a tiny apartment is not exactly cathartic, although it may be life-saving as far as someone like Marion is concerned.

The idea of an innocent party, someone born during or after the war, being a victim is not unique to Marie Suzin's text. Jacques Chessex published in 2009 *Un Juif pour l'exemple*. When Chessex was a child of eight, during the war, a group of young Nazi supporters in his little town, Payerne, murdered a Jewish merchant, someone chosen quite arbitrarily *pour l'exemple*. The question which appears to haunt Chessex is contained in the *pour l'exemple*. Could it really be that perennial anti-Semitic clichés could have such power as to result in the death of an Arthur Bloch, and even if that were the case, the murder was an example of what? The body was hidden, and no group claimed responsibility for the crime. But for the sheer stupidity of the perpetrators, Bloch might have simply become a missing person. These sorts of questions have haunted Chessex throughout his career. *Un Juif pour l'exemple* constitutes the fifth time he has written about this incident or alluded to it in a work of fiction.

A corollary of contemporary fiction's more modest approach to writing about the Second World War is that these novels tend to be tightly bound up with history. I am fully aware of how ridiculously self-evident the foregoing sentence must appear. How can any novel about the Second World War not be related to history? My point is that the strong involvement with historical incident ideally serves as a grounding device, a control that prevents the novel from venturing too far afield into realms where bombast and speculative flights upset the rhythm and development of the narrative, and move the story into melodrama. When most successful, the historical dimension and the fictional element proceed apace to describe in a calm manner often very emotional and distressful occurrences.

With regard to the relationship between historical and literary narrative, *Les Bienveillantes* provides an excellent example of what I maintain the contemporary novel is attempting to avoid. Jonathan Littell's work is well researched, but when combined with the Gothic dimension of Max Aue's personal life, the effect is jarring and often gives the impression of a baroque opera juxtaposed against a particularly ugly contemporary crime scene.

The relationship between history and fiction often found in the contemporary novel is one which gives predominance to the historical event and minimizes the literary pyrotechnics. Emotions, frequently very strong emotions, emerge from the artistic exploitation of the historical incident, rather than a novelist's purple prose, while events are discreetly manipulated for their maximum effect on the reader. A simple example is Chessex's *Un Juif pour l'exemple*. The author structures the novel in

such a way that the narrator *appears* to just be recounting what happened
in a sleepy Swiss town at the beginning of the war. The attitudes of the
young Nazi sympathizers are recorded with little or no commentary. The
events leading up to the murder and the consequences of Arthur Bloch's
death are described in a relatively straightforward manner. The horror,
indignation and ultimate inability to make sense out of the events emerge
from the reader and are not supplied by the writer. What Chessex provides is not history; it is fiction, since events are assembled and deployed
not simply to convey what occurred, but to invite an intellectual/
emotional reaction from an audience.

A much more elaborate example of the intertwining of fiction and
history is found in Yannick Haenel's *Jan Karski*. As previously mentioned,
Jan Karski (1914–2000) was a Polish diplomat who rallied to the Resistance after Poland's collapse, and was among the very first to report
to the Allies about the Warsaw Ghetto. In a note preceding the first
chapter Haenel explains that in some instances he has taken Karski's
words directly from an interview the latter gave to Claude Lanzmann
during the filming of *Shoah*, that chapter 2 is a résumé of Karski's
book, *Story of a Secret State*, and that while chapter 3 is fiction, it draws
on information gleaned from a biography of Karski. From the outset
the author wishes to underscore his fiction's involvement with the
historical record.

At the point in the novel where Karski eye-witnesses the Warsaw
Ghetto, the two Jews who have led him there insist that 'Il faut que
vous le disiez au monde' (p. 136). In the novel the Allied indifference to
the plight of the Jews will be excoriated: 'Ce n'est pas la Pologne qui a
abandonné les Juifs, ce sont les Alliés' (p. 181) but the more troubling
issue remains associated with the mission the two Polish Jews assigned
to Karski. The question for Karski, as it is for the contemporary novel,
is not just to report what he saw, but to do so in a way which will affect
the audience.

A scene between Karski and Justice Felix Frankfurter of the United
States Supreme Court illustrates the difficulty of this task. Frankfurter
tells Karski that he cannot believe what he is being told. Karski responds
heatedly by asking whether the judge thinks he is lying. Frankfurter
replies: 'Je n'ai pas dit que vous mentiez, j'ai dit que je ne peux pas le
croire' (p. 112). Haenel's *Jan Karski* very self-consciously mingles history
and imagination, in an extended meditation on the enormous difficulty
of satisfying this demand, of conveying the reality of the war's most
notorious event, the Nazi genocide, to a public whose education and

cultural background made it almost impossible for them to believe what they heard, namely that a nation which cradled the Enlightenment could commit crimes for which at the time there was not even a name.

The novel begins in 1984 where the elderly Karski is being interviewed by Claude Lanzmann for what will be the film, *Shoah*. Despite the passage of time, Karski has difficulty telling his story; he fumbles about and finally blurts out: 'Au milieu de l'année 1942, je décidai de reprendre ma mission d'agent entre la Résistance polonaise et le government polonais en exil' (p. 14). The narrator immediately pounces on the use of the quintessential literary tense, *le passé simple*, in the passage, and remarks: 'on se croirait au début de Dante, mais aussi dans un roman d'espionnage' (p. 14). To tell his story most effectively and also to protect himself from the memories it evokes, Haenel's Karski turns to a literary format which instinctively seems to him to have a better chance of conveying and containing the story he wishes to tell. Yet to assume, as Haenel does in this novel, that literature has the capacity to transfer the aspects of historical reality in ways perhaps stronger than direct historical narration, is to propose an approach, not to guarantee a successful conclusion. Haenel is all too aware that what provides the 'strength' of a literary text may have the unfortunate side effect of diverting readers from a novel's real theme. Two scenes in *Jan Karski* illustrate this danger.

A book, be it history or fiction, is a cultural artefact that must be to some degree marketable. The fictional Karski discovers this when he attempts to place his first manuscript with a publisher. Apparently the struggle to survive in Occupied Europe was not considered 'assez humain', so, at the editor's insistence, 'je fus obligé de modifier mon livre, afin de lui donner le piquant propre à satisfaire l'éditeur et ses puissants amis' (p. 144). The book, *Story of a Secret State*, published in 1944, turned out to be a best-seller thanks in part to the addition of an erotic subtext.

Even worse, the 'literary qualities' of *Story of a Secret State* end up having an extremely deleterious effect on what the author is trying to convey, 'une vieille dame couverte de perles et de rubis . . . s'est jetée sur moi pour me dire qu'elle venait de lire la scène où la Gestapo me torture, et qu'il y a rien de plus beau que cette scène: le moment où l'on me torture, c'était magnifique' (p. 147). Whereas the purpose of employing literary techniques had been to shock readers into a heightened sense of the reality of the Nazi Occupation, what the author has managed to provide, at least in one person's eyes, is a version of *grand guignol*.

Haenel's *Jan Karski* is very much concerned with the difficulty that attends creating literature about the Second World War. Yet there is an even more fundamental question that hovers in the background of any discussion of literature and the war, and which haunts any effort to write about the war. This question comes almost brutally to the fore in *Jan Karski* when the fictional Karski ruefully notes the influence his best-seller had on the injustice it described: 'le livre n'a rien changé . . . Mes paroles avaient échoué à transmettre le message, mon livre aussi' (p. 152). As far as Karski is concerned, he failed to deliver the message entrusted to him by the two Polish Jews.

In terms of social ramifications, Karski's best-seller was negligible, and this all too apparent truth necessarily leads us to wonder what is the purpose of persisting to write about the war, or as a character in Siegfried Lenz's *The German Lesson* so eloquently phrased it, why should we continue 'stirring around in all this crap'?[2] Why then do novelists persist in writing about events that took place over sixty years ago?

A common way of responding to this type of conundrum is to refer to the literary text's capacity to raise social consciousness, but I think most people who have undergone that uplifting experience already had their consciousness on the rise before they opened the book. Nor do I believe that the novel has any special claims to revealing historical truths. For the most part, historians do an excellent job providing us with history. Towards the end of *Jan Karski*, another approach to the issue is proposed, one that emphasizes the personal over the political.

Karski realizes that if at one historical moment his writings were a form of witnessing, that would no longer be sufficient: 'avec le temps, la nature du message avait changé: reprendre la parole serait une manière de rendre hommage aux Juifs d'Europe. . . . Et puis j'ai compris que moi-même, d'une manière plus mystérieuse, je faisais partie désormais de cette famille. Par la parole, j'étais entré dans le destin des Juifs d'Europe, dans la pensée qui les destine à la parole, dans le déploiement immense d'une meditation qui s'élargit à travers le temps' (p. 187). This is highly charged, emotionally fraught language, but except for the very last words cited, I do not think it really answers the question.

To identify with a people to the point of becoming one with them is an extremely individual act that may or may not have anything to do with writing. Indeed so powerful an empathy could well lead to rather melodramatic posturing and there is more than a little of that

---

[2] Siegfried Lenz, *The German Lesson*, tr. Ernest Kaiser and Eithne Wilkins (New York: Avon, 1971), p. 162.

towards the end of *Jan Karski*. However, 'le déploiement immense d'une méditation qui s'élargit à travers le temps' is another matter.

Every war is different, and so to argue for a hierarchy of awfulness, to claim one bloodbath was worse than another, is an academic exercise of the most sterile sort. Yet one can note features of a conflict which were, at least at the particular moment, somewhat unique. For instance, it remains essentially true that the First World War unleashed a level of firepower and mechanized warfare to a degree the world had never seen. The Second World War featured even deadlier weapons, but what stands out when we consider what took place between 1939 and 1945 is a different sort of intellectual and physical destruction. I am referring to the severe challenge to the Enlightenment heritage resulting from the Nazi genocide, the American dropping of the atomic bomb, and the terror bombing practised by the Axis and Allies during the war.

In his 'What is Enlightenment?' Foucault may well have provided an intellectual safety net for this heritage by arguing that Enlightenment is essentially techniques of thinking rather than a series of historically circumscribed ideas, but the Second World War undoubtedly undermined confidence in humanity's ability to restrain its darkest impulses, and made all too relevant the sorts of interrogations suggested by the title of Primo Levi's 1947 autobiography, *If This is a Man*.

In this essay I have argued that contemporary fiction's engagement with the war has much more to do with the present than what happened in the past, that the war experiences provide the backdrop, the shadow hanging over and influencing a meditation on what it means to be a human being today. The word 'meditation', which I took from the citation in *Jan Karski*, is particularly apt, since the war novel, for all the drama and violence it contains, is a very cerebral affair, one which deals with powerful emotions but is not governed by them. If I insist on the intellectual nature of this sort of novel, it is for the same reason I stress the bond with history; they are both means of asserting some control over the emotional volatility engendered by the peculiar ugliness of the Second World War.

In a conclusion which is necessarily tentative, I would like to suggest first of all that the serious contemporary novel about the Second World War will probably never have a vast audience, but it will have an audience of intelligent readers concerned by the questions this fiction constantly poses, questions which tend to be more focused on the nature of the individual than on vast political movements. This sort of novel is still sifting through the debris of a historically circumscribed past because in terms of understanding the self the Second World War opened some dark corridors in the human psyche whose existence and force cannot be denied. What I am saying here is in part a paraphrase of the argument Adorno and Horkheimer made in *The Dialectic of the Enlightenment*. For these authors the Enlightenment failed because it assigned insufficient importance to the power of the irrational. The Second World War exposed that error, and today's war fiction at its best is attempting to shed a little light on what can no longer be explained away or dismissed as the deviant conduct of a group or even a nation. Modest in the events it describes, faithful to the historical record, the contemporary war novel is ultimately quite ambitious since, with a minimum of fanfare, it has undertaken the exploration of, in the words of Goethe which D.M. Thomas cites, 'what unknown or neglected by men, walks in the night through the labyrinth of the heart'.[3]

---

[3] D.M. Thomas, *The White Hotel* (London: Penguin Books, 1981), p. 15.

Chapter 3

Getting at the truth: some issues of sources in the construction of an understanding of the Second World War and Occupation in France

Colin Nettelbeck

After more than sixty years of research and reflection, we now have a quite detailed understanding of how and why the French experience of the Second World War has been so difficult to come to terms with. But few, if any, would claim that the multiple traumas and complexities have been laid to rest. It is hard to imagine, for instance, the popular and commercial success of Irène Némirovsky's *Suite française*[1] or Jonathan Littell's *Les Bienveillantes*[2] without the background of a persisting general obsession with the period portrayed; or we might think of William Hitchcock's recent account[3] of the Allied Liberation of Europe from the perspective of the undertreated, but hugely significant, suffering and death of civilian populations; or again, we can cite Nadine Fresco's meditation on *La Mort des juifs*[4] as a sign of grief unassuaged and no doubt unassuageable. As researchers, we have a situation in which a large number of fields have been more or less delineated as quasi archeological sites: in some of them excavation is well advanced, in others much less so. Nothing is really finished: sifting continues and shards of information, testimony and understanding are painstakingly gathered and catalogued, in the hope that one day it will be possible to construct a scientifically sound and emotionally satisfying metanarrative that

[1] Paris: Gallimard, 2004.
[2] Paris: Gallimard, 2006.
[3] *Liberation: the Bitter Road to Freedom, Europe 1944–1945* (New York: Free Press, Simon and Schuster, 2008).
[4] Paris: Seuil, 2008.

makes all the interconnections. Despite scepticism about whether such a metanarrative could ever be definitive or singular, or whether it can transcend the relativities of its time and authorship, we are still driven to try.

This essay will make the case that such a metanarrative necessitates a variety of source materials of quite different orders: archival documents (including newspapers and newsreels), oral testimony, memorial accounts and fictional narratives (both literary and filmic). This approach is of course something of a trademark in the work of those French cultural historians who follow the mode of a Pascal Ory. It is not unproblematic, however, and the following discussion will seek to identify and confront some of the issues. The particular focus will be the uses of oral testimony on the one hand, and fictional cinema on the other. Both of the instances to be examined concern Vichy, and raise questions about the extent to which Vichy was a period of bracket and break, or a period of continuity. (Most would now agree that the continuity factors are significant, perhaps dominant, and the analysis will support this view.) The first example is a prominent and extreme political event, namely the assassination of Philippe Henriot, the Vichy Minister of Information and Propaganda; the second is a largely forgotten film, Richard Pottier's 1942 *Mademoiselle Swing*.

The 1980s and 1990s saw vigorous debate among French historians about the value of testimony in the construction of historical narratives. After Pierre Nora in *Les lieux de mémoire*,[5] Pierre Laborie took up the question in the specific context of the Resistance.[6] In 1998, Annette Wieviorka, in *L'Ere du témoin*,[7] focused on the Shoah, and the many thousands of testimonies gathered under the auspices of the 'devoir de mémoire'. She works very methodically and effectively through the different layers of the problem, from the question of reliability and the sheer impossibility of any single historian mastering the accumulated data, to the socio-political dilemmas arising from ambitions as vastly different as those of, say, the Yale University Fortunoff Video Archives for Holocaust Testimonies and of Spielberg's Visual History Archives.

---

[5] 'Entre Mémoire et Histoire: la problématique des lieux', in Pierre Nora (ed.), *Les Lieux de mémoire*, vol. 1, *La République* (Paris: Gallimard, 1997), pp. 25–43. The text dates from the original edition of 1984.

[6] Notably in P. Laborie and J.-M. Guillon (eds), *Mémoire et histoire: la Résistance* (Toulouse: Privat, 1995).

[7] Paris: Plon, 1998.

Wieviorka also maps the history of the process that has put individual testimony so much to the fore, beginning with the Eichmann trial of 1960. This movement gathered momentum with subsequent trials – those of Barbie, Touvier and Papon in particular – leading to a veritable historiographical crisis. Wieviorka quotes Frédéric Gaussen in *Le Monde* of 14 February 1982: 'L'idée s'est imposée que toutes les vies se valent et sont bonnes à raconter'. Her key point is that the recounting of individual stories may get in the way of, or even displace, archive-based historical accounts with etiological and general value. Nonetheless, like other historians, she appreciates the importance of oral testimony, and its impact as 'fire in the refrigerator of history',[8] as she puts it, citing Yale's Geoffrey Hartmann: 'C'est en quelque sorte une démocratisation des acteurs de l'histoire, qui veut qu'on donne désormais la parole aux exclus, aux sans-grade, aux sans-voix.'[9]

The idea of a 'democratization' of memory is brilliant and important: the concept of a 'devoir de mémoire' gives way to a kind of 'droit de mémoire' open to each and all. Wieviorka associates the trend with May '68 and its consequences, but it can be traced further back, to the aftermath of the First World War, with the emergence of such emblematic fictional figures as Céline's Bardamu or Renoir's Monsieur Lange, and the whole socio-political impetus leading up to the Popular Front. This perspective offers a further contextual explanation of why the French experience of the Second World War has been so hard to circumscribe: a dramatic intensification of the individual nature and perception of the experience generates an almost exponential pluralism that complicates enormously the historian's task. Democratization of memory can become a demagogic force.

It seems fair to say that testimony has ended up working its way into historical accounts, not as a replacement for archival documentary evidence, nor simply as a way of providing colour or warmth to the ice-tipped pen of the historian, but rather as an impulse to take at least some account of the democratization of experience that Wieviorka identifies. William Hitchcock, for instance, does not hesitate to call upon a Rotterdam tram conductor's diary to render the desperation of the starving Dutch in late 1944;[10] or to cite Duras's *La Douleur* when

---

[8] Wieviorka, *L'Ère du témoin*, p. 112.
[9] Wieviorka, *L'Ère du témoin*, p. 128.
[10] Hitchcock, *Liberation*, p. 114.

discussing the return to France of the concentration camp survivors.[11] We cannot but note, however, that the debate about testimony has focused essentially on those parts of the experience that concern heroes (the Resistance) or victims (starving Dutch civilians, Jews and other deportees). There is a certain amount of fictional work dealing with the experience of the other side – those we might call the 'perpetrators': one thinks of the last novels of Céline, for example, or works by Nimier or Laurent, and more recently of *Les Bienveillantes*, explicitly inspired by its author's desire to enter the mental world of an egregious perpetrator. But, as Claude Lanzmann pointed out in his critique of Littell, it is for obvious reasons no easy thing to get real perpetrators to talk: '[ils] n'ont pas de parole . . . Ils n'ont pas non plus de mémoire.'[12]

That, then, is the context for the first case study, which revolves around the assassination of Philippe Henriot on the morning of 28 June 1944. Why was Henriot executed when he was? The answer seems simple enough: very widely admired as a charismatic orator, he was fighting far too successfully in the 'war of the airwaves' launched at the time of his appointment in January, and carried out in his twice-daily radio broadcasts.[13] Along with Darnand and Déat, Henriot has proven to be one of the easier villains to classify in the story of Vichy France, one of those who constitute the hard core not just of collaborationism, but of ideologically committed French fascism. There is a famous photo of Henriot in the last phase of the Occupation.[14] It portrays him at the Gare de l'Est giving a smiling send-off to an LVF contingent heading for Russia. A litany of horribly eloquent slogans is chalked on the carriages of the train: 'A bas les Anglais', 'Mort aux Juifs', 'Mort aux Russes', 'Vive

---

[11] Hitchcock, *Liberation*, pp. 261–262.

[12] Marie-France Etchegoin, 'Lanzmann juge *Les Bienveillantes*', *Nouvel Observateur* (2006), 21 septembre; http://hebdo.nouvelobs.com/sommaire/dossier/067771/lanzmann-juge-les-bienveillantes.html (accessed 23 April 2010).

[13] Henriot's radio speeches, or 'editorials', as they were named, were published in brochure form for sale to the public. They were widely distributed, with print runs of 85,000, according to ministerial archives (Archives Nationales – henceforth AN – F41 290). Further evidence of Henriot's immense popularity can be adduced from a conversation reported to the present author by the philosopher and *académicien* Michel Serres with President François Mitterrand, when the two men agreed that Henriot was 'un des plus grands orateurs du 20e siècle'.

[14] It has been published, among other places, in Gilles Perrault's pictorial *Paris sous l'occupation* (Paris: Belfond, 1987), p. 171.

la Légion française', 'Vive Doriot', 'Vive Henriot', 'Heil Hitler', 'Vive la France'. This iconographic representation situates Henriot firmly in the gallery of the unredeemable.

Enter the witness. It was happenstance rather than deliberate research that led, in the mid-1990s, to a woman who shall be identified as Germaine X. She was within weeks of her death from cancer, but perfectly lucid. She had changed her public identity and her profession a half-century earlier, abandoning business personnel management for a completely new career as an art historian. For all but her closest friends, the part of her life that had historical significance was locked away, and understandably so, for she had been a significant, if minor, civil servant in the Vichy Ministry of Information and Propaganda, a person whose work and life had served ends repudiated by the whole post-war order.

It was apparent that in opening the hidden years of her life to historical inquiry, Germaine X was not motivated by regret, or any sense of youthful errors of judgement. Rather, she avowed herself frustrated by the seemingly irreducible gap between her experience and the ongoing series of historical reconstructions of the Vichy regime. Through her work as an art historian, she was conscious of the difficulty of retelling the past without falsifying it. However, as an eye-witness, she felt 'cheated' ('flouée') by accounts which shut out what she had subjectively experienced, or which, alternatively, gave credence to things that she believed not to be the case. In sum, if she finally spoke out about what she had kept so strictly private for fifty years, it was because she wanted there to be a chance, before she died, of getting her story into history.[15]

Any hint of self-justification from a former willing servant of the Vichy of the last days is bound to set alarm bells ringing in the mind of anyone familiar with the persistence and virulence of revisionist tendencies in post-war France. At the same time, no historian can afford to ignore material that may shed new light on a period that is notoriously full of shadows, and we shall see that Germaine X's testimony does indeed cast a certain amount of light.

Germaine X was recruited towards the beginning of the Occupation to manage the secretariat of the Paris branch of the Vichy Ministry of Propaganda, later the Ministry of Information and Propaganda. She had already established an impressive career in the private sector, and had

[15] The present author interviewed Germaine X in May 1997, and her secretary in February 1999.

been head of the administrative staff at Japy (best known for manu-
facturing typewriters, alarm clocks and household goods). It was in fact
through her general manager at Japy that she was given the Ministry
position. That manager was Pierre Pucheu. She was to remain close to
Pucheu until his ill-fated departure for Algeria in February 1943, while
she reported first to Paul Marion and then, after November 1943, to
Philippe Henriot.

According to her own account, her life was simple and routine. She
was well enough paid to be able to rent a comfortable apartment in the
fifteenth arrondissement; she bought decent clothing; she made the short
metro journey to work in the first-class carriages; her job allowed her to
eat lunch every day in one of the many restaurants between Solférino
and Saint-Germain-des-Prés; she found that, for a single woman, rations
were adequate, without having to stand in long queues, dine on rutabaga
or use the black market. Like many other Parisians, she went frequently
to the theatre and the cinema, adapting to the rules of curfew and not
feeling particularly threatened by the German patrols. She had no personal
relationship with any member of the occupying forces, but never saw a
German commit a reprehensible act. Her Paris was calm and quiet: she
kept to herself, enjoying her outings and the view over the pretty, well-
tended flowerbeds of the little square below her apartment window.

Her work, too, was straightforward. With no role in policy-making,
she kept the secretariat ticking over, protecting the Minister from
importunate visitors or receiving the numerous writers who came by
regularly – Brasillach, Drieu, Benoist-Méchin, Bardèche, Sacha Guitry,
Jacques Laurent-Cély. She was also charged with preparing the monthly
envelopes for those needy supporters whom the Minister favoured with
ex gratia payments from his secret funds.

When Philippe Henriot took up his position, Germaine X found herself more directly implicated in the Minister's private life. She liked him:
although she saw him as vain and gullible, she found him uncomplicated,
kind, generous, upright and sincere. His personal affairs were complicated
in that he was maintaining sentimental relationships over a distance with
both his wife and a much-cherished long-term mistress to whom he
wrote and spoke on the phone every day. Germaine X was thrust into
a kind of chief housekeeper role, and when Henriot was assassinated she
was called immediately by his wife to the scene, and then dispatched
to get the priest from the Invalides to bless the corpse. And it was to
Germaine X that Paul Marion gave the task of buying the wreath of red
roses that were 'his' contribution at the funeral.

It is disorienting to find, in the discourse of an aged and dying woman, this effort to reconstitute a veil, not perhaps of innocence, but of understandably human characteristics around a figure such as Henriot. She did not consider herself as a political person, although she readily acknowledged a leaning towards the Pétainist view that France was incapable of sustaining the fight and that an armistice was both unavoidable and legal – even a partial and largely ineffectual government being felt better than a 'gauleiter'. After the Liberation, she lost her job but was not otherwise punished. Obviously, this story had to be tested. This was done in two ways: one was through talks, after her death, with some of her close friends, who possessed a number of personal documents which they made available; the other was through the Archives nationales. Some interesting facts emerged, and a few discrepancies: for instance, Germaine X was not as far from power as she had suggested – she was the mistress of the director of Marion's cabinet, Maurice Touzé, and became herself the secretary of that cabinet;[16] and if she did not fear German patrols, it was because her position entitled her to a permanent pass. Generally, however, her story stands up well to scrutiny, and there are at least three ways in which it has a claim to historical interest. First, it offers a rare insider account of one of the Vichy regime's most notorious collaborationist figures,[17] as well as glimpses of others, such as Marion and Pucheu. Secondly, Germaine X's position in the bureaucracy invites further reflection on the relationship between structural and personal responsibilities within the authoritarian framework of Vichy, and her story provides significant insight into the detail of the post-Liberation purge of the civil service. Finally, her life as a successful professional woman during the Occupation requires some revisiting of the tension between Vichy's policies on women and the independence that some women, at least, were able to exert. For reasons of space, this chapter deals only with the last point.

As with many aspects of the period, the subject of the role of women under Vichy has suffered from historical stereotyping. The existence of repressive laws to push women out of the public service, or to make

---

[16] She was a 'Collaborateur Technique', promoted from third to second category on 1 May 1944, with a pay rise from 4000 to 5000 francs per month (AN F41 2674).

[17] The fact that she liked Henriot invites one to look for things that might make this plausible. In doing so, one discovers that, among other things, he looked after his staff very well: he was successful in securing a large pay rise for them and he deployed considerable stratagems to protect them from the STO (AN F41 3 and F41 4).

divorce and abortion more difficult, lend credence to the imagery of a reactionary and paternalistic state forcing women back into traditional roles, bound by motherhood and home duties. This is the picture painted, for example, by Francine Muel-Dreyfus.[18] Her central argument is that Vichy, reacting against the 1920s and 1930s advances of feminism and democracy, enacted laws to prevent dissent from the paradigmatic view of female 'destiny' being under the sign of submission and resignation; it resurrected the myth of the eternal feminine and, under the guise of a benign and banal projection of women as home-bodies, engaged in what was in fact legitimation of inequality, domination and exclusion.

It could be thought that the simple test of showing that the Muel-Dreyfus thesis does not, and cannot, account for the experience of Germaine X is inadequate: is not the case so exceptional as to be inapplicable to any more general understanding of the life of women under the Occupation? Dominique Veillon, in her study of women's daily life in the Vichy regime,[19] might think so. She evokes the existence of a 'privileged minority' who were able to continue life much as it was before the Occupation, but she believes that most women were adversely affected by the circumstances and by Vichy legislation. She does not tell us who the 'privileged minority' were, nor how numerous, nor whether their presence was sufficient to produce any change in our assessment of the bigger picture.

In this respect, the work of Hélène Eck[20] is more enlightening. Like the others, Eck castigates Vichy's repressive attitudes towards women, but she refines the account by showing that women had a significant presence in public life. Her research proves that, despite the Vichy laws, the number of women in the workforce was certainly maintained, and in fact probably increased, during the Occupation. Nor is this necessarily a paradox: the same regime that enacted laws preventing married women from working outside the home also set up (at the same time, in October 1940) the École nationale des cadres féminins at Écully, and by 1944 some 20,000 young women were

---

[18] *Vichy et l'éternel féminin* (Paris: Seuil, 1996).

[19] 'La Vie quotidienne des femmes', in Jean-Pierre Azéma and François Bédarida (eds); *Le Régime de Vichy et les Français* (Paris: Fayard, 1992), pp. 629–639.

[20] 'Les Françaises sous Vichy: femmes du désastre, citoyennes par le désastre', in Georges Duby and Michelle Perrot (eds), *Histoire des femmes en Occident*, 5, *Le XXè siècle* (Paris: Plon, 1992), pp. 185–211.

attending one or other of 345 professional training courses. Eck further reminds us that the Vichy government was planning to give women the vote.

Even more usefully, Eck contextualizes her analysis of Vichy in a wider temporal framework. If it is certain that Vichy made abortion and divorce more difficult, there was nothing new in the pressures for more women to embrace motherhood: France's demographic slide had made this a constant preoccupation of the inter-war period. As for the women of the bourgeoisie, Eck notes that from the time of the First World War, young women had to work and assume the responsibilities of a celibate life, even if marriage remained the ideal. And the 1930s saw the growth of an idea of womanhood that emphasized physical health, openness and independence. For Eck, if women did not come out of the war all that well, it was only in part due to Vichy-specific factors: women's contributions to the Resistance, for example, were marginalized as soon as the Resistance normalized its political structures, the male leadership being seemingly no more inclined towards real female emancipation than their Vichy predecessors.

Hélène Eck's framework, in demonstrating the gaps that often existed between the rhetoric of the National Revolution and what occurred in practice, points us towards a category of women who were not intellectual but enjoyed considerable autonomy; who lacked the high profile of actresses or society women but were trained and exercised significant responsibility; who certainly did not fit either the image of the worn-fingered, queue-haunting mother of six hungry children, nor that of the smiling, noble guardian of the happy hearth. Germaine X would seem to belong in such a grouping, part of the post-1919 society described by Eck, that brought its young women up to be independent and career-minded. It was that training that led Germaine X to her position at Japy before the war, and that allowed her to reorient her professional life so swiftly and so markedly afterwards.

The testimony of Germaine X does not elicit sympathy for her, or for Henriot and the regime he represented; it does refine our understanding, and it illustrates how much, despite the strength of the forces of reaction and repression, Vichy was the site of important socio-historical continuities. The same is true of our second case study, the film *Mademoiselle Swing*.

In the early 1980s, Marc Ferro lost his CNRS funding because the president of the contemporary history commission believed: 'Le cinéma, c'est pas sérieux!'[21] The intervening period has been marked by a wide, if gradual, acceptance of the use of cinematographic material in the construction of historical narratives, and even of cinema as a way of writing history. But the following analysis is more in the spirit of Ferro's exploration of the capacities of *fictional* cinema to transmit historically authentic reconstitutions of the past.[22] *Mademoiselle Swing* is not a historical reconstruction of life under Vichy, nor is it a cinematographic masterpiece like *L'Eternel retour* or *Le Corbeau*, but it is important – an excellent example of the tangled ambiguities of the cinema of the Occupation.[23]

For a long time there was a tendency, as with anything to do with Vichy, to place a bracket around the cinema of the period. The revision of this process of denial follows a chronology that parallels the political studies post-Paxton. In 1975, a collection of André Bazin's essays appeared under the title *Le Cinéma de l'occupation et de la résistance* (with a wittily irreverent preface by François Truffaut).[24] In 1981, Jacques Siclier published *La France de Pétain et son cinéma*[25] based on his own experience and on the thesis that cinematographic production of the Occupation years was a continuation of the 1930s – a point echoed by Jean-Pierre Jeancolas[26] and François Garçon.[27] By 1985, Evelyn Ehrlich could present a detailed study that showed not only the limitations of the resistance–collaboration paradigm, but that enough masterpieces had been created during this period for it to be seen as a point of new departure in the history of the French industry.[28] Alan Williams, in 1992, took Ehrlich's account a step further by bringing out links between films made under the Occupation and the post-war Tradition of Quality, thereby completing (once again in parallel to the political historiography) the process by

---

[21] Christian Delage and Vincent Guigueno, *L'Historien et le film* (Paris: Gallimard, 2004), p. 9.

[22] Marc Ferro, *Cinéma, une vision de l'histoire* (Paris: Le Chêne, 2003).

[23] I am grateful to Kate G. Seward for her assistance with the research associated with this part of the chapter, some of which was included in her unpublished *Zazou, Zazou Zazou-hé: a youth subculture in Vichy France, 1940–44*, Thesis (MA), University of Melbourne, School of Historical Studies, 2008.

[24] Paris: Union générale d'éditions, 1975.

[25] Paris: Henri Veyrier, 1981.

[26] *15 ans d'années trente: le cinema des Français, 1929–1944* (Paris: Stock, 1983).

[27] *De Blum à Pétain: cinéma et societé française 1936–1944* (Paris: Les Editions du Cerf, 1984).

[28] *Cinema of Paradox: French Filmmaking under the German Occupation* (New York: Columbia University Press, 1985).

which the Vichy period is seen as an integral part of France's cinema history and not apart from it.[29] In 1993, Colin Crisp, in his *The Classic French Cinema, 1930–1960*,[30] embedded the notion of continuity with an emphasis on Vichy's contribution to the ongoing institutional and economic organization of the cinema – a point brilliantly developed from archival sources in Laurent Creton's 2004 *Histoire économique du cinéma français: production et financement 1940–1959*.[31] Notwithstanding this evolution, broad agreement has remained about the detachment of the films from contemporary places and events. Julian Jackson, for example, observes that 'films of the occupation seem to exist in a time capsule . . . one could view most films without realising they were made while France was occupied'.[32] The cinema experience for the spectators of the time is thus seen as being essentially escapist.

Few cinema historians mention *Mademoiselle Swing*, and most who do only do so in passing.[33] Let us try to elucidate what they have over-looked. Shot in 1941,[34] the film was due for release in April 1942, but because of censorship problems it did not hit the screens until 10 June. It was a considerable success. We shall see shortly how right the censors were to be worried. But it is important to note at once the coincidence between the release date and that critical moment of Occupation history that saw the return of Pierre Laval as Head of Government and the subsequent ramping up of French collaborationism. Vichy-sponsored anti-Semitism was at its height, and Laval was about to declare his hope for a German victory. The Occupation was entering its darkest period. It was in particular a very difficult time for young people. In addition to suffering material deprivation and claustrophobic curfews, French youth, since the beginning of the Occupation, had been the subject of unremitting conflict between Vichy's attempts to herd them into a single youth movement (on the German and Italian models) and the Catholic Church's determination to maintain its own diversity of organized youth

---

[29] *Republic of Images: a History of French Filmmaking* (Cambridge, Mass.: Harvard University Press, 1992).

[30] Bloomington: Indiana University Press, 1993.

[31] Paris: CNRS Éditions, 2004.

[32] *France: the Dark Years, 1940–1944* (Oxford: Oxford University Press, 2001), p. 319.

[33] See, for instance, Noël Burch and Geneviève Sellier, *La Drôle de guerre des sexes du cinéma français (1930–1956)* (Paris: Nathan, 1996); Pierre Darmon, *Le Monde du cinéma sous l'occupation* (Paris: Editions Stock, 1997).

[34] Through a small production company, S.U.F. (Société Universelle de Films), which specialized in films about show-business.

movements. Both sides of this divide represented constraint and regi-
mentation that provoked increasing rebelliousness, manifest in sharply
rising rates of delinquency as well as in the peculiar phenomenon of the
Zazou subculture. At the time of the release of *Mademoiselle Swing*, media
and police attacks on the Zazous were at their most intense.

The action of *Mademoiselle Swing* begins in Angoulême, in the
palatial and architecturally modern home of a high-music composer,
Armand de Vincy. De Vincy looks upon his wife's and niece's love of
swing with good-humoured disparagement. The niece, Irène, dreams of
becoming a song and dance star. She is the Captain of the Angoulême
Swing Club, participating in a concert which includes a sweet-talking
singer and pianist, Pierre Dornier. In her attempt to smuggle her own
song composition, 'Quand viendra le jour', into Dornier's bag, Irène
becomes accidentally trapped on the train to Paris.

In the meantime, Dornier has found and adopted Irène's song, and
when she hears it on the radio, she seizes the initiative. That evening,
a mysterious figure bursts onto the dance floor. Irène, in a strapless
sequined black pant-suit and an eye-mask, styles herself 'Mademoiselle
Swing'. She is an instant celebrity, setting all Paris abuzz with rumour
and intrigue. The plot of the film twists more and more frenetically as
Irène plays out her different roles. Complications ensue in her relationship with her uncle, and especially in her romance with Dornier, but
everything is sorted out happily in the denouement: the family is united,
the young couple have declared their love and Irène has reached the
stardom to which she aspired.

The patent imitation of the Fred Astaire and Ginger Rogers romantic
Hollywood musical genre has led most commentators to dismiss the film
as a vapid entertainment.[35] Arguably, it is more subversive. If Irène's
'Quand viendra le jour' seems a fairly conventional and unthreatening
song about love and hope for a bright future, it could also be read as
something else. But the song 'Mademoiselle Swing' that she performs
with Dornier at the end of the film was what made the censors hesitate.
Its final verse was particularly pointed: 'Il faut braver le destin/En chant-
ant avec entrain/Ce refrain de demain/Le swing, le swing.' More telling
than these lyrics, moreover, is the fact that Irène's uncle, the distinguished
establishment composer and music publisher, finishes up classifying swing

---

[35] See, for instance, Darmon, *Le Monde du cinéma sous l'occupation*, p. 179. Darmon
echoes Jacques Siclier's earlier comments in *La France de Pétain*, p. 172.

music on the same level as his own, giving a stern lesson to the old guard surrounding him (whose likeness to Pétain and his world could hardly have been missed by contemporary audiences).

Towards the beginning of the film, there is a direct satire of the National Revolution's doctrine of return to the land. In the dance club at Angoulême, we are introduced to Irène in a quite hilarious mockery of the backward and narrow-minded mentality of French provincial life, with folksy caricatures of the dance and music cultures of Auvergne, Brittany, Berry and Poitou. The ghastly presentation is saved only when the folk music is turned into swing. The choice of Angoulême may not be by chance, either. Although it was in the Occupied zone, it was only just so, in an ambiguous space between Occupation and the greater autonomy of the Free zone. When the Occupation occurred, the Mayor and Church authorities issued an appeal typical of Pétainist resignation:

> Continuez vos occupations et vos travaux dans le calme, dans l'ordre. Observez scrupuleusement les mesures qui seront prises dans votre intérêt. Nous sommes convaincus de votre adhésion car nous savons que, tous, vous avez compris que notre affliction sera respectée si la paix intérieure est maintenue, si chacun reste calme, digne, confiant dans les Destins de la Patrie.[36]

Nothing could be further from this ethos of oppression, misery, stasis and affliction than the climate evoked by Irène, which is all about freedom, mobility and the future.

As a piece of cinema, too, *Mademoiselle Swing* asserts freedom and the individual values of contemporary art, as distinct from the stereotypical reactionism and authoritarianism associated with Vichy. This is illustrated through Irène's itinerary, through the Picasso-like painting of the family friend who gives her refuge in Paris, and through the architecture and décor of the de Vincy apartment. The dancing motif evokes a concept of turning limitation into the expression of virtuosity and liberation. The film is informed by a distinctly modernist aesthetic, emphasizing openness to the future and development, and the transformative power of the imagination: there is a stunning, almost surreal shot of a water droplet on the string of a violin, and a fantasy sequence in which an animated fairy sings and dances on the snow.

---

[36] Text available at: http://musee.delaresistance.free.fr/apropos/collections/documents/appel.jpg (accessed 24 April 2010).

All in all, the reading that imposes itself compellingly is that of a deliberate challenge to the social and artistic ideals of the Vichy regime, using lightness and romantic and comic stereotypes to deliver a message, if not of resistance, at least of rebelliousness, one that in the face of heavy resignation and intimations of national guilt extols youth and the vitality of popular culture. Significantly, Audiberti, writing in *Comoedia* at the time of the film's release, expressed surprise that a film extolling youth culture could be screening at a time when the Zazous were under especially targeted attack. In doing so, he acknowledged the unique role of the cinema in providing not escape but a means of expressing ideas and desires otherwise forbidden: 'Où le français ne va pas le gascon y aille, disait cet invraisemblable raseur appelé Montaigne. Le cinéma, lui-même, se permet des fantaisies où reculerait ce qui n'est pas lui. Sortir une brillante et retentissante "Mademoiselle Swing" au moment même où le swing est mal vu, seul le cinéma peut se le permettre.'[37]

In harmonizing high and popular culture, and emphasizing the attraction of a future built on the resilience and intrepidity of youth, the film challenges any notion of Vichy as a monolithic closed space in French cultural history. It also offers an example of continuities in the wider French cinema world. Two of its main actors, Saturnin Fabre and Jean Murat, had unbroken careers into the 1950s and 1960s respectively. As for the director, Richard Pottier, from the time of his arrival in France from Hungary in 1934 until his retirement in the mid-1960s, his prolific rhythm never faltered. His output of seven films during the Occupation was equalled by only one other director (Jean Boyer), and after the war he maintained his momentum at the rate of a film a year.

These examples of personal testimony and fictional film show how such sources can provide more nuanced understanding of the Occupation period. Notwithstanding the difficulties of interpretation that they present, the story of Germaine X and *Mademoiselle Swing* are more than splashes of colour or injections of human warmth for our attempts to compose an overview of the period. They are not a substitute for written archival documents. Indeed, cross-referencing with the relevant archives must remain a key condition of their validation and use, in order to protect the integrity of the historical enterprise. But, as we have seen, these sources can actually open our eyes to different ways of approaching the archives. Precisely because of their individual and subjective dimensions,

---

[37] Audiberti, 'Chronique des films', *Comoedia*, 27 juin 1942, p. 5.

they allow us to keep in mind not just that the collective aspects of the war and Occupation affected all sorts of individual lives, but that the construction of any metanarrative of the experience must take into account the broad process of democratization informing French culture over the course of the twentieth century. Only an inclusive approach to sources – audio-visual as well as written, fictional as well as factual, high culture as well as popular culture, religious as well as secular – combined with a rigorous use of archival materials, will satisfy our double need for scientific exactitude and affective understanding.

Chapter 4

La Main à plume: poetry under the Occupation

Nathalie Aubert

In historical terms, choice, or the ability or even the *obligation* to take sides, has been one of the characteristic features of French intellectual life since the time of the Dreyfus Affair, and it became more pronounced during the Second World War. It affected writers of all political persuasions. Montherlant, for instance, complained about the pressures that this state of affairs was bringing to bear on writers: 'Un peintre, un sculpteur, un compositeur de musique n'est pas tenu de *dire un mot*, à tout bout de champ, sur tout et sur rien . . . Mais un écrivain, oui bien. S'il y rechigne, il sera réputé manquer à son devoir.'[1]

The members of *La Main à plume*, a group of young surrealists who found in modern ideologies (communism, in their case) 'de quoi alimenter sa propension à la radicalisation politique',[2] were especially aware of how politics overdetermined all their activities at this time. Even so, the poets who became involved in the Resistance did not actually have to change the way they published their work to any great extent, given that they were used to small print-runs and little magazines, and this was particularly obvious in the case of this group, who published their work clandestinely. They were in fact 'prédisposés par leur pratique à la clandestinité et au secret'.[3] Although there are other variables pertaining to age, position within the literary field (genre, place of publication) and the adoption of an aesthetic or political stance, this is perhaps why, as Gisèle Sapiro has pointed out,[4] two thirds of all poets were involved in the Resistance, while two thirds of all novelists and half of all dramatists collaborated.

---

[1] Cited in Sapiro, *La Guerre des écrivains*, p. 70.
[2] Sapiro, *La Guerre des écrivains* 1940–1953 (Paris: Fayard, 1999), p. 80.
[3] Sapiro, *La Guerre des écrivains*, p. 90.
[4] Sapiro, *La Guerre des écrivains*, p. 90.

Whatever the truth of that claim, the fact is that these young poets, who were all almost unknown at the time, founded *La Main à plume* in response to the German invasion.[5]

The group originally consisted of former members of the 'Réverbères' group, which was established in 1938 in a milieu of painters and jazz lovers who shared a post-Dada taste for the ludic and a conviction that 'la poésie est partout'.[6] The declaration of war, mobilization, and then the debacle and the German invasion convinced some of its members (the youngest) that Dada activity was completely incompatible with the political situation and the reality of the Nazi Occupation. They included Jean-François Chabrun who, like Gérard de Sède, Jean-Claude Diamant Berger, Francis Crémieux and Noël Arnaud, was a *lycéen* in the French capital when Réverbères was established. It was Chabrun who felt the need to radicalize its position when the Munich Agreements were signed. 1938 was, of course, the year in which Breton and Trotsky wrote *Pour un art révolutionnaire indépendant*, which led to the founding of the FIARI (Fédération internationale de l'art révolutionnaire indépendant), and some members of the Réverbères group had begun to move closer to the surrealists, especially Péret, and Breton.

Establishing *La Main à plume* was thus a way of pursuing a surrealist activity *and* supporting a minimal political platform based upon anti-fascism and dialectical materialism. As one of its members, Jean Simonpoli, stated in 1943, it was important for them to distance themselves 'aussi loin de Péguy et d'Aragon [que de] Drieu la Rochelle'.[7] The first issue, which was entitled *La Main à plume*[8] and which

---

[5] Gérard de Sède found the group's name in Rimbaud's 'Mauvais Sang' (which is part of *Une Saison en enfer*): 'J'ai horreur de tous les métiers. Maîtres et ouvriers, tous paysans ignobles. La main à plume vaut la main à charrue. Quel siècle à mains! . . . moi, je suis intact, et ça m'est égal.' See M. Fauré, *Histoire du surréalisme sous l'occupation* (Paris: La Table ronde, 1982), p. 65.

[6] Fauré, *Histoire du surréalisme*, p. 24.

[7] This implied a refusal to join the PCF and to collaborate with the Occupation forces. Jean Simonpoli, 'A nos lecteurs', in *Le Surréalisme encore et toujours (1943)*, *La Main à plume. Anthologie du surréalisme sous l'occupation* (Paris: Syllepse, 2008), p. 179 (further references are given in text as MPA).

[8] In order to outwit the censors, who would not have allowed a magazine to be founded, each number had a different title: *Géographie nocturne* (September 1941), *Transfusion du verbe* (December 1941), *La Conquête du monde par l'image* (June 1942), *Le Surréalisme encore et toujours* (August 1943), *Quatre-vingt et un, Décentralisation surréaliste* (June–October 1943), *Informations surréalistes* (May 1944) and *L'Objet* (May 1944).

represented the de facto founding of the group in May 1941,[9] clearly
defined them as direct heirs to Breton, but also as poets writing in
occupied France:

> Nous nous refuserons toujours à fuir la poésie pour la réalité, mais nous
> nous refuserons toujours aussi à fuir la réalité pour la poésie
>
> . . .
>
> *Nous restons.*
>
> Et c'est-à-dire par là que nous ne renonçons ni à avancer dans le temps,
> ni à l'avancer. (MPA, p. 29)

Quite apart from the courage displayed in these lines (the insistence
on 'rester' and on producing poetry that was free without being detached
from reality), the final sentence is important as it reproduces the slogan
issued by Breton who, writing to Raoul Ubac in 1940, refused to allow
surrealism to 'survivre'.[10] At this time, a declaration of loyalty to surrealism meant inscribing oneself within a history; it was a way of declaring
one's opposition to the sickening climate of the times. And given the
circumstances, that was in itself an act of resistance. How, in these
conditions, was it possible to create the demanding poetry expected of
self-declared supporters of surrealism?

The first answer was by sticking to the principles of surrealism, as
defined in the strictest of senses: 'nous nous refuserons toujours à fuir
la poésie pour la réalité, mais nous nous refuserons toujours aussi à fuir
la réalité pour la poésie'. Poetry could, in other words, still be anything
but literature or a mere intellectual activity. Poetry was an objectification
of desire and must lead 'du connu à l'inconnu'.[11] The first issue therefore
offered a series of articles, poems and illustrations outlining a surrealist
position and a surrealist aesthetics. They were not signed, as the group
wished to make a collective statement. A few months later,[12] Jean-François

---

[9] Participants included Adolphe Acker, Christine Boumeester, Jean-François Chabrun,
Achille Chavée, Christian Dotrement, Emile Guikovaty, J.-C. Manuel, Marcel Mariën, Marc
Patin, Régine Raufast, Robert Rius, Hans Schoenhoff, Gérard Schneider, Ita (Edita Hirshowa)
and Gérard Vulliamy (Eluard's son-in-law).

[10] 'Se survivre . . . ce serait là l'illusion périlleuse entre toutes', letter to Ubac, cited in
Cinquante ans d'avant-garde 1917–1967, p. 134.

[11] Georges Bataille, 'Réponse à l'enquête sur la poésie lancée par *La Main à plume*'
(September 1942). See Fauré, *Histoire du surréalisme*, p. 120.

[12] In September 1941.

Chabrun recalled in 'Géographie nocturne' how important dreams and 'night' were to surrealist aesthetics. The entire text is constructed around a rejection of the Enlightenment rationalism against which Romanticism had already rebelled, but the article's author criticizes Romanticism for having symbolically associated night with death, whereas night was, for the surrealists, a 'concentration du désir' (MPA, p. 42). He also stresses the fact that the surrealists were looking towards a future that had yet to be built:

> [Le romantisme] n'a pas compris ce que nous qui sortons d'une Aufklärung, l'Aufklärung réaliste, sommes maintenant susceptibles de comprendre, à savoir que pour transformer la réalité il ne suffit pas de lui opposer une réalité anarchique mais de construire contre elle et grâce à elle, une sur-réalité qui sera la réalité de demain. (p. 42)

It was obvious to Chabrun and the group's members that constructing this 'réalité de demain' was their *responsibility*: 'Nous avons remarqué au cours de cette introduction que si la nuit nous contraignait à abandonner le sentiment de notre responsabilité, celle-ci n'en était pas moins engagée, que nous le voulions on non' (MPA, p. 43).

It seems to me highly significant that Chabrun should choose the word *responsabilité* (and the adjective *engagée*), as it demonstrates that the notions that Sartre was to theorize immediately after the war were already of interest to certain writers at the very beginning of the war. It was in fact difficult to sing the praises of a metaphorical 'night' when the daily lives of most people were dominated by a very real 'night', when democracy was a thing of the past and when the German Occupation was a palpable reality. In its early stages there had, in Breton's view, been an ethical dimension to surrealism, even though it was grounded in democratic society, which was of course the very society it was rebelling against; the death of democracy displaced the immediacy of these ethical and aesthetic issues, in favour of the political demands for effective action, to which they could not remain insensitive.

'Mais la guerre vint'

Transfusion du verbe is in that sense exemplary. The text begins by once more evoking the 'sujet rêvant' (MPA, p. 51), which is the anchoring point for surrealism's 'merveilleux', but it also attempts to establish a link between the 'merveilleux' and action by endorsing Breton's attacks on the novel and realism. Current events proved Breton right in that so many novelists had become collaborators: Drieu la Rochelle, for example, had for a very long time been a personal friend of Aragon's, but had become editorial director of the *NRF* under the Occupation. Chabrun therefore had good reason to write:

> Un peu de talent et beaucoup de concessions font l'affaire. C'est de cette étoffe dont on fait des hommes de paille des apparences que sont les hommes de lettres, et, plus que tous les autres, à quelque espèce qu'ils appartiennent, les romanciers. (MPA, p. 53)

His entire argument is articulated around the notion of choice: *either* poetry serves to 'charmer les *récréations* que nous laisse une vie en tout point absorbantes' *or* 'la poésie représente un besoin d'agir sur la réalité' (MPA, p. 54), which implies that 'équation poétique ne se pose vraiment [pour eux] que si les données sont à la fois d'ordre esthétique et d'ordre éthique' (MPA, p. 54). In the first part of the text, the question of choice is located within the sphere of 'ethics', but it is quickly displaced on to the political level by the irruption of history. And the text in fact reproduces that irruption by interpolating the phrase 'mais la guerre vint', which marks the transition to an autobiographical narrative. In the second part of the text, Chabrun describes how everyone became scattered after the mobilization of 1940 and admits that he was 'isolated'. The transition towards the biographical, which serves to discredit the fictional aspect of the novel, is also designed to demonstrate that subjectivity has nothing to do with the 'pratiques solitaires de l'individualisme' (MPA, p. 57). On the contrary, Chabrun sees the collective practice of art as one of the new possible ways of escaping despondency. The members of *La Main à plume* found in the 'Usine à poèmes'[13] an original solution, a way of 'faire commun' that had nothing to do with committed poetry of any kind. Adopting Lautrémont as a tutelary figure, they contended that 'la poésie personnelle a fait son temps de jongleries relatives et de contorsions contingentes. Reprenons le fil indestructible de la poésie impersonnelle',[14] and the poems produced by the 'Usine à poèmes' are spontaneous works in the pre-war surrealist tradition. One detects no or few references to the historical situation, but the influence of love poetry is everywhere:

---

[13] A writing technique introduced in 'Géographie nocturne' and used until 'La Conquête du monde par l'image'. Neither the texts nor the drawings were signed.
[14] *Poésies I, Œuvres completes* (Paris: Gallimard, Edition de la Pléiade, 1970), p. 268.

Fillette aux sens d'hermine
un galop de fourmis m'émerveille.
Un œuf s'ouvre doucement
sous les doigts bagués de noir d'une vierge
belle comme le mot savane
comme un sauvage frais
comme l'eau bleue d'une bouche

Des icebergs de velours gris
glissent entre deux rangs de miroirs charnels
qui se battent dans une hutte de chaume rouge
(MPA, p. 68)

This poem, which is entitled *Le Matin*, is one of a series of seven. They are all short, and the titles and subject matter vary considerably (*Eau morte, Notre femme, Musique, Automne, Faible*). As in most of the output of this group of young poets, the intertext relates to a corpus of images and themes found throughout the work of the fathers of the surrealist movement (and especially Breton). The 'galop de fourmis' recalls Luis Buñuel's *Un Chien andalou* while the 'l'oeuf [qui] s'ouvre doucement' evokes the image of the eye in the same film. The 'doigts bagués' and the hint of 'velours gris' evoke both the defiant gesture of Dora Maar who, when Picasso saw her for the first time, was sitting alone at a table in Les Deux Magots and passing the time by stabbing a knife into the table between the splayed fingers of her gloved hand, and Breton's description of one of Nadja's drawings in the eponymous novel. The poems are therefore a further attempt to demonstrate that it is forms rather than ideas that make art subversive, and to that extent they are true to Breton who, on the eve of war, clearly declared his support for 'un art révolutionnaire indépendant' that saw the political system and intellectual creativity as two different realms:

L'art véritable, c'est-à-dire celui qui ne se contente pas de variations sur des modèles tout faits, mais s'efforce de donner une expression aux besoins intérieurs de l'homme et de l'humanité d'aujourd'hui. Ne peut pas ne pas être révolutionnaire, c'est-à-dire ne pas aspirer à une reconstruction complète et radicale de la société . . .

Si, pour le développement des forces productives matérielles, la révolution est tenue d'ériger un système socialiste de plan centralisé, pour la création intellectuelle elle doit dès le début même établir et assurer un régime *anarchiste de liberté individuelle*.[15]

---

[15] André Breton and Léon Trotsky, *Pour un art révolutionnaire indépendant*, 25 July 1938, http://www.marxists.org/francais/trotsky/oeuvres/ (accessed April 2010).

The theory that individual freedom can be based upon the 'anarchist' practice of systematically seeking and discovering 'the new' is obviously incompatible with what political commitment is usually understood to mean. But as early as September 1941, Chabrun gave this 'régime anarchiste de liberté individuelle' a slightly different meaning in 'Géographie nocturne': under the Occupation, freedom is something that has to be *won*: 'Pour transformer la réalité il ne suffit pas de lui opposer une réalité anarchique mais de construire contre elle et grâce à elle, une sur-réalité qui sera la réalité de demain' (MPA, p. 42). All the texts in the various issues published by the group were to concentrate more and more on realizing this ambition.

La Conquête du monde par l'image

A major change of direction that affected the whole movement can be observed in the issue entitled *La Conquête du monde par l'image* (1942), which inaugurated a debate about the very basis of surrealist aesthetics, namely the image. The war and increasingly difficult living conditions meant that 1942 was a transitional year for the group, not least because the German noose was tightening. Ever since it had been founded, the magazine had succeeded in outwitting the censor but the decree of 27 April 1942 introduced a new constraint: publishers had to officially apply for the coupons that allowed them to obtain paper. This was a thinly disguised form of censorship. At the time some of the group's members had either been arrested (the painter Tita, a Jewish artist of Czech origin, had been denounced and deported to the camps), had been forced to flee to the Free Zone (Chabrun) or were being held prisoner in Germany (Léo Malet). It was therefore not in its interests to draw attention to its publications, which were full of references not only to Breton but also to Marx and Lenin who, even though they were not mentioned by name, were readily identified by the quotations drawn from their works.

It was under these conditions that, in the spring of 1942, the members of *La Main à plume* came up with the idea of devoting a whole issue to the surrealist image. And yet, as we shall see, the issue actually focused on the question of commitment. Paul Eluard's contribution, which was entitled 'Poésie involontaire et poésie intentionnelle', should be seen in this context. The poet declares that 'nous sommes des êtres moraux et nous nous situons dans la foule'.[16] He makes it clear that, for him,

---

[16] Cited in, Fauré, *Histoire du surréalisme*, p. 125.

commitment was the order of the day. It should also be emphasized that this was also the year in which *La Main à plume* published *Poésie et vérité* and the poem 'Liberté'. The question of 'committed' poetry therefore takes an unexpected turn and, perhaps less predictably, the surrealist image is modified accordingly. The liberation referred to in 'Liberté' is purely *literal*. Now that it is confronted with the new temporality of the 'moment' and the need for action, the surrealist image is no longer the image of the blinding quality of the instant that had from the very beginning been one of surrealism's anchoring points: the ever deeper investigation into what creates the link between the physical world and the way it is represented in the immediacy that surrealism wanted so much. What is being disputed in this issue is the notion that, while the surrealist image must try to establish relations that have a certain depth (given that it is bound up with the unconscious), it must do so 'à la manière d'un excitant' and not 'd'un stupéfiant'. Jean-François Chabrun's text 'Image-Image' rejects that notion without further ado: 'Nous ne croyons pas en effet, suivant les termes du premier Manifeste surréaliste de Breton, encore teinté d'idéalisme, que la poésie, donc l'image poétique doive agir à la manière d'un stupéfiant, mais tout au contraire, à la manière d'un excitant' (MPA, p. 89).

This was a decisive turning point: Breton accepts that his definition of the image is contradictory in that it is described both as a pure revelation that is *passively* received and as an investigative *technique*. Here, there is no longer any question of 'passivity': the image is now something to be *conquered* and the poet has the ability to grasp the moment, orientated by the force of circumstances and by the way society is evolving. While no concessions can be made to reality, it is essential to join in the struggle. The word 'liberté' therefore appears more and more frequently in the poems written by the group's members, especially after the turning point of Eluard's poem. In a poem dedicated to Noël Arnaud, André Stil quietly questions the power of the poetic word:

> L'Encre pâlit les plumes tombent à l'automne du vol
> les murs sont hauts Qui comprendra le reste.
> (MPA, p. 186)

It is true that surrealist poetry is not easily accessible and always has to be decoded by a reader who has to play an active role. As Eluard understood very clearly, it was therefore open to challenge at a time when the important thing was to keep hope alive. It is therefore no accident that the final word of Stil's poem should be 'liberté'.

Ever since the 1920s, the links between surrealism and political activity had been seen as a way of avoiding the divorce between art and life, as a way of filling the gap between the a priori world of the mind and the material world of factuality, and it was because they were close to Breton that the *Main à plume* group thought that they should forge ties with the PCF. And yet it is important to understand the pressure they were under, now that they had resolved to stay and *precisely* because they saw surrealism not as one more artistic movement, but as a way of influencing life, it was becoming more and more difficult for these young poets and artists to remain outside the field of action as the war went on. While writing committed poetry was out of the question, the conflict was a forceful demonstration that words had no power. After the collapse of the German–Soviet pact, some members of the group saw the PCF as the only viable alternative to doing nothing, as they wanted not only to join the Resistance but to take to the *maquis* and fight.

And it was indeed the question of politics that decided the group's fate. In 1943, all of them, including the Trotskyists, had become convinced that joining the PCF was the most effective form of action. Some, however, wished to retain a certain degree of independence and it was the dispute between them and the supporters of unconditional loyalty to groups under the control of the PCF that caused the group to break up in the spring of 1944.[17] *La Main à plume* paid a heavy price for its members' theoretical and political commitment during the Occupation: eight of its twenty long-term members did not live to see the end of the war.[18] Quite apart from the human cost (which in itself says a lot about the risks these young people were running and about their total commitment to the anti-fascist struggle), it is to *La Main à plume*'s credit that it raised high the banner of poetry. And theirs was a demanding poetry that remained free of any subservience to any political system.

---

[17] Picasso, who was one of those who remained in Paris during the war, and had been one of the group's main financial backers, was expelled when he joined the PCF in 1944.

[18] Diamant-Berger, who was one of the founders of *La Main à plume*, escaped to London and joined the FFI. He was killed in action near Caen on 18 July 1944; the fifteen-year-old Jean-Pierre Mulotte was shot on the pont d'Austerlitz (he had just killed a German soldier in the street); Jean Simonpoli (a member of the PCF), Rius (former secretary to Aragon) and the eighteen-year-old Marco Ménegoz were shot near Arbonne (Seine-et-Marne); all three had joined a *maquis* operating in Fontainebleau Forest; Tita, who was denounced and deported, vanished into the camps; Marc Patin died of pneumonia in Berlin; Hans Schoenhoff was deported in 1942. See MPA, p. 295.

Chapter 5

A reading of Genet's adaptations from the Russian novel in his Occupation narratives

Thomas Newman

Recent critics have sought to look at source material for Genet's Occupation narrative, *Pompes funèbres*, and have done so by privileging historical sources. We will look at the way certain critics' claims to illuminate enigmatic texts using the cold objective light of historical context can fall short of convincing criticism, especially when there are key literary sources to be explored. We begin with a discussion of the influences Genet has drawn from the Russian novel, especially those of Dostoevsky and Tolstoy, and move from there to historical sources and comparisons, with a view to illuminating the discursive complexity of Genet's writing.

We first turn to an episode from *Pompes funèbres* based on the Santé Prison Rebellion of 14 July 1944. A riot broke out which the *Milice* put down. In the novel, a boy-thief, Pierrot, must denounce the ringleaders to save himself, but he instead falsely denounces prisoners of his own age whom he simply dislikes. Twenty-eight prisoners are shot by firing squad. Genet compares Pierrot's role in the prison to the role of the *Milice* in France generally.[1] That is to say, a thug on a prison wing is compared to the criminality of the *Milice* holding sway over an occupied nation. The supervising captain of the militia cannot repress a certain grudging affection for the boy when he understands what he is doing: 'Quelle petite salope que ce môme!'[2]

---

[1] *Pompes funèbres* in *Jean Genet: Œuvres complètes*, Vol. 3, A. Dichy (ed.) (Paris: Gallimard, 1953), pp. 145–148.

[2] *Pompes funèbres*, p. 146.

Harry E. Stewart, in *Jean Genet: from Fascism to Nihilism*, in examining the episode, never seems to recover from his discovery of its basis in historical reality: the number executed in the novel is the same in fact.[3] Although he is careful to note that Genet, having been released a few months earlier, could not have been a first-hand witness, the fact that he did not undergo the ordeal of the events assumes for Stewart the proportions of the worst kind of guilt. He speculates that Genet's information was obtained directly from the militia, perhaps from its leaders or from Vichy police officials: 'perhaps Toesca, Dubois or Buissière himself.'[4] While the truth of the situation cannot be known, if it were true, the terrible irony of its retelling by Genet would be all the more far-reaching, as, by December 1943, due to his latest act of book theft and a new law introduced to combat recidivism and vagrancy, the narrator himself was at mortal risk of being deported to a concentration camp.[5]

We take another example from Eric Marty's 2006 book, *Jean Genet: Post-scriptum*, in which he discusses Genet's betrayal of the memory of Jean Decarnin, who is the subject of *Pompes funèbres*. The conceit at the centre of the controversy, which Marty traces, not unreasonably, back to Genet, is that he was excused on the grounds that he had confessed to a crime committed by the *résistant* Decarnin in order that the war hero's name 'ne reçoive aucune tache'.[6] Marty contends that Genet used Decarnin's memory to his own advantage with the probable foreknowledge and cognizance of Sartre and Cocteau, who drafted a letter appealing against his tenth strike and sentence to life imprisonment. Marty goes on to argue that if Genet does not respect Decarnin's memory in the non-fictional world, then *Pompes funèbres* is just a fantasized confession of his true sympathies and erotic attraction to the Gestapo and the *Milice*, or, as Stewart puts it, 'men made to Genet's order'.[7] He does not accept the complication of viewpoint between occupier and occupied dramatized through a dead Resistance fighter and a moribund occupying force.

---

[3] London: Peter Lang, 1994, p. 78; referring to the passage in *Pompes funèbres*, pp. 136–147.

[4] Stewart, *Fascism to Nihilism*, p. 78, referring to *Pompes funèbres*, pp. 136–147.

[5] See J. Genet, *Lettres à Olga et Marc Barbezat* (Paris: L'Arbalète, 1988), pp. 22–23 and E. White, *Jean Genet*, trans. P. Delamare (Paris: Gallimard, 1993), p. 247.

[6] *Jean Genet, post-scriptum* (Paris: Verdier, 2006), pp. 114–115.

[7] Stewart, *Fascism to Nihilism*, p. 78.

It would however be reductive to claim that such pragmatic hypocrisy on Genet's part would be equivalent to that of the book as a whole, with Genet merely changing his stripes with the change in political fortune at the Liberation. Instead, it is in order to escape the, much discussed, work of mourning Decarnin, that Genet, through use of inversion, glorifies the *Milice*. We bear in mind that Genet's understanding of such inversions earned him an advisory role on the Louis Malle film *Lacombe Lucien*.[8]

Critics have consistently run the risk of attributing directly to Genet positions that he is, instead, exposing and re-inflecting through the processes of his stylization. The examinations of Nazism we find especially in *Pompes funèbres* (1948) and *Un captif amoureux* (1986) are so disturbing as to make it understandable that a critic might lose heart and write off the whole œuvre as being the product of moral turpitude. We remember that, as early as *Saint Genet* (1952), Sartre pointed out that Genet's writing sought to expose 'la mauvaise conscience secrète de la bonne conscience', and to test the ethical consistency of the reader.[9] Genet's interest in betrayal can thus be understood largely as an exercise in style – betraying lack of rigour in his reader, placing unsuspected responsibilities along their path, as well as forming his subject matter.

The Russian novels we will look at allow us to examine such instances of betrayal and to deterritorialize different notions of occupation: looking at Germany occupying France, and France occupying both Russia (1812) and Jaffa (1799) during Napoleon's Egyptian campaign. The figure of Napoleon is important as both a historical and psychological metonym. W.G. Sebald, in an interview published ten days after his death, dates the genocidal potential of Europe as originating 'with Napoleon at the latest'; a possibility that may be discerned in Napoleon's colonial and technological dream of 'turning this very disorderly continent of Europe into something much more orderly, rule-governed, thoroughly organized, powerful'.[10] Dostoevsky and Tolstoy in these respects each had premonitions concerning Napoleon and his impact upon the European psyche.

---

[8] P. Billard, *Louis Malle: Le rebelle solitaire* (Paris: Plon, 2003), pp. 337–338.

[9] J.-P. Sartre, *Saint Genet* (Paris: Gallimard, 1952), p. 610.

[10] Quoted by R. Sheppard in 'Dexter – Sinister: some Observations on Decrypting the Morse Code in the Work of W.G. Sebald', *Journal of European Studies*, 35 (2005), 422.

In Dostoevsky's *Crime and Punishment*, Raskalnikov wants to commit murder and arrives at the hypothesis that if the good of mankind depended on one murder (in this case that of a miser), then that murder would not only be permissible but a duty. As we know, Raskalnikov is later paralysed by guilt. He confides to Sonia Marmelodova the reason his plot became an obsession: 'I knew perfectly well I was not a Napoleon . . . I wanted to murder, . . . for my own satisfaction, *for myself alone*.'[11] Although some of Genet's characters are persecuted by their consciences (e.g. Ange Soleil and Yeux Verts), Genet's narrative voice exercises a kind of infallibility, whereby the generalized destructiveness of crime is taken for gratifying outcome in a logic of *qui perd gagne*. Sartre explains it thus: 'Si le criminel . . . a la tête solide, il voudra jusqu'au bout demeurer méchant. Cela veut dire qu'il bâtira un système pour justifier la violence: seulement du coup celle-ci perdra sa souveraineté.'[12] Bataille, who agrees with this part of the argument, names this loss of sovereignty in Genet 'souveraineté dérisoire'.[13] This motif of self-defeating sovereignty, and of betrayal, stretches deep into Genet's writing which he uses, superficially at least, as a way of avenging himself for his position as an outcast: abandoned child, kleptomaniac and homosexual. Since there is no real question of Genet thinking that he is Napoleon who could take the world by storm, he instead proceeds covertly. Stating his hatred of France arising from his humiliation as an *enfant de l'assistance publique* in Morvan, he discreetly correlates his references to *The Brothers Karamazov*, a novel about the Karamazov family centred around the murder of the father, with his own life.

Genet, who was usually so dismissive of attempts to find his sources, instead cultivating the mystique of someone who came into the world poetically fully armed, is kind enough to leave us a text dating from 1981, set aside for publication at the same time as *Un captif amoureux*, 'Les Frères Karamazov'.[14] He points out that the brothers are four in number, including Smerdyakov, the illegitimate son who serves the father as a lackey. The potential for betrayal in Smerdyakov's criminality finds echoes in Genet. In the interview with Hubert Fichte (1975) we read:

[11] *Crime and Punishment*, trans. D. Magarshak (London: Penguin, 1951), p. 432.

[12] G. Bataille, 'Genet', *La Littérature et le mal* (Paris: Flammarion/Coll. folio, 1990), p. 130, quoting Sartre, *Saint Genet*, p. 267.

[13] Bataille, 'Genet', p. 267.

[14] In A. Dichy (ed.), *Jean Genet: Œuvres complètes, Vol. 6: L'Ennemi déclaré* (Paris: Gallimard, 1991), p. 216.

'Le fait que l'armée française, ce qu'il y avait de plus prestigieux au monde il y a trente ans, ait capitulé devant les troupes d'un caporal autrichien, eh bien ça m'a ravi.'[15] And once again, ten years later, in a comment to Nigel Williams (1985): 'Elle était battue par les Allemands, elle a été battue par Hitler, j'étais content.'[16]

In an uncanny crossing between fiction and supposedly reliable spoken discourse we can see that Genet adapted these lines from the Smerdyakov character.[17] If we go back to the serenade scene in *The Brothers Karamazov*, Smerdyakov exclaims, 'I hate all Russia my dear . . . It would have been a good thing if them Frenchies had conquered us. A clever nation, my dear, would have conquered a stupid one and annexed it. Things would have been different then.'[18] Genet thus adapts Smerdyakov's description of the Napoleonic invasion of Russia of 1812 into positions in relation to the German invasion of France.

It is worth repeating, then, that Genet's positions are not straight-forward conceptual assertions, but discursive conceits. It displays once again the 'derisory sovereignty' pointed out by Bataille whereby domina-tion even of oneself or one's nation is welcomed.

Genet's work continues to bring up memories of the *années noires* in post-war France, often in the guise of aesthetic commentary. We think notably of 'L'Enfant criminel' (1949), which examines the identity of the torturer, and the theoretical text *L'Etrange mot d'* . . . (1968). In the latter text, through a musing on the nature of urbanism and the theatre, Genet discusses the city ridding itself of its unwanted inhabitants by creating a theatre-crematorium.[19] From the late 1960s Genet's increasingly direct concern through more current affairs-based political writings with, among others, the Black Panthers, the Palestinians and the Baader-Meinhof gang, ultimately do not lead to a calming of his aesthetic, as the oneiric elements and nightmare visions of the Holocaust in his final work, *Un captif amoureux*, show.

In that final work, Genet incorporates a rewritten version of his article 'Quatre heures à Chatila' on the aftermath of the Sabra and Shatila

---

[15] Dichy, *Jean Genet*, p. 149.

[16] Dichy, *Jean Genet*, p. 301.

[17] D. Eddé also notices the adaptation in *Le Crime de Jean Genet* (Paris: Seuil, 2007), pp. 40–41.

[18] F. Dostoevsky, *The Brothers Karamazov*, Vol. I trans. D. MaGarshack (Harmondsworth: Penguin, 1958), p. 262.

[19] 'L'Étrange mot d' . . .', *Jean Genet: Œuvres complètes, Vol. 4*, A. Dichy (ed.) (Paris: Gallimard, 1968).

massacre committed between 16 and 18 September 1982.[20] Palestinians
and Syrians were killed by Pierre Gemayal's Phalangists, under Israeli
guard, in revenge for the assassination two days earlier of Bashir Gemayal,
the Lebanese president elect. Sharon was forced to resign after the Kahan
Commission found Israel partially responsible and Sharon personally
responsible for not preventing the bloodshed. The massacre has often
served as a pretext for anti-Semitic remarks or revisionism. Hadrien
Laroche formulates thus the specious mental shorthand which may result:
*that if the former victims of the Holocaust are now involved in victimiza-
tion themselves, and if I do not feel beholden to the new victims, then it
is as though there are no victims – salving the conscience.*[21]

Genet's writing is not reducible to this position. His vision instead
disturbs categories by illuminating broader responsibility. We take a
relatively controlled example from *Un captif amoureux*. Genet and *fedai*
Abou Omar know a Palestinian leader who was blinded in one eye by
an Israeli parcel bomb. Genet wishes to be sure of precisely which eye
was blinded, and in which eye Moshe Dayan, politician and former Chief
of Staff of Israeli defence forces, still had vision. Abou Omar, startled,
confesses that while he regrets the Palestinian's injury, he does not regret
that of Dayan.[22] Genet's choice of Moshe Dayan is not, however, innocent
or accidental. Although unmentioned in the text, it transpires that Dayan
was blinded in one eye fighting alongside the British against Vichy in
Lebanon during the Second World War.[23] Other figures are also related
to Nazism, though not as victims, including Pierre Gemayal's Christian
Maronite Phalangists, who were based in part on the Italian and Spanish
fascists, and the Grand Mufti of Jerusalem, who met with Nazi chiefs
in March 1941.[24] The present tense of a Near East conflict is being read
by Genet in relation to the Europe of the Second World War and other
conflicts, demanding the examination of dozens of individual readings
and points of view to endow them with meaning. This complex set of
references to the Second World War marks the whole of Genet's final
period.

[20] J. Genet, 'Quatre heures à Chatila', *Jean Genet: Œuvres complètes, Vol. 6: L'Ennemi
déclaré*, A. Dichy (ed.) (Paris: Gallimard, 1991).
[21] *Le Dernier Genet: Histoire des hommes infâmes* (Paris: Seuil, 1997), p. 202.
[22] J. Genet, *Un captif amoureux* (Paris: Gollimard, 1986), pp. 313–314.
[23] *Moshe Dayan, Story of My Life* (New York: William Morrow and Company, 1976),
p. 70.
[24] The first Arab soldiers entering the war on the side of Germany in November 1943
in Bosnia. Laroche, *Le Dernier Genet*, p. 191.

While the multi-layered referencing of his style may be, at points, bewildering, it does refer to real events and produce unexpected though illuminating comparisons. Marty suspects Genet of displacing meaning away from the representation of the true victim in a writing process tacitly approved by the reader who, unable to ascribe meaning to Genet's wilder moments, then simply skates over them and observes a taboo. For Marty, this taboo is anti-Semitism, which the reader tacitly supports through a 'malentendu latent'.[25]

One particular quotation to which Marty refers, though fails to interpret adequately, is found at the end of 'Souvenirs I', in which Genet attributes glory to El Cid and greatness of soul to Hitler. With one embracing a leper and the other the muzzle of a wolfhound, Genet states that the only things to have remained of them apart from the delicacy of the caress are a tragedy which lasted a few centuries (perhaps Corneille's play) and the extermination of the Jews. He refers to a time in which 'seul demeure la caresse éternellement visible, c'est-à-dire, presque sans soutien, la grandeur d'âme, la preuve grâce à laquelle cette grandeur d'âme sera toujours vivante'.[26]

But this 'grandeur d'âme' proves to be an adaptation from *War and Peace*. In the first scene, which takes place in 1805, Pierre refers to the judicial murder of the duc d'Enghien (1804) as 'political necessity': ' "and I consider", says he, "that Napoleon showed nobility of soul in not hesitating to assume full responsibility for it" '.[27] We know this is the very same term taken up by Genet because in the Russian text it appears first as 'velitchye douchi', and then, as befits the aristocratic characters involved, in French as 'grandeur d'âme'.[28] If we look to the end of Tolstoy's novel, he returns to greatness of soul and attacks it, arguing that 'when an action flagrantly contradicts all that humanity calls good and even right, the historians fetch out the saving idea of greatness.'[29] Where Tolstoy applies this to Napoleon, Genet applies it to Hitler. To return to Sebald's remark, Napoleon is a precursor to the extremes of the twentieth century by the scale of his ambition. For Tolstoy, as an exponent of the Russian as both victim and hero, Napoleon's greatness of soul is

[25] Marty, *Post-scriptum*, p. 82.
[26] Genet, *Un captif*, p. 320.
[27] Leo Tolstoy, *War and Peace*, trans. R. Edmonds (London: Penguin, 1957), pp. 20–21.
[28] Lise: 'Comment, M. Pierre, vous trouvez que l'assassinat est grandeur d'âme?', *War and Peace*, pp. 20–21.
[29] *War and Peace*, p. 1267.

debunked, but this is not necessarily the case for the French historian.[30] In associating Napoleon with Hitler, Genet creates a complicity that no one could defend, which forces us to read further.

As Genet explains, 'Evidemment sous mon récit un autre pousse et voudrait venir au monde.'[31] In Tolstoy, Prince Andrei will come to Pierre's aid: 'one must admit . . . that Napoleon on the bridge at Arcola [1797] or in the hospital at Jaffa when he gave his hand to the plague stricken is a great man; but there are other things it would be difficult to justify.'[32] It is only via the embrace of the leper by the Cid, originally recounted in a fourteenth-century Spanish text, that these lines can be understood.[33] This embrace is being compared to Napoleon embracing his sick men at the plague hospital in Jaffa on 11 March 1799, as in the painting by Antoine-Jean Gros, in which he can be seen touching a bubo. Genet ironically implies they are each using royal touch, thought to be healing. However, according to Miot, two days previously, on 9 March 1799, after the siege of Jaffa, the surrendered Turkish soldiers had been massacred by bullet, sword and bayonet to the number of 2500. Henry Laurens argues that Napoleon modelled this massacre on the one perpetrated in 1776 by Abu Dahab, the Mamluk warlord.[34] Volney tells us this massacre was of men, women and children. As an act of terrorism, Genet seems to sense in it a precursor to Sabra and Shatila, which was also committed punitively. So Genet lays together the bodies of the Jews whose killing was commissioned by Hitler, the Palestinians killed by the Lebanese Phalangists, and now the Turkish soldiers in Jaffa killed by the French. All these acts were committed without apparent loss of countenance for the aggressor.[35]

Genet's comparisons reveal not a removal of responsibility, but an obsessional French responsibility. There remains, however, the glaring

---

[30] Or novelist. See Stendhal's *Le Rouge et le noir* (Paris: Gallimard, 2000), and his posthumously published historical biographies *Vie de Napoléon* (Castelnau-le-Lez: Climats, 1998) and *Mémoires sur Napoléon* (Castelnau-le-Lez: Climats, 1998), all of which refer to 'grandeur d'âme'.

[31] Genet, *Un captif*, p. 320.

[32] Genet, *Un captif*, p. 23 (translation altered).

[33] *Las mocedades de Rodrigo/The Youthful Exploits of Rodrigo*; ed. and trans. M. Bailey (Toronto: Toronto University Press, 2007), pp. 82–83, ll. 636–655.

[34] *L'Expédition d'Egypte 1798–1801* (Paris: Seuil, 1997), pp. 266–269.

[35] Desgenettes, the chief French army doctor, also features within Genet's comparison and merits further exposition.

disparity in the numbers of people killed. It would take a longer piece of work to determine the ultimate significance of Genet's critique of the genocidal impulse in European culture. I hope I have said enough to show that Genet discerns historical warnings and repetitions, in which the disparity between the events referred to emphasizes their scandalous nature, and presents them as events whose motivating factors must be rejected and combated.

Chapter 6

Private and public places and spaces in Jonathan Littell's *Les Bienveillantes*

Peter Tame

This chapter examines the interaction of people, places and spaces in two major areas that feature in Jonathan Littell's *Les Bienveillantes*.[1] The action takes place in multiple locations since the narrator, the fictitious Maximilien Aue, travels widely in his function as member of the SS (*Schutzstaffel*) *Einsatzgruppen* that accompany and occasionally precede the *Wehrmacht* in its invasive action in the Soviet Union, beginning in the summer of 1941. However, this chapter focuses on one area in the East (the Ukraine) and the other in the West (France) of Europe. It will examine and analyse these areas in terms of what we call isotopias, namely places and spaces as they are represented in fiction.[2] In this way, the chapter will demonstrate the importance of the relationships between Aue and the locations in which he finds himself. The latter appear as different types of literary space in the novel, whether this be thematized in dream or dream-like sequences ('oneirotopias'), erotic fantasies ('erotopias') or scenes depicting death ('thanatopias'). References to other, more 'politicized', spaces – utopias and dystopias – will be included, as will the individual's own imaginary 'psychotopia' in the form of Aue's personal 'world'.

---

[1] Paris: Gallimard, 2006. All further references in text are to this edition.

[2] The concept of literary isotopia does not derive from Algirdas Greimas's linguistic 'isotopie', although the two concepts share some similarities; one, for example, is the notion of a modified parallelism, either between two words (linguistic) or two spaces/places (literary). We use the term 'space' here in a generic or abstract sense, while the term 'place' will refer to specific, defined and named spaces in the narrative.

The narrator and 'framer of the tale'

Maximilien Aue is a psychopath and a homosexual. As such, he suffers feelings of guilt in his relations with other characters, notably his National Socialist comrades. He is persecuted by manifestations of the 'Bienveillantes' or the Kindly Ones, those vengeful deities also known as the Furies, who pursue mortals who have committed serious crimes, particularly family murders. One of his homosexual companions confides in him, telling him that, as a child, his father 'disait que les homosexuels allaient en enfer' (p. 185). Aue's own 'hell' is the 'psychotopia', his inner world, in which he is condemned to live, together with the awful events of his life as an SS officer. Frequently, his 'internal hell' is matched by the location in which he finds himself; at other times, it is the location that exacerbates his inner self-loathing.[3] Whether internal or external, places and spaces play a vital role in identifying the narrator, his hopes and fears, together with his ideology. They 'frame' his action throughout the novel. These places may be the scenes of Aue's war crimes, the towns and regions that he visits on his very extensive and intensive travels in Europe, or they may be spaces in his imagination. Part of Littell's skill consists of a regular merging of the 'real' with the imaginary (the 'microtopia'/'psychotopia' or inner world of the character) to the extent that the reader is frequently unable to distinguish the two. One of the primary components of the narrative frame is the senses – the narrator appeals to the reader through a sensual matrix that informs the novel.[4] In geographical terms, the USSR and France provide the spatial framework, the outer limits and the twin poles of the action in the novel. East and West thus frame Aue's activities, representing in broad cultural terms

[3] Littell transgresses the pattern established by Propp in the context of the folk-tale in that he fuses the 'function' of the 'aggressor' with that of the 'hero'. They become one and the same, along with the narrator, Aue, who describes himself at the outset as 'un bien méchant homme' (p. 23). (Cf. Vladimir Propp, *Morphologie du conte* (Paris: Seuil, 1970), p. 96.)

[4] The name chosen by Littell for Aue's brother-in-law, the crippled Great War veteran, is Berndt von Uexküll. This is clearly referential in the broader context of the novel since Jacob von Uexküll (1864–1944) was a well-known contemporary biologist who studied the role of the senses in animals, their inner world and their environment. He influenced a number of scientists and philosophers, particularly in the fields of cybernetics, phenomenology and hermeneutics. Like his fictional double, he was opposed to Germany's National Socialist regime. For a summary of Uexküll's theories, see Stephen Kern, *The Culture of Time and Space 1880–1918* (Cambridge, Mass.: Harvard University Press, 1983), pp. 136–137.

Asiatic barbarism on the one hand contrasted with Western civilization on the other. As we shall see, however, this distinction becomes increasingly blurred as the novel proceeds.

The USSR

As a member of one of the National Socialist State Security Service's 'action groups' (*Einsatzgruppen*), Aue's mission is essentially military, necessitating the 'ethnic cleansing' of the *Ostland* territories in order to make them Jew-free (*judenrein* or *judenfrei*). This mission has as its aim the founding of a National Socialist 'utopia' in the West of Russia. From any other point of view, this region was to become a hell, a dystopia, in which Aue is obliged (he has twinges of conscience) to participate in the massacre of large numbers of Ukrainian Jews so as to fulfil the quotas imposed by the policy-makers of the SS, such as Heinrich Himmler, on the *Einsatzgruppen*.

In the course of his duty in the Western USSR, Aue is therefore charged with organizing pogroms, engaging in the most horrific assassinations and burials of executed Jews. During one of the first mass execution scenes, Littell's theory of liquefaction of the fascist forces in the Soviet Union is proleptically illustrated by the water-filled mass-graves into which the Jews tumble after being shot and into which the collaborating Ukrainians are ordered to descend in order to finish off wounded victims.[5] Water, blood and alcohol combine in a nightmare of chaotically organized slaughter. Moreover, the Germans discover mass-graves dug previously by the Soviets before their retreat, thanatopic hecatombs that compete for space with the German graves in the woods. Burial space is here clearly at a premium, although the Germans do not miss the opportunity of noting the location of the earlier graves left by the Soviet secret police, the NKVD, 'au cas où il s'agirait de revenir pour une investigation' (p. 84).

The National Socialist credo included a Nietzschean transgression of limitations, leading to excess and megalomania. In the USSR, the moral limits of the human and the humane are certainly exceeded by the *Einsatzgruppen* who transform hangings into a spectacle for the

---

[5] Littell claims that *Les Bienveillantes* illustrates the theory of German sociologist Klaus Theweleit that typifies fascism as 'dry', 'solid', 'rigid' and 'masculine' while anti-fascism is characterized by wet, damp, humidity and the feminine. See Jonathan Littell, *Le Sec et l'humide* (Paris: L'Arbalète Gallimard, 2008).

Wehrmacht, perfect the *Sardinenpackungen* of Jewish victims in order to economize on space, and even find that they are obliged to execute their own soldiers (p. 105). In Aue's individual case, he informs us that he has always been haunted by a passion for the absolute and for a 'dépasse-ment des limites' which has led him to the edge of the mass-graves in the Ukraine (p. 95). As he implies in his omniscient narrative, such fanaticism and obedience to orders inevitably ends in self-destruction, although, as has been pointed out, he exercises a paradoxically critical and distanced judgement on many of the methodological aspects of the genocide.[6]

Little by little, Aue finds himself dispossessed of his humanity in the degrading activities of genocide. His childhood memories of playing Tarzan in the forests that represented freedom and erotic fantasies to him are transformed into nightmarish hauntings of executions in the woods – even the vocabulary used here moves subtly from 'forêts', the oneiric erotopias of his childhood roamings, to the 'bois' that harbour mass-graves. In Zhitomir, Aue dreams of attempting to leave his office, when he is confronted by an old woman who, barring his way, exhorts him to stay and write. He turns round to find a man in his chair typing. In his library, someone is nonchalantly tearing up his books. After resist-ing a naked nymphomaniac in his bed, he tries to escape by the window but it jams. He finally withdraws to the w.c., the only unoccupied space. Clearly, Aue's private, personal spaces are under threat from various forms of 'Bienveillantes'; his grim daily work is slowly robbing him of the last vestiges of humanity and civilization (p. 109).

Babi Yar

One of the most unpleasant sequences in the novel relates Aue's involve-ment in the massacre of Jews at Babi Yar – never actually named as such – just outside Kiev in the Ukraine. Crowds of Jewish citizens are herded from the city by the *Einsatzgruppen* and the *Wehrmacht* on the pretext of providing resettlement for them. They are ordered to leave behind belongings including family photographs and memories of happier times, that incite Aue to further hatred of the Jews since his own family life had been so dysfunctional. He glances at a 'prise de vue

---

[6] Margaret-Anne Hutton, 'Jonathan Littell's *Les Bienveillantes*: Ethics, Aesthetics and the Subject of Judgment', *Modern and Contemporary France*, 18:1 (2010), 5. Here, Aue is described as 'a complex literary construct occupying a number of subject positions'.

de vacances, du bonheur et de la normalité de leur vie d'avant tout ça'
(p. 122). It reminds him of a photograph of another anonymous happy
family that he had kept religiously as a child to remind him of how things
might have been for him. Like Rudolf Lang, the principal character of
Robert Merle's *La Mort est mon métier*, Aue envies happier families.
It is clearly this negative motivation, originating in a dystopic family
environment, that Littell and Merle offer as explanations for the driving
force of such fictional, sadistic fascists.

Blood and excrement mingle with the little stream that runs at the
bottom of the ravine. Aue feels as though he is drowning in a sea of
blood and mud. This 'nécropole', or thanatopia, is only made bearable
for the SS by their liberal consumption of alcohol. Once again, the themes
of deliquescence and of 'dépassement des limites' recur, with Aue who,
musing on a quotation from Chesterton, compares war to 'un pays des
fées perverti, le terrain de jeux d'un enfant dément' (p. 127). As we shall
see, he subsequently makes a similar ludic comparison in his narrative
on the Battle of Stalingrad.

With a hint of irony in his tone, Aue describes the visit made by
Heinrich Himmler to their *Sonderkommando* in October 1941, following
the Babi Yar massacre. The *Reichsführer* 'gratifies' the SS officers with his
vision of the future of the area. With a Sparta-like society, a *Slavland*
'rump' beyond the Urals, holiday camps replacing the frightful Russian
industrial towns, all this interlinked by giant express railways, Himmler's
dream is compared to the 'fantastiques utopies d'un Jules Verne'. According to Aue, this was the 'final objective' that would build on the 'Final
Solution' (p. 129). Such an 'oneirotopia' seems out of all proportion,
a product of the tentacular Third Reich's particular *hubris* – out of all
proportion, but not incredible, since it matches some of Hitler's other
known megalomaniac ambitions.

Stalingrad

Aue is eventually sent to Stalingrad, where the crucial battle between the
Germans and the Russians takes place during the winter of 1942. While
engaged in the fighting in and around the city, Aue has the distinct
impression, as he did at Babi Yar, of a huge 'children's game', that:

> tout ceci était un vaste jeu d'enfants, un terrain d'aventure formidable
> comme on en rêve à huit ans, avec des bruitages, des effets, des passages
> mystérieux, et j'en riais presque de plaisir, pris que j'étais dans cette idée
> qui me ramenait à mes jeux les plus anciens. (p. 336)

This somewhat surreal vision is partly inspired by his childhood passion for the adventures of Tarzan, with whom he readily identifies, as we have seen, around which he constructs personal fantasies, and to which he frequently refers throughout the narrative.

Unlike the majority of historical and fictional accounts of house-to-house fighting between the *Wehrmacht* and the Red Army, the description of the Battle of Stalingrad in *Les Bienveillantes* gives an impression of spaciousness, of open fields covered in snow, and of a hallucinatory emptiness.[7] When interiors are described, they frequently consist of seemingly endless corridors and doors that lead nowhere, as in dreams and particularly in nightmares. A 'Rattenkrieg', a 'guerre des rats', it may be, but it is presented in a relatively detached manner as a space 'où l'on perdait toute notion du temps et de l'espace et où la guerre devenait presque un jeu d'échec [*sic*] abstrait, à trois dimensions' (p. 369). The ludic and the spatial appear therefore as constants in such descriptions. Notwithstanding, the situation of the German army is desperate; hemmed in on all sides by the Red Army, they are vulnerable targets and death is everywhere present. Stalingrad is a thanatopia *par excellence*. Aue himself is badly wounded by a bullet that penetrates his skull. It is unclear to what extent his injury at Stalingrad changes his perspective on the war. He himself describes the 'hole' as 'un étroit corridor circulaire, un puits fabuleux, fermé, inaccessible à la pensée, . . . et plus rien ne sera jamais pareil' (p. 404). There is, however, no doubt that the shot to his head opens up what he calls a 'third eye', the pineal gland, with which he is apparently enabled to see things that had hitherto remained hidden or obscure to him. Later in the novel, for example in beleaguered Berlin, his new vision allows him clear prescience of Germany's imminent defeat in the war.

Paris

After convalescing in Usedom and in Berlin, Aue visits German-occupied Paris in 1943. Born in Alsace, Aue attended school in France. His mother is French and he has French friends, mostly *bourgeois*, who are typical products of the Grandes Ecoles system of education. Some of them turn

---

[7] Compare, for example, the descriptions of life, existence and survival during the Battle of Stalingrad in one of the principal fictional precursors of *Les Bienveillantes*, Vassily Grossman's *Life and Fate* (London: The Harvil Press, 1985), which concentrate on the essentially claustrophobic experiences of Russian soldiers in the ruined houses of the city.

out to be quite famous, even notorious, such as the collaborators Robert Brasillach and Lucien Rebatet. Aue returns to visit them in the spring of 1943, shortly after the Battle of Stalingrad. There follow some 'mises en scène' of reconciliation with friends from the heady, utopian French capital of culture in 1932. Many of them are now collaborators, both heterosexual and homosexual. Aue understandably tries to obtain a permanent post with the German forces in occupied France, with little success. In psychotopic terms, that is to say in terms of Aue's personal inner world, the long-desired Paris that appeared, from the contrasting point of view of the trauma of Russia and Stalingrad, as a utopia transforms itself for this German officer into a dystopia.

Disappointed, Aue seeks refuge in a further homosexual erotopia that repeats many of the stock images already established in similar preceding episodes. The mirror in his hotel room reflects his face, swollen with desire, which is then effaced by that of his beloved twin-sister, Una, in true Lacanian fashion. Suddenly, the face of his hated mother interposes itself, causing Aue to smash the mirror, drawing blood. He retires to the bathroom to wash, the wan light of a street-lamp illuminating the room. It is at this low point, apparently, that he conceives the desire to assassinate his mother. From an erotopia, the narrator has therefore moved in characteristically violent behaviour, via symbolic lustration or a kind of self-purging, to the state of vengefulness and thanatopia, by contemplating matricide.

Antibes

A second-hand copy of Maurice Blanchot's *Faux Pas* purchased by Aue in Paris and containing a review of Sartre's *Les Mouches* functions as a 'generator', to use the terminology of the *Nouveau Roman*, for the Oresteian act of parricide committed by the narrator in Antibes in the section that follows his stay in Paris. In a similar fashion, a bronze statue of the young Apollo inspires in Aue a desire for a brief homosexual encounter. The situations in which Aue finds himself are thus rarely random; on the contrary, throughout the novel, Littell takes care to prepare the narrative ground and the situations for scenes to come.

Aue's subsequent actions illustrate, as Littell has confirmed elsewhere, Deleuze and Guattari's concept of anti-Oedipus, the man who kills his mother whom he suspects of betraying his real father, her first husband. On his arrival in Antibes, where his mother, Héloïse, lives with her second husband, Aristide Moreau, a businessman and collaborator, Aue makes a point of changing from his civilian clothes into his SS uniform, a gesture whose purpose is twofold, namely to act as a reminder to his mother of his status as a German supporter of the National Socialist regime, but also as a token of his allegiance to his father, her first husband, a hero of the German *Freikorps*. Aue returns home as an avenger, like Orestes, since he believes that his mother was indirectly responsible for his father's death. The family house, where he grew up and in whose corridors he wanders, destabilized, as previously in the corridors of houses in Stalingrad, now appears unfamiliar and unwelcoming to him. Aue's parricide, situated as it is at the climactic mid-point in the novel and after the decisive defeat of Germany at the Battle of Stalingrad, may here be interpreted as a liquidation of his French connections, a repudiation of the culture in which he was brought up and, by extension, of Western civilization in favour of the barbarism that has become ingrained in him as a National Socialist officer in the SS who has been involved in the 'Final Solution'. The conclusion of his account descends into anarchic confusion and even a kind of bestiality, when the Berliners are overrun by the Red Army and flee alongside the animals, disgorged by the zoo that has been smashed by Allied bombing, in the streets of the dystopic capital.

Conclusion

As far as utopias and dystopias are concerned, Littell clearly takes advantage of post-war knowledge of the 'ideal' state planned by the National Socialists during the Occupation of territories east of Germany in the Second World War by inserting some of his own invention or modifications of plans for such communities recorded by some of the Reich's most notorious luminaries. *Les Bienveillantes* therefore presents a mixture of Aue's personal fantasies, based on his childhood reading, much of it of dubious literary value, together with components of the Third Reich's official plans for the future. The way in which these two kinds of visions are mixed in the novel, just as history and fiction are mixed, is problematic. In the double perspective presented here, these plans are either utopian or dystopian, depending on whose viewpoint is adopted. Clearly, the planned *Ostland* may have been regarded as some sort of utopia by the Nazis, but for virtually everyone else, they were dystopias of the most awful kind. In this sense, what Littell is presenting in *Les Bienveillantes*, therefore, is a double portrait, in keeping with the novel's overarching theme of twinhood, that consists of two sides of the same *hubris*, or arrogant, ambitious pride. As for the West, Aue's narrative gives the distinct impression that, at this point in twentieth-century European history, the concept of Western civilization is problematic, if not illusory. This impression may, however, be partly accounted for by the fact that Littell, as the author who distances himself considerably from his hero, is clearly exploiting and illustrating the notion of the 'Holocaust as a demonstration of the failure of culture'.[8]

Some scenes and images in the novel are worthy of Dante, Milton or Bosch. Littell excels at portraying space and in describing real and fictitious places, frequently in a ludic or ironic perspective. He has an acute sense of the places of war and memory that he succeeds in conveying with great narrative power, versatility in the representation of shifting points of view, and a talent for theatricalization. Moreover, he manages to parallel the exteriorization of scenes with their interiorization in the soul and mind of his principal character, or, in other words, in Aue's 'psychotopia'.[9] It is in this sense that we cannot follow François Regnault's somewhat artificial separation of what he calls 'l'envers' (Aue's dark and secret private life) and 'l'endroit' (his public life) in Les Bienveillantes.[10] Though the distinction may hold intratextually in the case of Aue's relationships with his colleagues from whom he hides his private life, from the point of view of the reader, who becomes *volens nolens* a more or less complicit *voyeur*, seeing into the depths of the narrator's soul, the two 'worlds' are consistently conflated.

The majority of the locations in which Aue functions as principal character are nightmarish dystopias, with extensive empty spaces or menacing buildings in which dark, damp corridors, tunnels and passages lead nowhere or to abyssal voids, as at Babi Yar, in Stalingrad and in Berlin at the end of the war. Recurring nightmares of the Paris *métro*, particularly frequent in the 'Stalingrad' sequence, reinforce Aue's dizzying loss of a sense of balance and of landmarks as he moves haphazardly through dark, vertiginous and labyrinthine spaces in his imagination, frequently adopting multiple viewpoints in description and narration. Lastly, one of the most powerful features of the novel consists of Littell's subtle narrative connections between the oneiric scenes and the other self-indulgent fantasies of his (anti)hero, and scenes that reflect the ominous and ubiquitous presence of violent death, an inevitable series of thanatopias that prefigure the novel's final *Götterdämmerung*.

---

[8] Hutton, 'Jonathan Littell's *Les Bienveillantes*', p. 3.

[9] It is likely that Littell is illustrating here Jacob von Uexküll's biosemiotic theory of the relations between a subject's *Innenwelt* (interior world) and its *Umwelt* (environment). See Jacob von Uexküll, *Umwelt und Innenwelt der Tiere* (Berlin: Springer, 1909).

[10] François Regnault, 'Hypocrite lecteur: l'envers de l'histoire nazie', *Les Temps modernes*, 655 (septembre–octobre 2009), 38–39.

Chapter 7

Henry Bauchau's *Le Boulevard périphérique*: the war story as clarification and investigation of the present

Béatrice Damamme-Gilbert

Henry Bauchau is an interesting example of a writer who asks what the Second World War, and by implication the First, can still mean to debates about the present at the beginning of the twenty-first century. A French-speaking Belgian writer born in 1913, he published his novel *Le Boulevard périphérique* in 2008, at the age of eighty-five.[1] The novel's narrative structure is organized around two stories: that of the aged narrator who lives in the Paris of the 1980s and who goes every day to visit his daughter-in-law Paule, who has cancer, in hospital, and the 1940s story of a friend in the Resistance who died in mysterious circumstances at the hands of a German officer the narrator met just after the war. That the novel was awarded the Prix Inter and was very well received by the press demonstrate that it has found a contemporary audience. Bauchau is a rare example of a writer who has lived through almost the whole of the twentieth century, who has been greatly influenced by both world wars and who is perhaps therefore in a better position than most to give us a sense of the memorial and narrative issues that are at stake in the interval that separates the Second World War from its literary represen-tations. His longevity means that when he writes about the war in 2008, he is still reworking his own lived experience and not, at first sight, transmitting or rediscovering a family heritage or looking at history

---

[1] Arles: Actes Sud, 2008.

through the intermediary of a purely fictional narrative. The work of memory and writing implies, however, an element of fiction, and the writer is, like anyone else, affected by a collective vision of the past and of history that influences his representation thereof, even though it is based upon his personal memories. As Bauchau has explained, both the war story and the story from the 1980s are drawn from episodes in his own life, and the character of Stéphane, the *résistant* friend who died in 1944, is based upon a real friend.[2] It is well known that old age tends to encourage old people's memories of their youth to return, and that the great temporal distance involved does nothing to invalidate the clarity or power of the vision they recover (on the contrary), but it is legitimate to ask how this is transfigured. We will therefore be looking on the one hand at how lived experience is represented in this war story and, on the other, the way in which it is contrasted with everyday life in the contemporary period, and at the meaning Bauchau extracts from the contrast between the two. We will begin by looking briefly at the genesis of the novel and at various aspects of Bauchau's biographical and literary trajectory, and especially the role of the war, before looking more closely at the text of the novel itself.

Bauchau wrote a first draft of the novel in the early 1980s. For reasons that he discusses at several points in his writing, he states that he 'resisted' this first manuscript, which was written during a period of deep despondency. He also speaks of an 'acte manqué': he had been hoping to work on the manuscript during his holidays, but left one of his notebooks in Paris.[3] The word 'resistance', defined in its psychoanalytic sense, is used deliberately; psychoanalysis played an important role in Bauchau's emergence as a writer, and he actually became a psychoanalyst late in life. It would appear that he always wanted to write about the Second World War but that it took a long time for the project to come to anything. This suggests a need to distance himself from an episode or subject that may have been too painful or that he resisted the idea. It also means that we have to rethink the very concept of resistance and combat that is so central to his imaginary world and which obviously also alludes to the Resistance. Bauchau in fact wrote repeatedly about the idea and theme of war, and Watthee-Delmotte speaks of his

[2] See O. Rogeau, 'Jusqu'au bout de ses forces – Entretien – Henry Bauchau', *Le Vif/L'Express*, 14 December 2007, p. 96.
[3] In this context, it is worth noting the title of O. Ammour-Mayeur's thesis: *Une écriture en résistance* (Paris: L'Harmattan, 2006).

'imaginaire guerrier'.[4] In 1972, he published a historical novel entitled *Le Régiment noir*,[5] which is set during the American Civil War, but he had never written about his own experience of war. In 1983, he wrote in his diary:

> Dans une lettre, André Molitor me rappelle mon ancien projet d'écrire un roman sur la période de guerre et ce qui l'a précédée et suivie . . . J'ai senti une sorte d'appel faisant écho à celui de L. pour que je reprenne ce projet, auquel en profondeur je n'ai jamais cessé de penser.
>
> Je pense au manuscrit de la première version de *La Mort par le boulevard périphérique*, roman qu'à ma grande surprise je n'ai jamais pu reprendre ni même relire jusqu'ici.[6]

He did not go back to the project at the time. In 2004, he did, however, publish a novel entitled *L'Enfant bleu*,[7] which was based upon some fifty pages from the abandoned manuscript. The remainder, which was slowly reworked at great length and whose very genesis incorporated layers of memory and resistance, eventually became *Le Boulevard périphérique* twenty-six years after it was first conceived. Bauchau feels very little of the nostalgia that is sometimes associated with extreme old age because the past is the site of his 'déchirure', a term used repeatedly in his work to refer to an old wound that appears to have affected his whole being and which the discovery of writing, which came much later, helped him over- come. Wounds and resistance are therefore central to Bauchau's world, to the autobiographical construct we glimpse in his diaries and to his fiction.[8] Death is also of central importance to *Le Boulevard périphérique*, and this has something to do with the age of the writer: how does one come to terms with death? And which death are we talking about – that of a young man who died during war, or that of a young woman who is dying in hospital in the present day? Or that of a man dying of old age? These are some of the questions raised, and they are based upon incidents in the author's life. Is the memory of the war still at work here?

---

[4]   M. Watthee-Delmotte, 'Sens et contresens d'un imaginaire guerrier: l'œuvre d'Henry Bauchau', in L. Van Ypersele (ed.), *Imaginaires de guerre: l'histoire entre mythe et réalité*, Actes du colloque, Louvain-La-Neuve, 3–5 mai 2001 (Louvain-La-Neuve: Académie Bruylant and Presses de l'Université de Louvain UCL, 2003), pp. 451–466.

[5]   Paris, Gallimard, 1972; Arles: Actes Sud, 2000.

[6]   *Jour après jour: Journal d'Oedipe sur la route (1983–1898)* (Arles: Actes Sur, coll. Babel no. 588, 2003), p. 12.

[7]   Arles: Actes Sud, 2004.

[8]   Henry Bauchau's first novel was entitled *La Déchirure* (Paris: Gallimard, 1966).

The diaries Bauchau kept as he wrote his fiction and poetry reveal him to be a writer who is acutely aware of the contemporary context in which he is writing and of a modern world that asks us questions and challenges us in very different ways from the world of our parents and grandparents. The choice of a title symbolizing the growth of the Paris of the *trente glorieuses* is not accidental. The past and memory are evoked primarily as a way of asking how we should go on living in the present and in the future. The past is depicted as a potential source of self-knowledge while war – the two world wars – represents the foundations on which our contemporary world is built. They can therefore shed light on the challenges of the present. While Bauchau obviously writes for personal reasons and because it is writing that allows him to go on living rather than succumbing to the despair and humiliations of old age, the human profundity of these questions gives them a much wider import. Bauchau, who came to writing through psychoanalysis, draws very heavily on the resources of the unconscious, but it is the unconscious of an entire society that he is addressing. The meanings he extracts from it are of general interest at a time when our actual contact with the events of the war is becoming blurred. The unconscious gives us access not only to our individual past but, at a deeper level, to the mythical dimension of humanity's past, as war is one of the archetypes that humanity has always used to express itself. The point of this war story, which is grounded in the memory of the years of defeat and Occupation in Belgium, is not that it raises yet again the issue of the veracity and accuracy of the personal or historical events it describes, even though they are recognizable, but that it goes beyond them in order to discover a human meaning that is at once cultural and philosophical. Referring to Bauchau, Myriam Watthee-Delmotte speaks of 'une création qui se profile sur un horizon défini par l'Histoire et surtout par les représentations dont celle-ci a fait l'objet.'[9]

Bauchau explains that as a young man he saw himself as a man of action who was involved in the contemporary world.[10] But his life was also a series of traumatic moments and failures until psychoanalysis allowed him to discover literary writing. His family was profoundly affected by the destruction, pillaging and burning of Louvain in 1914 (a well-known and especially atrocious war crime). Bauchau himself was

---

[9] Watthee-Delmotte, 'Sens et contresens', p. 451.
[10] On the life of Henry Bauchau, see M. Watthee-Delmotte (ed.), *Bauchau avant Bauchau: en amont de l'œuvre littéraire* (Louvain-La-Neuve: Academic Bruylant, 2001).

only eighteen months old at the time, but narrowly escaped death and was then separated from his mother for two or three months. He never recovered from this early disaster. Born into a bourgeois Belgian family, Bauchau was involved in the Christian youth movements that were so active in Belgium in the 1930s. He did his military service at the age of twenty in 1933 and was called up on several occasions in the 1930s before taking part in the eighteen-days campaign of 1940. He experienced defeat as a great humiliation. In 1940, he and a few others founded the Volontaires du Travail Wallon movement, a Christian-inspired social experiment aimed at young men who were in danger of being sent to the STO (forced labour). The experiment lasted until 1943, when it was taken over by the Germans. At that point, Bauchau resigned from it. He then joined the Resistance in the Ardennes and in London, but a wound prevented him from playing a fully active role. At the Liberation, his involvement in social action during the early years of the war led to the accusation that he had been close to collaborationist milieus. The accusation was proved to be unfounded – even though he now describes his ideological commitments of the time as an 'erreur généreuse'.[11] He emerged from this period exonerated but very humiliated and bitter, went into exile in Paris and worked in the French-language publishing industry. That experience also ended in failure. It was at this point that he first went into analysis while suffering a serious bout of depression. He himself became a psychoanalyst when he was over sixty. In the meantime, he began to write. From 1958 onwards, he wrote volumes of poetry before turning to plays, novels and journals but did not enjoy any success until the 1990s. On more than one occasion, his past therefore proves to have been a series of traumas, some relating to history and others to unsuccessful career choices. Writing poems and fiction was for Bauchau an arena in which he could work through his fears and failures and arrive at an understanding of both the past and the world by writing. Bauchau's originality and strength stem, however, from the way in which his writing draws upon the unconscious and from the fact that the images he produces have the pared-down simplicity that is often characteristic of dreams but which also gives the reader access to a universal depth

---

[11] See Watthee-Delmotte (ed.), *Bauchau avant Bauchau*; A. Morelli, 'La Guerre dans l'œuvre et la vie d'Henry Bauchau', in Marcel Van de Kerckhove (ed.), *Henry Bauchau: un écrivain, une œuvre*, Terzio Deminario Internazionale Noci 8/10, November 1991, Congrès la littérature belge (Bologna: CLUEB, coll, Beloeil, 3, 1993), pp. 23–28, and especially Bauchau's 'Note sur la communication de Madame Anne Morelli', ibid., pp. 39–42.

of meaning that puts us in touch with mythic structures.[12] As we have already said, he is also a writer who works for the present. He describes himself as an 'écrivain par espérance',[13] and sees life as an initiatory journey in which surviving ordeals gives access to a richer inner life. He is completely open to the problems of the contemporary world: what new meanings does the world around us have to offer, and how are we to integrate them into our individual and collective histories? This helps to explain the autobiographical and poetic genesis of *Le Boulevard périphérique*, in which he juxtaposes a war story born of his personal memory and a tragically banal contemporary story about the death of a young woman in a Parisian hospital that serves as an emblem of the hostility of the urban world.

In *Le Boulevard périphérique*, Bauchau describes an aging narrator who has a lot in common with the author. Every day, he crosses Paris to be at the bedside of his daughter-in-law Paule, of whom he is very fond. She is suffering from cancer, and no one knows if she will recover. How can he not panic? The narrator lists the exits from the *périphérique* as though they were the beads of a rosary. On the days when he takes the metro, the RER and the bus, 'Je m'engouffre dans le corridors que je connais jusqu'à l'écœurement' (p. 13). The narrator describes the details of this daily Way of the Cross, on which he sometimes sees a friendly or hostile face, an immigrant lost in his thoughts or the rhododendrons in flower in the Luxembourg glimpsed in the distance. As well as being emblematic of the post-war development of Paris, the boulevard périphérique of the title symbolizes the way we are trapped in a contemporary world in which every gesture is repeated *ad infinitum*. In the hospital, he describes the day-to-day ups and downs of Paule's treatment, the presence or absence of the oxygen mask, the disappointments and insane hopes of the patient's existence, the ulcers invading her mouth: another rosary of despair. Paule's mother is always there: an immoveable and hieratic presence who clings to the need to cheer up her daughter. The novel therefore records the cruelty of modern death and of the urban environment, and does so in a style that, by describing in detail the impersonal world of the hospital and the ordeal of these daily visits, paints a forceful picture of the conditions of our modernity: 'un monde

---

[12] His writings that deal directly with mythological subjects include a novel about the figure of Oedipus, a novel about Antigone and a play about Genghis Khan.

[13] The expression is cited in Nathalie Crom's review, 'L'Ecriture à l'écoute', *La Croix*, 22 June 2000, p. 17.

plein de goulets d'étranglement, de bouchons. De forces saisies par l'ennui, l'énervement et l'épouvante de ne plus trouver d'issue' (p. 188).

We follow the narrator as he becomes caught up in endless traffic jams, always aware that the young woman might die, and the memory of another death emerges from the depths of his memory. He met his friend Stéphane in the early years of the war, and Stéphane's death is the subject of a narrative that alternates with the main narrative. The narrator sets out to re-explore Stéphane's death, which remains a mystery. It is the way he reconstructs it on his exhausting trips across Paris that gives the novel its rhythm and form. A number of powerful, and almost over-symbolic, scenes typify the story he remembers. There is, for instance, the story of how the narrator learned to rock-climb during the early years of the war, with Stéphane acting as his teacher and guide. The risks the two friends take as they climb, roped together to symbolize their burgeoning friendship, capture the issues that come to the fore in wartime: danger, courage and the desire to surpass oneself. Every hold and every move are crucial if they are to avoid falling, and Stéphane is described as a God gifted with an incomparable lightness who can inspire courage in a narrator who is usually weak. All Bauchau's work reveals his fascination with heroic figures like Stéphane, who later becomes a peerless Resistance fighter because he was able to operate alone. But it is not so much the heroism of these heroes that fascinates Bauchau as their vulnerability and failures: understanding how the seemingly invulnerable Stéphane died becomes the narrator's major preoccupation as Paule herself fights her cancer and sinks towards death.

The last two thirds of the narrative therefore alternate between the phases of the young woman's battle against cancer and the story of the *résistant* Stéphane, whose corpse was found in a pond whereas the other captured fighters were shot. The narrator gradually becomes obsessed with the mysterious circumstances surrounding his death. He has to go back beyond the death of Stéphane and look at the Nazi officer known as Shadow, into whose hands Stéphane had fallen. The narrator actually met Shadow at the end of the war when Shadow was a prisoner in the hands of the Americans, shortly before his death. Shadow is in a sense the black knight to Stéphane's white knight. Bauchau briefly reconstructs the childhood of this manipulative monster, and the reasons why he came to be ruling over 'un château de merde' (p. 159). He uses antithetical, Manichaean images to describe the encounter between the *résistant* and the Nazi, one blessed with an almost supernatural lightness and the other cursed with the heaviness of a stone. Shadow is nonetheless fascinated by the prisoner over whom he had no hold, so much so that he becomes obsessed with his memory as he waits to die in captivity. It is through an almost wordless dialogue with Shadow that takes place at the end of the war and that comes back to haunt his memory that the narrator finally succeeds in reconstructing what happened when the Nazis liquidated all their prisoners before fleeing in the face of the American advance. He explores the possible circumstances of Stéphane's death: he chose to throw himself, 'd'un mouvement superbe' (p. 247), into the water he feared so much. Stéphane's one weakness is that he cannot swim and is in fact terrified of even going into the water. He therefore escapes from Shadow because he has the courage to confront his own weakness. Speaking of the figure of Oedipus, Myriam Watthée-Delmotte evokes 'the unexpected strength of weakness'.[14] The formula could equally be applied to Stéphane.

The war story therefore makes a major contribution to the quest for meaning that played such a major role in Bauchau's emergence as a writer, and evokes what Marc Augé sees as a need to give meaning to the world in what he called the excess of our 'supermodernité'.[15] Compared with the three novels that deal directly with mythical figures,[16] *Le Boulevard périphérique*, which was begun earlier and to which Bauchau went back much later, adopts a hybrid mode of representation. The lived origins of the narrative, which emerges from the depths of the author's memory, are as crucial as the temporal distance that separates him from the events he describes. The period of the war meant a great deal to the author-narrator. His representation of heroism, in particular, strikes a chord in his imagination that can be traced back to those years, but the text uses a stylized mode of expression that reworks the real. It is concerned with neither realism nor autobiographical truth but achieves a mythic level, as in the crowd scene describing the intervention of the women.[17] While it does not rely upon what might be called psychoanalytic writing – dream narratives and images drawn from

[14] Watthee-Delmotte (ed.), 'Sens et contre-sens', p. 466.

[15] Marc Augé, *Non-lieu: Introduction à une anthropologie de la supermodernité* (Paris: Seuil, 1992), pp. 41–42.

[16] *Oedipe sur la route* (Arles: Actes Sud, 1990), *Diotime et les lions* (Arles: Actes Sud, 1991), *Antigone* (Arles: Actes Sud, 1997).

[17] The novel describes at length a dramatic incident in which the collective and vocal intervention of a group of women helps to keep apart a group of workers looking for trouble and a group of prisoners who are leaving for the STO under Nazi guard, thus preventing a probable massacre. See *Le Boulevard périphérique*, pp. 38–49.

the unconscious – to the same extent as his first novel in particular, the war story that the narrator constructs inside his head in 1980 can still be interpreted as an image of the dialogue that takes place during psychoanalysis: it is by using past events and his memories to reconstruct meaning and a narrative that the patient can recover and find reasons to go on living. In the novel, Paule dies but the narrator goes on living. His success in elucidating the past by giving a meaning to Stéphane's death and discovering unsuspected aspects of their relationship[18] helps him to live through the ordeal of his daughter-in-law's death in the present, and to come to terms with his own imminent death.

[18] The narrator discovers, for instance, that Stéphane loved him.

Part 2

Representation and reception

Introduction

'Representation and reception' focuses on the role of the reader, actual and implied, in the formation of the narrative of the war, investigating the ways in which these narratives interact with the expectations and assumptions of their public, how they shape them and how they are in their turn shaped by them. Beginning with Richard J. Golsan's analysis of the complexities of representation of memory in recent narratives, Part 2 then concentrates on the dialogue that develops between established views, received ideas and new kinds of representations, as writers, artists and directors work within and against their audiences' preconceptions.

Golsan's critical account of 'le devoir de mémoire' and current theoretical and historiographical debates on memory frames his contrasting analysis of the multi-layered novels *Le Village de l'Allemand* and *Les Bienveillantes*. Examining the ways in which the trials of the 1980s engineered a public reading of behaviour under the Occupation as wholly good or wholly bad, he argues that while *Les Bienveillantes*, far from the nuanced historical status to which it aspires, endorses this Manichean reading, the multiple voices, from France, Germany and North Africa, of Sansal's novel demonstrate the problematic consequences of genocide and totalitarian oppression.

Debra Kelly discusses English-language translations of Agnès Humbert's *Notre Guerre* and Berr's *Journal*, to explore the power of existing cultural preconceptions of the unmediated nature of personal experience in writing, and the economic and commercial infrastructure in their reception both in France and in the UK, as well as the discursive figures of memory that emerge across a large variety of texts. Angela Kershaw examines the context of production and reception of Irène Némirovsky's novel *Suite française*, analysing the many readings which have so often placed the text in a testimonial frame with its own markers and values, and which tend to oversimplify the discourses of both fiction and testimony in the process. Virginie Sansico raises interesting questions of verisimilitude and plausibility in her analysis of texts of false resisters and false Holocaust victims, setting them within the historiographical context of hegemonic portrayals of Resistance figures, and noting the cultural dynamics which differentiate literary and filmic or televisual discourses.

Penny Brown's subject is children's literature and the generic constraints and imaginative solutions involved in presenting the bleak and distressing stories, particularly of Jewish children and their families deported to Auschwitz, to a young public. Angela O'Flaherty gives a detailed reading of *Les Bagages de sable* and traces the 'non-dit', the unsayable feelings of the wider national community, in the gaps in representation in the text, underlining the isolation of the survivor and the dramatization of the difficulty of communication, both individual and collective, that she experiences, symbolizing a wider social ostracism of the survivor and her pain. Luc Rasson's comparative study of three perpetrators, in novels by Merle, Rachline and Littell, considers the tensions involved in first-person narratives of monstrosity for the implied reader, the stereotypical traits involved and the possible challenges to such stereotypes played out through the narratives.

Sartre's famous comment that literature, like bananas, needs to be consumed immediately, highlights the importance of understanding the conditions of a text's reception, but less helpfully implies that there is one singular moment of truth in the text/reader relationship. As we can see from the readings in this section, however, Occupation narratives and their readers (or viewers) engage with and shape a longer-term process of cultural and historical understanding in many different ways.

Chapter 8

Corruptions of memory: some reflections on history, representation and *le devoir de mémoire* in France today

Richard J. Golsan

In 1993 the American historian Charles Maier published his influential essay, 'A Surfeit of Memory: Reflections on History, Melancholy and Denial'.[1] In his essay, Maier voiced growing concerns over what he perceived to be a widespread cult of memory, or, as he phrased it more pointedly, an 'addiction to memory' in contemporary society. Maier articulated these concerns along several lines. In the postmodern era, the addiction to memory had come to represent in effect a dangerous retreat from the more rigorous practice of the discipline of history. Contrasting history and memory, Maier wrote:

> History, I believe, must be reflective and inevitably discordant and plural . . . historians must at least presuppose different life situations; they must assume that individuals and groups bring limited perspectives to any conflict. Historians, moreover, must reconstruct causal sequences; they tell stories of before and after and explain events and their antecedents. But the retriever of memory does not have the same responsibility to establish causal sequencing. Triumphs, traumas, national catastrophes make their presence felt precisely by their re-presence and representation. Memories are to be retrieved and relived, not explained. (p. 143)

In his essay Maier was equally concerned with the reason or reasons *why* memory had become an 'addiction' and, in many circumstances, a replacement of or substitute for history. First, he argued that in general

---

[1] 'A Surfeit of Memory', *History and Memory*, 5:2 (1993), 136–151. Subsequent references are given in text when a work is repeatedly cited.

terms memory presupposes a form of melancholy, or 'sweet sadness', that has its own seductions. But more specifically – and crucially – in the current climate, the addiction to memory signalled a generalized 'loss of faith' and the advent of 'an age of failing expectations'. As Maier phrased it: 'In the twilight of Enlightenment aspirations to collective institutions, we build museums to memory, our memory' (p. 151). At least implicitly, then, memory constituted not only a dubious and dangerous substitute for history, but a convenient means of avoiding coming to grips with the present and future. For all of these reasons Maier concluded his essay by expressing the hope that memory be 'kept in its place as servant, not master' of our understanding of the past, and that it be understood as a 'reflection on experience, and not experience as a whole' (p. 151).

In the years since the publication of Maier's essay, any number of historians, philosophers and others on both sides of the Atlantic have voiced mounting concerns over the insidious implications and impact of our 'addiction to memory' in contemporary Western culture. All the while memory – in the sense that Maier conceives it – has only expanded its domain in political and cultural terms as well as in legal practices and institutions. The results of this expansion of memory, or what Tony Judt has more recently and colourfully labelled 'mis-memory', include a troubling obscurity where the past is actually concerned, coupled with the 'incessant' invocation of its 'lessons' which, Judt claims, are nevertheless 'ignored and untaught'.[2] Judt argues in 'The World We Have Lost' – the appropriately entitled introduction of his book *Reappraisals* – that this ignorance of and indifference to the past are accompanied, ironically, by a veritable compulsion to commemorate and memorialize, especially where the twentieth century is concerned: 'We have memorialized it everywhere: museums, shrines, inscriptions, "heritage sites", even historical theme parks are all public reminders of "the Past".' But, he adds, 'there is a strikingly selective quality to the twentieth century that we have chosen to commemorate. The overwhelming majority of places of official twentieth-century memory are either avowedly nostalgio-triumphalist – praising famous men and celebrating famous victories – or else, and increasingly, opportunities for the acknowledgment and recollection of collective suffering' (p. 3). The result of all this, Judt concludes, is the creation not of a coherent Past with a capital 'P' that binds the national community together, but the multiplication of

---

[2] Tony Judt, *Reappraisals: Reflections on the Forgotten Twentieth Century* (New York: The Penguin Press, 2008).

'fragments of separate pasts, each of them . . . marked by their own distinctive and assertive victimhood' (p. 4). For Judt, as for Maier before
him, the 'addiction to mis-memory', to combine the expressions of both
historians, implies the loss of a coherent binding, communal – if not
national – narrative which itself is a necessary precondition to progress
and faith in a democratic future.

What of the French context? Given that one characteristic commonly
associated with *l'exception française* is a fascination with, celebration of
or, conversely, to quote Henry Rousso, an *hantise du passé*, the problem
of memory is understandably equally apparent and arguably more vexed.
The issues and concerns noted by Maier and Judt have of course been
acknowledged by French historians and intellectuals. But given the
specificities as well as complexities of the French case, there are other
complications and problems as well. As an example of at least some
of these, it is worth considering the debates and controversies generated
by the most recent of the so-called 'trials of memory', that of Maurice
Papon on charges of crimes against humanity in 1997–98.

Shortly after the conclusion of the Papon trial, Jean de Maillard argued
in the pages of *Le Débat* that the fulfilment of the so-called 'devoir
de mémoire' in trying Papon had not only produced unsatisfying legal
and moral results but, at least as importantly, it had been predicated on,
and in turn propagated, a completely false understanding of the history
of Nazism and of the Second World War. According to that understanding, 'all that existed, on one side, were the Nazis and their accomplices,
all of whose efforts were given over to the elimination of the Jews and
their friends. For all those [living at the time] no one could escape the
obligation of choosing one side or the other, with a full and complete
understanding of the stakes involved, and no one could escape the consequences of his or her choice.'[3]

In an essay on the declining role and importance of the historian in
contemporary France, Henry Rousso[4] echoes Maillard's concerns that
the trials for crimes against humanity distorted our understanding of

---

[3] Jean de Maillard, 'A quoi sert le procès Papon?', *Le Débat* 32 (November 1998),
pp. 32–42.
[4] Henry Rousso, 'A-t-on besoin des historiens? Exception française et rapport
contemporain au passé', in Marc Dambre and Richard J. Golsan (eds), *L'Exception et la
France contemporaine: histoire, imaginaire, littérature* (Paris: Presses Sorbonne Nouvelle,
2010).

history, but in different ways. First, to maintain as was the case in these trials that one can fulfil a 'duty to memory' and repair the crimes of the past implies that the past can somehow be remade, that its crimes can essentially be purged. For Rousso, this constitutes nothing less than an effort to 'whitewash history'. Secondly, in subjecting the interpretation of the past to the vicissitudes of the courtroom, one removes it from what Rousso calls the 'scientific judgement' of the academy and places it instead at the mercy of the legal give-and-take of lawyers. The latter are, of course, less intent on establishing truth than in vanquishing their adversary and having their partial and perhaps skewed version of the past prevail. Finally, Rousso argues, the very notion of the imprescriptability of crimes against humanity imposes upon these crimes what he calls 'un caractère inachevé'. The result is a dangerous 'abolition de la distance temporelle avec le passé' that further undermines a full and accurate understanding of the historical events themselves. This direct and unmediated recovery of the past in the courtroom constitutes, in fact, less the recovery of historical truth than the retrieval of memories that Charles Maier reminds us, are 'relived, not explained'.

In a lecture delivered at the University of California-Berkeley in May 2009, Tzvetan Todorov underscored different, but equally problematic, aspects of the French 'trials for memory', as well as others like them, not only where history is concerned but where morality and human psychology are at issue as well. In his lecture, entitled appropriately 'Memory, a Remedy for Evil?',[5] Todorov argues that the trials of figures like Klaus Barbie, Paul Touvier and Maurice Papon impose a historically, morally and psychologically false narrative on events and individuals by assigning simplistic, and ultimately profoundly inaccurate, roles to all the major players. According to Todorov, in these trials only four historical roles are possible. First there is the couplet of 'the *villain* and his [or] her *victim*. Then there is the *hero* and his or her *beneficiary*.' Since history is never entirely black or white and cannot be understood in such Manichean terms, the four roles the court assigns are inherently false, because they imply precisely such dichotomies. Moreover, the trials are ultimately very damaging in the larger society in which they take place in that they imply that evil belongs exclusively to the villains, the historical monsters who carry out these crimes, and not to others,

---

[5] Todorov's lecture has been published in French as 'La mémoire remède contre le mal', in *La Signature humaine* (Paris: Seuil, 2009), pp. 251–276.

to us. *We* are innocent, whereas *they*, the villains, are entirely culpable and evil.

But of course, as any number of historical experiences teach us – and Todorov cites the example of Khmer Rouge crimes as well as those occurring in Apartheid South Africa – the *bourreaux* (the torturers and executioners) are ultimately not that different from the rest of us, if they are different at all. Moreover, the 'heroes' in these circumstances are not always entirely 'good'. Todorov notes that in South Africa, the 'heroes' of the ANC were hardly heroic in all circumstances, and indeed criminal in some instances. The truth is that in certain extreme situations anyone can assume any, and indeed all, of these roles, even simultaneously. As long as the trials for memory – as well as the French 'lois mémorielles' for that matter – do not come to terms with these realities, Todorov argues that they will be ineffective in preventing similar crimes in the present and future. Rather than 'delivering us from Evil' in this fashion, 'memory', through the instruments Todorov describes, ironically perpetuates it among us by denying its pervasiveness and ubiquity.

Todorov's pessimistic take on 'memory' misconstrued, as a moral – and moralizing – force for good and cast on a global level is entirely appropriate to the French context for several reasons. First, among French intellectuals and philosophers, Todorov is by no means alone in seeing memory, or the 'duty' to it as manifested in the French context, as essentially a negative and even divisive force which in no way prevents or impedes evil in the form of mass crimes from occurring in the present. In his 2006 essay, *La Tyrannie de la pénitence*, Pascal Bruckner anticipates many of Todorov's criticisms of memory, and goes further. For Bruckner, the cult of memory, and especially the incessant evocation and remembrance of the crimes of the past, constitutes a form of masochism as well as the expression of a thinly disguised arrogance or *suffisance*. Those French and Europeans who harp on Europe's past crimes and preach the duty to memory are referred to derisively by Bruckner as *les fonctionnaires du péché originel*. They proclaim themselves 'des rois de l'infâme' who, through their infamy, aspire to remain 'au cime de l'histoire'.[6] They claim memory and the understanding of true barbarism as their exclusive domain, and condescendingly lecture others about it. In focusing on the horrors of the past rather than the problems of the present, the *fontionnaires du péché originel* embrace 'culpability' over 'responsibility'.

---

[6] Pascal Bruckner, *La Tyrannie de la pénitence* (Paris: Grasset, 2006), pp. 35, 50.

Moreover, Bruckner continues, the 'duty to memory' itself in this context no longer constitutes merely a respect for the dead, as Primo Levi intended it to be in coining the phrase in the first place. Rather, it has been transformed into a 'morale de vigilance: notre conscience doit rester aux aguets, prévenir à tout moment le retour de l'horreur' (p. 182). But because few crimes and genocides measure up in horror and scale to the principal foci of the 'duty to memory', the Holocaust and the crimes of colonialism and decolonization, the functionaries of original sin as well as Europeans in general dismiss or ignore them. Bruckner asserts, 'Seule l'épouvante d'hier nous mobilise et nous donne le droit d'écarter tout ce qui n'est pas elle' (p. 182).

For Bruckner, ultimately, the memory that is embraced and indeed sacralized in this process is a sclerotic one, one that seeks to 'intimidate, condemn, and strike down' rather than to 'desacralize, explain, and provide detail', which is, of course, the true work of history. And the memory in question, Bruckner continues, composed principally as noted of the crimes of the Holocaust as well as those of colonialism, implicitly proposes dangerous analogies and causal linkages that are historically false and in fact smack of revisionism. In this context in *La Tyrannie de la pénitence* Bruckner is especially critical of historians and others who in his view indulge in what he labels 'the sin of retrospective intentions'. These individuals claim to 'discover in the European colonial adventure the antecedents of the totalitarian regimes of the twentieth century' (p. 142). Indeed, Bruckner suggests, some wish to imply that the crimes of colonialism are in fact *worse* than the crimes of the Nazis and their allies in that they are the *original crimes*, a sort of blueprint or prototype of what was to follow. And this form of revisionism is far from innocent. According to Bruckner, it allows, for example, for the condemnation of Israel's excesses in 'colonizing' the occupied territories as essentially the same as the crimes Hitler perpetrated against European Jews. The Israeli Jews are thereby transformed into latter-day Nazis, and the culpability of *today's* vigilant European where the crimes of the Nazis and their accomplices are concerned is thereby happily diminished. Indeed, those familiar with Roger Garaudy's scandalous reprise of *négationnisme* in the mid-1990s[7] and Ernst Nolte's attempts to lessen German guilt during the 1980s German historians' debate will recognize the strategies

---

[7] For discussions of Garaudy and the abbé Pierre affair, see my 'Denying the Holocaust in France: The Past and Present of an Illusion', in my *Vichy's Afterlife: History and Counter-history in Postwar France* (Lincoln: University of Nebraska Press, 2000), pp. 124–142.

of diminishing the weight of the Holocaust either by comparing Nazi crimes favourably to the crimes of colonialism (colonialism was far worse, with many millions more victims) or by arguing that they were only a pale copy or sequel to the 'originary' crimes of Stalinism.

Bruckner's critique in *La Tyrannie de la pénitence* of the corrosive and indeed corrupting power of memory in historical, cultural, political, moral and psychological terms is deliberately provocative. Nevertheless, in his essay Bruckner obviously shares and pursues the concerns raised by Maier, Judt, Rousso and Todorov that I have alluded to here as well as those of others. Moreover, his arguments underscore another, equally problematic aspect of the nature of memory in contemporary society, and that is what Rousso calls its *mondialisation*, or globalization. This is evident, in the first instance, in the linkage and occasionally the conflation of the crimes of the past, for example those of the Nazis and the Vichy regime during the Second World War and those of Fourth-Republic France in Algeria and elsewhere in the post-war years. Striking examples of this are visible not only in what Bruckner sees as the tarring of Israel with the brush of colonialism alluded to earlier, but, in a specifically French context, the conflation of Papon's crimes against the Jews in deporting them from Bordeaux during the Occupation and those he committed against Algerians in the post-war years, and especially in the streets of Paris in October 1961. Early in the trial, in fact, Pierre Vidal-Naquet created shock waves by labelling *both* as crimes against humanity, a highly problematic claim, certainly in legal terms. But Rousso makes the point that this conflation and overlapping of the memories of crimes go even further than this. In the late 1990s the crimes of Nazism and communism were scandalously equated by the historian Stéphane Courtois and much debated during the heated controversy following the publication of *The Black Book of Communism* in the autumn of 1997.[8] And as far afield as South Korea, Rousso points out, recent debates over Korean collaboration with the Japanese invader bear a striking resemblance to debates over collaboration in European countries with the Nazi occupier more than a half-century before. The result of all this is, he observes, '[de mettre] en cause la domination traditionnelle de l'histoire nationale' (p. 5). It is also, he continues, to further complicate

---

[8]   For a discussion of the controversy, and its links to Nolte and the German 'historians' debate' of the 1980s, see my 'Historical Revisionism and *The Black Book of Communism* Controversy', in my *French Writers and the Politics of Complicity* (Baltimore: Johns Hopkins University Press, 2006), pp. 143–162.

'l'évolution incertaine, intrigante, voire inquiétante de notre relation à l'histoire' (p. 10).

If, over the past two decades memory has increasingly come to be seen in many quarters as a highly problematic and indeed dangerously corrupting phenomenon that bleeds into the present and undermines a rigorous and objective historical understanding of the past, while at the same time crippling our moral understanding of ourselves as well as what is essentially 'human' in us,[9] what role has literature played in this process? More specifically for my purposes here, how has the contemporary French novel represented, or perhaps refined or even challenged, France's addiction to 'mis-memory' with all of its pitfalls? The number of novels and writers to be examined in this general context is, of course, extraordinarily large and quite daunting. Therefore I will limit my remarks to two recent and I believe emblematic works, Boualem Sansal's 2008 novel *Le Village de l'Allemand ou le journal des frères Schiller* and Jonathan Littell's 2006 Prix Goncourt-winning *Les Bienveillantes*. From the perspectives on memory developed here, these are, I will argue, diametrically opposed works. While Sansal's novel dramatizes and explores the impact and destructive power of memory in the present, ultimately it construes memory more positively as a means not only of understanding the past but as a force for good in the present. By contrast, both in its representation of the past and in the novel's highly problematic and controversial reception, *Les Bienveillantes* not only recapitulates the worst features of an 'addiction to mis-memory', but it also succumbs to its inherent corruptions.

Le Village de l'Allemand ou le journal des frères Schiller is composed of the alternating diary entries of two brothers, Rachel and Malrich, both Algerian immigrants living in Paris. But the brothers are highly unusual, in that while their mother is a native Algerian, their father Hans Schiller is German. More specifically, he is a former SS officer who had fled Europe with the downfall of the Third Reich, and in the immediate post-war years had been shunted through Egypt by the Nasser regime to serve as an advisor to the FLN. Following Algeria's independence, Schiller had settled in a small village, Aïn Deb, to raise a family. The brutal murder

---

[9] For a much more positive discussion of the interplay of divergent memories and their competing demands, primarily in the French context, see Michael Rothberg's excellent recent book, *Multidirectional Memory: Remembering the Holocaust in the Age of Decolonization* (Stanford: Stanford University Press, 2009).

by the GIA in 1994 of Schiller and his wife and most of the villagers of Aïn Deb leads the older brother Rachel to return to Algeria where, to his utter horror, he learns for the first time of his father's Nazi past. After returning to France, Rachel's life begins to unravel. He loses his wife and job and sets out on a journey across Europe and North Africa in an effort to understand his father, the latter's allegiance to Nazism and the horrendous crimes that Hitlerism perpetrated. His travels take him to Germany, Poland and Auschwitz, Turkey and Egypt. Rachel's journal describes his travels, his readings and meditations on Nazism, genocide and evil itself. But most of all it describes his growing horror in the face of his father's crimes which, ultimately, he can neither comprehend nor expiate. In despair, he takes his own life.

Although interspersed in the text with Rachel's diary entries, the younger brother Malrich's journal entries begin only after his brother's death, and upon reading the latter's journal. Malrich's journal reflects on his father and his crimes and also the tragic fate of his brother. But, unlike the older sibling, through his writings Malrich engages much more directly with the present. While Rachel describes himself as 'un mort qui avait trop vu', Malrich, who lives in the *cité* and daily experiences its abuses and injustices, is less concerned with meditating on the past and on Nazism's crimes than he is in understanding the dangers of the present through the prism of that past. Like his brother, Malrich also goes to Algeria, whose oppressive regime with all its abuses is terribly reminiscent for him of totalitarianisms past. His father's double past as both SS officer and FLN advisor sets the stage, of course, for Malrich's reflections.

But even more so than the oppressive regime in North Africa, it is the reign of the most extreme forms of Islamic fundamentalism in the *cité* in Paris that brings comparisons between past and present into sharpest focus. Of the *cité*, Malrich writes: 'Les islamistes ont colonisé notre cité et nous mènent la vie dure. Ce n'est pas un camp d'extermination nazi, mais c'est déjà un camp de concentration, *ein Konzentrationlager* comme on disait sous le Troisième Reich.'[10] But lest one assume that Islamist *colons* are incapable of the worst crimes of Nazism, Malrich writes elsewhere: 'Je me dis que c'est impossible mais quand je vois ce que les islamistes font chez nous et ailleurs, je me dis qu'ils dépasseront les nazis si un jour ils ont le pouvoir. Ils sont trop pleins de haine et de prétention pour se contenter de nous gazer' (p. 222). Enlightened at the

---

[10] Paris, Gallimard, 2008, p. 231.

novel's end about the dangers of the present and future by what he has learned from the past, Malrich resolves not to be destroyed by memory like his brother but to fight against what he sees as Nazism's successors in the present. Memory serves, in effect, as his inspiration.

It could be argued that the weight of memory in *Le Village de l'Allemand* proves ultimately destructive and indeed divisive in the lives of the two brothers, in that it literally kills Rachel and serves to alienate Malrich from his own community, such as it is. If this is the case, then memory's toxic and corrosive effects are entirely in keeping with those of an 'addiction to mis-memory'. More importantly for our purposes here, Sansal's novel arguably casts in sharp relief the dangers alluded to by Pascal Bruckner and others of conflating criminal moments in the past and then applying their lessons willy-nilly to the present, thus obscuring or skewing historical as well as current realities. Although Malrich's passion is compelling, he is, one might claim, only an angry and uneducated youth from the *cité*, and for this reason perhaps, misuses the past to justify his rage against the Islamic fundamentalists in the present.

But it is also possible – and more plausible in my view – to read *Le Village de l'Allemand* as ultimately a *positive* meditation on memory not only as a means of gaining access to historical truth but also as a tool for understanding goodness and evil in human terms. It is also possible to argue that the novel suggests that the memory and comparison of crimes from the past can indeed have a positive impact on the present. Despite Rachel's final despair, at the end of his terrible journey not only does he comprehend the historical realities of Nazism, he understands that good and evil are not abstract or metaphysical entities, they are human. Evil, moreover, is itself not in the exclusive purview of what Todorov describes as memory's 'villains'. Rachel affirms: 'L'humanité est une . . . et le mal est en elle, dans sa moelle' (p. 96). It follows, Rachel reasons, that were he to respond to Primo Levi's question in *If This is a Man* he would state that *both* victim *and* executioner are men. What separates them is the choices they make, and Rachel affirms, surprisingly optimistically: 'tout le choix nous appartient, à chaque instant' (p. 262).

As if responding to Rachel's affirmation that humans can choose, and at every moment, Malrich *chooses* to transform memory into action, not in the name of vengeance of past injustices done to him, but in the name of those around him whom he knows to be the victims of abuses and crimes committed by the mullahs. To invoke an important distinction made by Todorov in *Les Abus de la mémoire* (1995): Malrich's memory thus becomes *paradigmatic*, not *literal*. Rather than becoming a paralysing and sterile personal obsession, a 'literal memory', it becomes 'paradigmatic': even in its militancy it is transformed into a force of good for others in the present and future.

I will not rehearse the action of Jonathan Littell's massive novel, *Les Bienveillantes*, nor for that matter, the broader controversies and debates swirling around it since its publication. Given the enormous coverage the work has received, one would be hard pressed *not* to be familiar with both. Suffice to say that Littell's protagonist and narrator, SS officer Maximilien Aue, is, as has been noted, a 'Nazi Zelig'. He is present everywhere from the Nazi invasion of Russia in 1941, to occupied Paris and its collaborationist intellectual circles, to the Battle of Stalingrad, to Auschwitz, and finally to Hitler's bunker and the fall of Berlin.

Aue's adventures during the war are recounted in retrospect several decades after the war, when the narrator is retired and living under a false identity in France. This allows Aue to reflect and moralize on the nature and implications of his experiences. We are thus supposedly given privileged access to the mysteries of the torturer's psychology. But if we are given this access, it is disappointing certainly to the extent that it – along with the novel itself – articulates and indeed validates many of the preoccupations and misconceptions associated with an 'addiction to mis-memory' described earlier. In the first instance, in representing the past *Les Bienveillantes*'s offers for the most part only a seemingly endless series of graphic and lurid descriptions of crimes, brutality and perversion. And yet, through the voice of its narrator the novel aspires to the status of history. Buttressed by a healthy diet of post-war reading in history and historical interpretation, Aue's retrospective ruminations pretend to explain Nazism and its major figures, as well as more broadly totalitarianism in general. In Stalingrad, Aue and a captured Soviet officer compare Nazism and communism, and in this way the novel proposes to explain both. But while these discussions are occasionally compelling, they offer nothing profoundly new or original. As Rousso notes in the essay cited earlier, the scholarship on which Littell bases Aue's ruminations is more than a decade old. And ultimately, the novel teaches us little if anything, in terms of what Maier calls 'causal sequences' and the nature of events as well as their antecedents, which is, he argues, the real work of history. Yet one of the more disturbing aspects of the critical reception and adulation of *Les Bienveillantes* has been precisely that it was taken to be historically ground-breaking in any number of ways.[11] For example, Pierre Nora claimed in highly laudatory comments in the pages of *Le Débat* that the publication of the novel was an extraordinary 'literary *and* historical event' and a remarkable *exposé d'historien*.[12] Moreover, it enlightened the French public in historical terms, Nora claimed, by reinserting the Shoah 'dans l'ensemble de la guerre' (p. 37). Historians and others might well challenge Nora's claim here. But in a very real sense, it implies that memory, and *fictional* memory at that, can take the place of history.

In at least one other important respect Littell's novel validates the problematic and indeed skewed perspectives associated with mis-memory. In the person of the protagonist himself as well as other characters, Littell appears to reinforce precisely the distribution of stereotypical roles and even the moral Manichaeism that Todorov associates with the politics and practice of the 'duty to memory' in recent trials for crimes against humanity, among other phenomena. The Nazi villains in the novel, and Aue in the lead, are almost entirely all evil, grotesque and indeed monstrous, and their adversaries in their great majority exclusively innocent victims. Aue himself is of course a murderer, a matricide as well as a sadomasochist whose great passion is an incestuous involvement with his sister. Aue's assertions throughout *Les Bienveillantes* that he is as normal, as human, as the reader whom he claims famously in the first sentence to be his 'brother' only serve paradoxically to remind the reader how false and misguided the claim is. As several American reviewers of the novel have written, Aue is not even a normal *Nazi*.

Finally, in this regard, it is worth noting, as have Edouard Husson and Michel Tereschenko in their highly critical book devoted to *Les Bienveillantes* and its reception in France,[13] that the obsessive eroticism and perversions that characterize Max Aue are strikingly reminiscent of characterizations of Nazis and Nazism from the early 1970s in films like Visconti's *The Damned* and Cavani's *The Night Porter*, and in France, in *mode rétro* works like Tournier's *Le Roi des Aulnes*. In an interview in *Les Cahiers du cinéma*, Michel Foucault largely debunked these stereotypes while exposing their political implications in the

---

[11] This has proven to be the case more in France than elsewhere, especially the US. For a discussion of the American reception of *The Kindly Ones*, see my forthcoming essay in *Substance*, 'Max Aue in America'.

[12] *Le Débat* 144 (March–April 2007), p. 25.

[13] *Les Complaisantes. Jonathan Littell et l'écriture du mal* (Paris: François-Xavier de Guibert, 2007).

post-war period.[14] To the degree that *Les Bienveillantes* reprises these same stereotypes, it turns out to be the memory of a memory, already shown to be false.

It is one of the strengths of Sansal's remarkable *Le Village de l'Allemand* that it can explore the problematic nature of memory, its corruptions but also its potential virtues, in an open, and even perhaps open-ended, fashion. Moreover, in the novel 'memory' is composed of different voices, different perspectives and different experiences. In this sense it is essentially 'discordant and plural' – like history itself, according to Maier. If this is the case, then Sansal's novel offers a refreshing challenge to the absolute opposition of history and memory and the corruptions and dangers of the latter sketched out earlier. Unfortuately, the same cannot be said of *Les Bienveillantes*. Praised precisely as a work where history emerges from memory, Aue's narrative ultimately submerges both in a criminalized and corrupting past. Moreover, the protagonist seems to have learned nothing from his experiences, even decades later, other than the absurd and false lesson that he is the same as other human beings, and they are the same as he. In this sense, Max Aue ultimately rejects Todorov's four roles and proposes something equally, if not more, misleading, and morally much worse. Now there aren't villains and victims, heroes and beneficiaries, because *all humans* are the villains. We don't need to acknowledge evil among us, because evil *is us, all of us, all the time.*

To conclude: what both novels confirm, most obviously, is that memory is a crucial and indeed troubling and troubled issue in our time. But on a much less grandiose scale, what they also confirm is that in France at least, whether succumbing to memory's 'corruptions' or exploring memory's potential for understanding the past and improving the present, the novel has an important and, in some instances even perhaps a vital and creative, role to play in ongoing debates. In this sense, to revise Charles Maier's claim made at the outset, memory *through literature* can be viewed as a valued 'servant', but not the 'master', of our understanding of the past.

---

[14] The interview has been translated as 'Film and Popular Memory' and published in *Foucault Live: Collected Interviews, 1961–1984* ed. Sylvère Lotringer (New York: Semiotext(e), 1996), pp. 122–132.

Chapter 9

Lived experience past/reading experience present: figures of memory in life-writing narratives of the Occupation

Debra Kelly

The study of memory turns academics into concerned citizens who share the burdens of contemporary memory crises.[1]

Texts, titles and cultural assumptions

Focusing on two recently published life-writing narratives concerned with experiences of the Occupation, this chapter has two main aims. It proposes some ideas concerning their reception by a range of French and (in translation) English-speaking readerships, addressing questions of what these reading experiences in the present might further tell us about cultural assumptions concerning lived experience in the past (specifically during the Second World War) and about life-writing narratives and their authors. Secondly, it suggests some tentative ways to analyse three recurring tropes evident in these (and indeed in some other narratives of the period) when ephemeral lived experience is transposed into enduring narrative form, thereby constructing 'figures of memory' in the written word.

The first text is published in English (in the UK) in hardback as *Résistance: A Woman's Journal of Struggle and Defiance in Occupied France*, and in paperback as *Résistance: Memoirs of Occupied France* (both Bloomsbury, 2008; translated by Barbara Mellor). Originally published

---

[1] Wulf Kansteiner, 'Finding Meaning in Memory: a Methodological Critique of Collective Memory Studies', *History and Theory*, 41:2 (2002), 179.

in France in 1946, and then re-published in 2004 by Tallandier,[2] the title of Agnès Humbert's *Notre Guerre: Souvenirs de Résistance* clearly underwent interesting changes for the English-speaking market, already suggesting assumptions concerning readership(s) and reception. The title of any literary work clearly has a highly symbolic value and function given that it is the first site of interaction between text and reader, and is the designation by which it functions in the literary 'system'.[3] It also has, of course, an important economic function within the contemporary publishing/marketing world. In French, first published just after the war, Humbert's title would seem to play wholly into the post-war Gaullist myth of the Occupation as part of a war in which the majority of French citizens participated – on the side of the Resistance. In 2004, following the work of historians, film-makers and writers and the various 'memory wars' (notably, for example, the Klaus Barbie and Maurice Papon trials) which have challenged the immediate post-war history of the Occupation experience over the last three decades or so, the title resonates very differently across the generations. In English, to keep the accented 'é' of 'Résistance', makes explicit an editorial decision to mark out the 'French-ness' of the text, thereby suggesting a clearly designated readership, playing on romanticized British perceptions of the French Resistance still nourished by cinema and literature which the echoes of those 'memory wars' finally do little to disturb in the popular imagination. For the American readership it changes its title yet again, dropping the accent (less understood by the reading public?), but reinstating the 'French-woman' while replacing the specifics of the Occupation (again less well known as a reference?) with the more general 'war': *Resistance: A French-woman's Journal of the War.* For the UK market, there is a notable change of emphasis in the second part of the title for the paperback edition, from the specific female experience to more general 'memoir', suggesting a concern for the gendering of the text and its readership (and therefore for sales), implicitly acknowledging the enduring perception in the publishing establishment that while male writers convey 'universal' experience, women's experience is just that (although interestingly the American title risks it). The book was launched in the UK at the French

---

[2] In an edition overseen by the author's grandson Antoine Sabbagh; for both the Humbert and Berr texts the intervention of the family in the story of their publication goes beyond the anecdotal to become an important element in that process.

[3] For a study of the ways in which titles and subtitles function, see Gérard Genette in, for example, *Seuils* (Paris: Seuil, 1987).

Institute in London in June 2008, and was listed by *The Sunday Times* as one of the history books of the year (30 November 2008), again suggesting a certain type of reading and categorization, that is to say that this is a factual work of history and not a work of literary status. The difference becomes important when compared with the reception of Marguerite Duras's *Wartime Notebooks* (published in France in 2006 and in English in 2008, the same year as the Humbert and Berr texts) and Duras provides an important counterpoint, as will be discussed.

The second text is Hélène Berr's *Journal*, translated into English by David Bellos, published by MacLehose Press in autumn 2008, and again receiving a launch in the UK at the French Institute a few months later in February 2009. The French edition (January 2008) has a foreword by the well-known writer Patrick Modiano which does not appear in the English version, which instead features an introduction and an essay, both by the translator, on the position of the Jews in France prior to and during the Occupation, again suggesting very different assumptions concerning readership and their knowledge/relationship to the text. Frequently described as a 'publishing sensation', its publication in France, even before the English version was available, was seen as meriting reporting in the British press (e.g. in *The Observer*, 20 January 2008). Such acknowledgement needs to be seen against the annual statistics for the publication of translated works in the UK, which is around three per cent.

The publisher, the market and the text

A concern with the cultural assumptions surrounding texts written during the Occupation requires preliminary examination of two contexts both linked to lived experience, but in different ways and from different perspectives. The first concerns the publishing world, constituted here both by the conditions in which a text comes to be published and disseminated to its reading publics, and by a specific type of response of one of those reading publics in the form of press reviews. The second concerns the theoretical framework within which texts which deal with the lived experience of war may be read by academics and other cultural commentators – that of memory studies.

As previously noted, in France the two texts are published/re-published by the same publisher, a scholarly press, with the Humbert text preceding the Berr text by some four years. The issue of timing of publication in English and of the launches in the UK is rather different, with the

Humbert text appearing just a few months before Berr's *Journal*, and by very different publishing houses. Berr's British publisher registered some dissatisfaction with the way in which Tallandier dealt (or rather did not deal) with this fact, noting that the *Journal* did not receive press reviews in all the publications whose attention it might have been expected to attract. There is a suggestion that there may have been some press fatigue concerning 'another' Frenchwoman's war memoir after fairly extensive coverage for Humbert's work, but most essentially after the earlier huge international publishing success of Irène Némirovsky's *Suite française* published in France in 2004 and in English in 2006. Although a work of fiction, this was of course also concerned with the experiences of those caught up in the events of the Occupation, and the attendant focus on the fate of the author herself blurred the distinction between fiction and lived experience. The critical and public reception of Némirovsky's work both inside and outside France provides an important context for the readings of all other recently published texts situated during the Occupation – and especially those written by women. Some commentators already saw Humbert's text as the 'next Némirovsky'. As for Berr, it is clear that Tallandier felt that it had an international best-seller on its list, and the rights to Berr's *Journal* had already been sold in fifteen countries before it was even published in France.

One might have expected some joint reviews given the striking contrast which the books provide. Of all the British press reviews which may have taken such an approach, it was the *Daily Mail* (4 December 2008) which reviewed the two texts together under the title 'The Extraordinary Courage of Women who Resisted', noting that: 'Read together, they give a vivid picture of the confusion and complexity of war' (suggesting that they do offer something more 'universal' while also emphasizing the female experience). A further flavour of British press reception can be gauged from other brief extracts; both Humbert and Berr are likened to previous female 'wartime' writers: 'Bloomsbury finds "real-life" *Suite française*' (Humbert described in the *Bookseller*, 11 October 2007), followed by a gushing interview with (Bloomsbury's editor-in-chief); 'France Finds its Own Anne Frank as Young Jewish Woman's War Diary Hits the Shelves' (*Observer*, 20 October 2008). Berr is subsequently billed in numerous reviews as the 'French Anne Frank' and, journalistic shorthand apart, while hers and Frank's texts are clearly very different, there is a connection. Both died at Bergen-Belsen in 1945, Berr dying within a month of Anne Frank, beaten to death for being too weak from typhus to rise from her bunk, just five days before the camp was liberated. Writing about Humbert, Carmen Callil (herself author of *Bad Faith: A Forgotten History of Family and Fatherland*) reminds or informs the reader of the less-well-known suffering of those deported for slave labour by the Nazis in her article 'Testament to that Other Holocaust' (*Guardian*, 6 September 2008). Callil welcomes a 'timely' translation of a 'heroine's war journal', also emphasizing the place of the trained art historian's eye in the (re)construction of experience in the written word. The education, background and influences (hence implicitly the writing style) of both authors form an important element of the reception of each of these texts, as will be further discussed.

The witness, the reader and the text

Working broadly within the approaches developed (and being developed) within memory studies, the underlying premise here is that both these texts are 'witness' texts in that although they recount (in part) traumatic experiences, they are not 'trauma texts' in the general understanding of the term, given that the authors are reacting immediately (on the whole) to those experiences and commit them to writing within a short space of time, rather than 'uncovering' them at a later stage.[4] Modiano's foreword to the French edition stresses 'Hélène' as a voice and a presence that 'will accompany' us for the rest of our lives. The diarist is herself fully conscious of her status as witness: 'I have a duty to write because people must know . . . I am still trying to make the painful effort to *tell the story*. Because it is a duty, it is maybe the only one I can fulfil.'[5] Felman and Laub in their founding text on narrative testimony note that:

> the act of bearing witness is not the communication of a truth that is already known, but its actual production through this performative act. In this process the listener becomes a witness to the witness, not only facilitating the very possibility of testimony, but also subsequently sharing its burden. That is to say, the listener assumes the responsibility to perpetuate the imperative to bear witness to the historical trauma for the sake of collective memory.[6]

[4] The place of trauma theory within memory studies is becoming increasingly problematized. See, for example, the special issue of the *Journal of Romance Studies*, 'The Witness and the Text', 9:3 (2009) edited by D. Kelly and G. Rye.

[5] Hélène Berr, *Journal* (Paris: Tallandier, 2008); trans. David Bellos (London: MacLehose Press, 2008), pb. p. 157.

[6] Shoshana Felman and Dori Laub, *Testimony: Crises of Witnessing in Literature, Psychoanalysis and History* (London: Routledge, 1992), p. 11.

Derrida's much-quoted intervention on the poetics and politics of witnessing raises many of the complexities and ambiguities of witnessing
– whether the concept of bearing witness is compatible with a 'value of
certainty', of assurance and even 'knowing', reminding us that 'whoever
bears witness does not bring a proof', and further raising the problematic
notions of truth-value.[7] These 'witness texts' are, of course, just that –
'texts' – constructed representations of 'reality' and 'lived experience', and
cannot be read at face value as 'documents'. The reader must tolerate the
uncertainties of the 'text as literature', even as s/he accepts the 'truth' of
the account sealed by the 'autobiographical pact' offered by the author.[8]
This renders the reading experience complex and the relationship of
the reader to the text ambiguous – some reader responses suggest that
this is a difficult process. This apparent unfettered access to 'reality' and
issues concerning the emotional individualization of history come with
a further caveat, as articulated by Susannah Radstone. She points out the
dangers of contemporary emphasis on the 'processes of identification
with suffering' and of 'taking the memoir's realism at face value', thereby
'producing a literal reading that assumes that the subjects inscribed
by memoirs are coincident with and can be mapped straightforwardly
onto suffering "persons" or "individuals" with whom readers can then
identify'.

Radstone goes on to note the importance of 'adequate attention to the
literary as literary' and to 'the complex play of tropes, narration, point
of view and address that together constitute the complexity of texts and
the reading experiences that they offer'.[9] I would further suggest that
Humbert's and, to an even greater degree, Berr's narrative, is taken at
face value because they are not '*writers*', as evidenced in the contrast in
press reviews to Marguerite Duras's *Wartime Notebooks*.[10] In Duras's case,
on the other hand, the nascent novelist receives considerable attention,

[7] Jacques Derrida, '"A Self-unsealing Poetic Text": Poetics and Politics of Witnessing',
trans. Rachel Bowlby, in Michael P. Clark (ed.), *Revenge of the Aesthetic: The Place of
Literature in Theory Today* (Berkeley: University of California Press, 2000), pp. 180–207,
p. 190.

[8] Philippe Lejeune, *Le Pacte autobiographique* (Paris: Seuil, 1975).

[9] Susannah Radstone, 'Memory Studies: For and Against', *Memory Studies*, 1:1
(2008), 34.

[10] It also needs to be noted, however, that some reviews in the French press suggest
(sometimes implicitly) the idea that had Berr lived she might have become a writer. This
is an important element in the general appreciation of the 'literary quality' of the diary
which is prized by a number of reviewers.

and this changes the emphasis of the *Notebooks'* reception. Aamer Hussein in *The Independent* (15 February 2008; Hussein also reviewed Humbert two weeks later) asks: 'was the unconscious novelist in Duras already turning the events of her life into fiction?' For *The Times Literary Supplement* (25 July 2007, reviewing the French text): 'In these notebooks one can observe the nascent writer at work, someone compelled to write in order to make sense of her thoughts and experience' (although Berr is arguably also doing this). *The Observer* (20 January 2008) echoes this: 'What it most strikingly reveals is the process by which life is transformed into art.' Carmen Callil, who reviewed both Humbert and Berr, writes in *The Guardian* (12 January 2008): 'the publication of her *Wartime Notebooks*, written between 1943 and 1949, before she had published her first novel, is a marvellous introduction to what is best in her writing.' Notably, the novelist Michèle Roberts in *The Sunday Times* (2 March 2008) writes: 'Anyone interested in the process of writing, of revision and re-writing, will find these notebooks intriguing. Duras helped pioneer our contemporary fascination with the overlaps between fiction and autobiography: her work simultaneously asserts the difficulty of pinning down anything called truth – and yet the obligation to pursue it.' The memoirist and the diarist, then (as Humbert and Berr are marketed), occupy a different place from the professional novelist with regard to their historical moment and their lived experience. This is particularly striking given that Duras is perhaps the writer who has dealt most insistently, if not consistently, with France's post-war memory, or rather its post-war amnesia – consciously interweaving 'fiction' with 'truth' in order to reveal the gravity of dealing with history and one's own history.

Figures of memory: the lost manuscript, the 'handwritingness' of history and the broken narrative[11]

This final section sketches out what further close textual readings of Humbert and Berr might yield by means of three tropes identified as common to both texts – the story of the lost manuscript and how it came to be found, read, disseminated and finally published; the value placed on the handwriting of the author as a physical link to history; and the status of the narrative that is in some way 'broken', being either interrupted or left unfinished due to events. These three tropes could equally

[11] Special acknowledgement is due here to the artist Jinny Rawlings, who suggested these three tropes with reference to her own work dealing with war and memory.

be applied to Némirovsky's *Suite française*, previously evoked as central
to the reception of Humbert and Berr, and to Duras's *Wartime Notebooks*
which provides, as has been discussed, an interesting comparison in
terms of the perceived 'status' of the authors. A further 'meta-trope' is
that of the 'woman who has experienced war' (notwithstanding earlier
remarks concerning gender and 'universal' experience); all four writers
may be considered themselves to be 'figures of memory' in that they
have come to embody the historical moment they lived and wrote
about. Perhaps the female experience of war exerts a particular type
of fascination on their reading publics in the twenty-first century, or is
more palatable to contemporary tastes which prefer the history of the
victim rather than that of the perpetrator?

Humbert's memoir may not appear at first sight to be a 'lost manuscript', but it was known only to historians and scholars of the period,
not to the larger reading public, and so still 'lost' to the wider cultural
landscape. It is, however, truly a lost manuscript since the original
manuscript vanished without trace.[12] As a journal in its original form,
it participates in what we will call here the 'handwritingness of History',
although it does not reach what might be termed the 'sacred' (fetishized?)
status of the manuscripts of Berr and Némirovsky.[13] The conditions
of the text's production were complex, and it is a 'broken narrative' due
to the author's imprisonment and deportation.[14] How, then, was this
text received in the British press, within a national culture that conceives
of the Second World War as a victory and tends broadly to a one-
dimensional view of the 'heroics' of the French Resistance, ably abetted
of course by the British Secret Services and then the British military
(with some help from the Americans, eventually)? Most reviewers note
the harrowing read: 'You have to force yourself to go on ... so vile
are the conditions she describes and the conduct of those in authority'

---

[12] Regarding reference to the disappearance of the original manuscript, *The Washington
Post* (30 November 2008), for example, notes that we will never know whether or not
Humbert revised the original diary entries before publication.

[13] Indeed the fascination with the original version of Némirovsky's *Suite française*: the
'lost' (or rather 'hidden') manuscript and other objects pertaining to it were eventually put
on public display in an exhibition, intensifying their quasi-sacred nature. In both Berr's
Journal and Némirovsky's *Suite française* the author's handwriting figures in facsimile in
the published versions as a page inside the text, and for the English hardback of Némirovsky
as the back/front cover.

[14] The details of these events are available in Allan Massie's review, 'Paris under the
Swastika' for *The Literary Review*, September 2008.

(Allan Massie, *The Literary Review*, September 2008). This is a typical 'evaluative' reading of the sort contained in several reviews, focusing on Humbert's own strength of character: 'Her generosity of spirit is as remarkable as her courage and endurance.'[15]

Mariette Job, the niece of Hélène Berr, was instrumental in bringing her diary to publication. She first saw the original, handwritten version of her aunt's diary in 1992, fifty years after it was written on a set of sheets from a student notepad: 'When I took hold of the diary, it was very moving. *When you see the actual handwriting, that really is life.* She has precise, beautiful handwriting and crossed out very little' (my emphasis).[16] Job's response to the fifty-year-old manuscript returns us fully to the tropes of the story of the lost manuscript, of the 'hand-writingness' of history and of the broken narrative – again broken by deportation, but also by death. The diary is also a broken narrative within itself (just as is Humbert's during the period of slave labour) since Berr stopped writing at one point for some ten months. Job had read a typed version of the diary when she was fifteen (it was originally typed up by an employee of the firm of which Hélène's father was managing director at the request of her elder brother). She recounts that for years, Jean Morawiecki (the intended recipient, then a young man with whom Berr was in love) could only read the typed copy because the handwriting 'emphasised the cruelty of her absence' and was like a 'frozen hand' reaching out to him (*The Telegraph*, 30 October 2008). Much of the French press review reception emphasizes the literary and intellectual qualities of the writing by the young woman who studied Russian and English at the Sorbonne: Antoine Sabbagh, the editor, tells *Der Spiegel* on-line (9 September 2008) that he was certain from the first pages that this was the 'work of an intellectual' and a 'literary description of life in Occupied Paris'. Revealingly, the word 'Jewish' is rarely used either with reference to the collective experience of 'life in Occupied Paris' or to the individual young (Jewish) woman's experience, although *Libération* (20 December 2007) astonishingly suggests that 'on a l'impression de comprendre *pour la première fois* l'horreur et l'absurdité de la vie quotidienne des Juifs dans Paris occupé'.

---

[15] See also *The Spectator* (17 September 2008) and *The Washington Post* (30 November 2008).

[16] Gerald Jacobs, 'How France Discovered its own Anne Frank', *Jewish Chronicle* 13 November 2008.

We will therefore end by once again situating the two texts within memory studies as suggested above, and precisely within three of its linked features as defined by Radstone: urgent and committed engagement with varied instances of contemporary and historical violence; close ties with questions of identity and, relatedly, with identity politics; and bridging of the domains of the personal and the public, the individual and the social.[17] Both writers felt compelled by the urgency of their experience in the Second World War and of varied forms of violence perpetrated on them and on those around them to keep a written record. While it would be anachronistic to think of them as being concerned with 'identity politics', both were certainly aware of their own 'identity' and of the position of their gender within the society in which they were living and, again, within the events to which they bore witness (indeed in the case of Humbert, her gender leads to deportation rather than execution). Berr obviously becomes increasingly aware of her status as Jew. Both become increasingly aware of the identity of the citizen under Occupation and his or her relationship to the power of the occupier. Both authors write at the intersection of the personal and the public, examining their own feelings and reactions within the broader spectrum of the immediate and of the larger society in which they live, and within the historical circumstances that they experience. Without indulging in the types of facile identification with the victim against which Radstone warns it may be that, if we are mindful of readings of the sort she advocates, more dynamic, if necessarily more fragile, identities that connect us with the histories that we seek to know may come into being. Agnès Humbert and Hélène Berr offer us the possibility of just such connecting identities. Life-writing provides another lens through which to view our relationship to the past, to the identities and experiences of those who lived it, and to our own needs, desires and identities in the present as we read.

[17] Radstone, 'Memory Studies', 34.

Chapter 10

Fictions of testimony: Irène Némirovsky and *Suite française*

Angela Kershaw

One of the reasons for the enormous success of Irène Némirovsky's post-humously published *Suite française* was its perceived value and status as a true testimony of the French experience of the Occupation. The fact that *Suite française* has become a best-seller is closely related to the continuing cultural dominance of the notion that post-Holocaust literature must – and should – fulfil a testimonial function. The 'age of testimony', in which the task of writing is to deal with the trauma of the war, was, for Shoshana Felman, inaugurated by Camus's *La Peste* (1947). Felman's reading insists on the complexity – or even 'crisis' – of witnessing: Camus's *La Chute* (1956) continues to affirm the necessity of witnessing, present in his earlier novel, but also demonstrates its impossibility.[1] Elie Wiesel's *La Nuit*, published in French in 1958, proves Felman's point – though recognized as a crucially important testimony of the camps, it struggled to find a readership in the late 1950s.[2] Wiesel has nonetheless continued to assert the importance of testimony. In 1977, he suggested that, after Auschwitz, testimony has taken over from literature because literature is no longer adequate: 'But then there are the witnesses and there is their testimony. If the Greeks invented tragedy, the Romans the epistle, and the Renaissance the sonnet, our generation invented a new literature, that of testimony. We have all been witnesses and we all feel we have to bear testimony for the future.' For Wiesel, giving and receiving testimony is a moral requirement: 'Anyone who does not actively,

---

[1] Shoshana Felman and Dori Laub, *Testimony: Crises of Witnessing in Literature, Psychoanalysis and History* (New York and London: Routledge, 1992), chapter 4, 'Camus' *The Plague*, or a Monument to Witnessing' and chapter 6, 'The Betrayal of the Witness: Camus' *The Fall*', pp. 93–119 and 165–203.

[2] Elie Wiesel, preface, *La Nuit* (Paris: Les Editions de minuit, 1958/2007), p. 21.

constantly engage in remembering and in making others remember is an accomplice of the enemy. Conversely, whoever opposes the enemy must take the side of his victims and communicate their tales, tales of solitude and despair, tales of silence and defiance'.[3] In 1998, Annette Wieviorka defined contemporary culture as 'the era of testimony', citing the Yale Fortunoff Video Archive and Spielberg's Survivors of the Shoah Visual History Foundation as evidence of an 'explosion du témoignage'.[4] Given the incremental importance of testimony through the second half of the twentieth century, it is not surprising that, in 2004, the last surviving manuscript of a Holocaust victim should be received by modern critics and readers as the author's attempt to bear witness to her own direct experience of the *années noires*.

Olivier le Naire's definition of *Suite française* as 'témoignage' and 'testament' in his review of the novel in *L'Express* is typical of the discussion the book generated.[5] Némirovsky's novel has been received as a witness statement and a bequest, as a true account of historical events and a literary legacy. It has also been understood figuratively as a 'testament' to Némirovsky's talent, as the culmination of her *œuvre*. There are important distinctions to be drawn between testimony and testament, yet their convergence is indicated by their shared etymological root in the Latin *testis*: whether it is understood as testimony or as testament, *Suite française* has defined Némirovsky as witness. In law, a testimony before a court and a last will and testament are validated by the same procedure – an individual declaration of authenticity. A testimony in a court of law must be validated by an oath before it is presented to the judge and jury as a genuine account of what the witness knows. Similarly, a will is a mutual act of witnessing whereby the testator testifies before a third party that the document is a genuine account of his or her intentions. The mutual natures of witnessing – the testimony/testament of the witness must be witnessed by others if it is to be accepted as an act of witness – points to the importance of reception in the study of the literature of testimony. The reception of *Suite française* as testimony

---

[3] Elie Wiesel (ed.), 'The Holocaust as Literary Imagination', in *Dimensions of the Holocaust: Lectures at Northwestern University* (Evanston, Illinois: Northwestern University Press, 1977), pp. 5–19 (pp. 9, 16).

[4] *L'Ere du témoin* (Paris: Plon, 1998), p. 176.

[5] 'La passion d'Irène', *L'Express*, 27 September 2004. I am grateful to Susan Suleiman for drawing to my attention the multiple meanings generated by the semantic proximity of 'testimony' (bearing witness) and 'testament' (a bequest).

is to a certain extent appropriate – the novel certainly does draw on Némirovksy's personal experience of exile in rural France, chased from Paris to the village of Issy l'Evêque in 1940 by the increasing climate of hostility towards foreign Jews[6] – but it is also problematic. The twenty-first-century reader has certain expectations of writers who bear witness to the Occupation and the Holocaust that *Suite française* cannot necessarily fulfil, first because it is a work of fiction composed *before* the 'era of testimony', and secondly because, tragically interrupted in July 1942, it cannot represent the Occupation from the post-Holocaust perspective familiar to modern readers. The modern reception of Némirovsky's last novel thus raises difficult questions about the relationship between fiction and truth and about the retrospective judging of the writer. The fiction of testimony of my title is, then, a reading effect: it has nothing to do with Derrida's opposition between a text presented in good faith and a lie.[7]

Now that the immediate excitement of Némirovsky's rediscovery is past, it is the task of critics and readers to achieve a fuller and more nuanced understanding of Némirovsky and her work. It is only by paying close attention to the contexts of production and of reception that we can understand how and why certain types of value have – or have not – been ascribed to Némirovsky's novels. Shoshana Felman and Dori Laub preface their influential study of testimony and the Holocaust with a call for contextualization, not to restate the idea that there is mutual reflection between 'history' and 'text', but rather to try to understand 'how issues of biography and history are neither simply represented nor simply reflected, but are reinscribed, translated, radically rethought and fundamentally worked over by the text'.[8] To achieve this, they propose, we must not only *contextualize the text*, but also *textualize the context*.[9] This is particularly important in the case of *Suite française* because of the temporal and political gap between the context of production and the context of reception. In an attempt to bridge that gap, *Suite française*

[6] As an émigrée who had left Russia as an opponent of the revolution, Némirovsky was a stateless person. She applied (unsuccessfully) for French nationality only in the late 1930s. See Olivier Philipponnat and Patrick Lienhardt, *La Vie d'Irène Némirovsky* (Paris: Grasset/Denoël, 2007), pp. 268–269, pp. 308–309; and Jonathan Weiss, *Irène Némirovsky* (Paris: Editions du Félin, 2005).

[7] Jacques Derrida, *Demeure: Fiction and Testimony*, trans by Elizabeth Rottehberg (Stanford: Stanford University Press, 2000), pp. 35–36.

[8] Felman and Laub, *Testimony*, pp. xiv–xv.

[9] Felman and Laub, *Testimony*, p. xv.

was published with substantial accompanying paratextual material. At one level, Myriam Anissimov's biographical preface and the notes and correspondence reproduced in the annexes to the novel are an attempt to supply the context of production for the modern reader unfamiliar with the life and times of an unknown writer. However, they also supply the twenty-first-century context of reception insofar as the paratextual material aligns *Suite française* with currently dominant cultural discourses of the French Occupation and the Holocaust. The preface frames the text in terms of Jewish memory of the Occupation by virtue of being written by a child of Holocaust survivors who is a well-known French Jewish novelist and also the biographer of Primo Levi and Romain Gary. The inclusion of the extracts from Némirovsky's notebooks and correspondence, and from Michael Epstein's correspondence after his wife's arrest, defines the novel as the legacy of a Jewish deportee. *Suite française* is not an autobiography, but Anissimov's preface operates as a surrogate autobiographical pact which invokes, in James E. Young's words, 'the empirical bond that has indeed existed between a writer and events in his narrative'.[10] It is in the preface and the annexes, rather than in the fictional text itself, that we find the individual declaration of authenticity which validates the text as testimony and testament. Anissimov describes *Suite française* as 'une photo prise sur le vif de la France et des Français'. The metaphor of Némirovsky as photographer links events and text via the author's *presence*: the text only exists because Némirovsky *was there* and because she *saw*.[11] The impetus behind such a presentation of the text is positive and laudable: it is an attempt to ascribe value to the text. Denise Epstein is perfectly justified in calling *Suite française* 'le journal de bord de ma mère',[12] and I do not wish to deny the existence of an autobiographical link between author and text. But it is important to be clear about the effects of this type of discourse: it transforms Némirovsky from novelist to witness.

In a cultural context in which the Holocaust has become the dominant point of reference for representations of the Occupation, the witness's text has become a privileged text. 'Holocaust literature' has been celebrated for its eye-witness value,[13] and, as Michael André Bernstein points

---

[10] James E. Young, *Writing and Rewriting the Holocaust: Narrative and the Consequences of Interpretation* (Bloomington: Indiana University Press, 1988), p. 24.

[11] Irène Némirovsky, *Suite française* (Paris: Denoël, 2004), p. 24.

[12] Le Naire, 'La passion d'Irène'.

[13] Le Naire, 'La passion d'Irène'.

out, after Auschwitz, the 'I' of the eye-witness is deemed infallible.[14] The
text written at the time is privileged over the text written with hindsight.
As Young writes of the Holocaust diarists, 'Because the diarists write
from within the whirlwind, the degree of authority in their accounts is
perceived by readers to be stronger than that of the texts shaped through
hindsight.'[15] By contrast, in a retrospective account, 'the survivor necessarily unifies his vision in the knowledge of its outcome',[16] and therefore
readers become suspicious of reconstructions after the fact. The proximity
between the time of writing and the events narrated has frequently been
cited by Némirovsky's critics as proof that *Suite française* is an example
of *unmediated* testimony, uncontaminated by the distortions of hindsight.
In an article significantly entitled 'Radiographie de la débâcle française',
Le Temps described how Némirovsky wrote the first two parts of the
novel 'à chaud' as events were unfolding.[17] According to *Le Point*, 'une
mouche chargée d'encre semble composer en temps réel la partition du
désastre'.[18] These and many other similar formulations depict Némirovsky
as a neutral vehicle transcribing contemporary events. But there is no such
thing as unmediated testimony: as Young's study of Holocaust writing
demonstrates, and as the reviews of *Suite française* illustrate, *authenticity*
can easily be confused with *factuality* and *authority*. Némirovsky's novel
is certainly authentic, but this does not make it a historically verifiable
and reliable account of the past. The reviews illustrate contemporary
desire for such an account, but the textual reality of the novel demonstrates its impossibility. It is this fundamental conflict between a cultural
need for testimony and the incapacity of narrative to provide it that
Shoshana Felman and Dori Laub have termed a 'crisis of testimony'.

Studies of Holocaust writing have demonstrated the difficulty of
distinguishing between testimony and literature. As Colin Davis writes,
'the truth of testimony positively requires the artifice of literature';
this is what Young calls the 'rhetoric of fact'.[19] Analysis of Némirovsky's

---

[14] *Foregone Conclusions: Against Apocalyptic History* (Berkeley and London: University
of California Press, 1994), p. 47.

[15] Young, *Writing and Rewriting the Holocaust*, p. 25.

[16] Young, *Writing and Rewriting the Holocaust*, p. 30.

[17] 'Radiographie de la débâcle française', *Le Temps*, 6 November 2004.

[18] Claude Arnaud, 'Irène Némirovsky: Le manuscrit retrouvé', *Le Point*, 30 September
2004.

[19] Colin Davis, 'Rewriting Memory: Wiesel, Testimony and Self-reading', in Helmut Peitsch,
Charles Burdett and Claire Gorrara (eds), *European Memories of the Second World War* (Oxford:
Berghahn, 1998), pp. 122–130 (p. 124); Young, *Writing and Rewriting the Holocaust*, p. 62.

narrative technique soon reveals the text's very *literary* quality, as Nathan
Bracher's recent discussion of shifting point of view in 'Tempête en juin'
shows: it is precisely through *literary* artifice that Némirovsky is able to
represent history.[20] Christopher Lloyd is less convinced than Bracher by
the text's literary qualities, expressing his 'reservations about the book's
form and construction' and preferring to concentrate on its 'documentary
interest'.[21] Indeed, it is quite a straightforward matter to demonstrate,
as Bracher does, by reference to works of history, that *Suite française* is
an accurate account of the events described.[22] What interests me is the
possibility that *Suite française* has been received as testimony not only
because it fulfils the contextual criteria of testimony as an accurate
account of lived experience, but also because it contains certain textual
tropes which twenty-first-century readers associate with testimony. *Suite
française* reads like testimony because it individuates history, notably via
representations of the quotidian and of suffering. This is what Martin
Crowley, discussing Robert Antelme's use of scenes of physical abjection
in *L'Espèce humaine*, calls 'testimonial frankness'.[23] Individuation occurs
in *Suite française* not so much through the characters, which we know
to be fictional, but rather through evocations of place. The narrative
centre of each of the two parts of the text is spatial: 'Tempête en juin'
derives its coherence from the geographical trajectories of the characters,
while 'Dolce' is focused on the village. Characters are always located with
spatial precision: for example, the fictional Péricands live on the very
real boulevard Delessert.[24] Paris is evoked through spatial detail: near
the avenue de l'Opéra, the reader sees and hears iron shutters closing:
'Les rues étaient vides. On fermait les volets de fer des magasins. On
n'entendait dans le silence que leur bruit métallique'. On the road, south
of Orléans, the reader smells '[u]ne faible odeur de fraise' mingled with
'les vapeurs de pétrole et de fumée' and sees women washing their clothes
in the river.[25] Such details are 'testimonial' insofar as they appear to be

---

[20] Nathan Bracher, 'Le fin mot de l'histoire: La Tempête en juin et les perspectives de
Némirovsky', *Modern and Contemporary France*, 16:3 (2008), 265–277.

[21] Christopher Lloyd, 'Irène Némirovsky's *Suite française* and the Crisis of Rights and
Identity', *Contemporary French Civilization*, 31 (2007), 161–182 (169).

[22] Bracher refers to Hanna Diamond's *Fleeing Hitler: France 1940* (Oxford and New
York: Oxford University Press, 2007).

[23] Martin Crowley, 'Remaining Human: Robert Antelme's *L'Espèce humaine*', *French
Studies*, 56:4 (2002), 471–482 (473 n.4).

[24] Némirovsky, *Suite française*, p. 31.

[25] Némirovsky, *Suite française*, pp. 51, 93.

so precise that only a witness could convey them. The suffering of the *exode* is evoked through graphic descriptions of injured bodies which, as Crowley's reading of Antelme suggests, we have come to associate with testimonial writing:

> Leurs corps étaient déchiquetés et par hasard leurs trois visages demeuraient intacts, de si mornes, de si ordinaires visages, avec une expression étonnée, appliquée et stupide . . . (p. 82)

> Ce sang chaud avait giclé sur la robe de Jeanne, sur ses bas et ses souliers. (p. 84)

These examples could be multiplied. I am not suggesting that we can know whether Némirovsky actually witnessed these details of daily life and of suffering under the Occupation – most probably she did not – but rather that they function within the narrative to connote 'testimony'; because readers potentially receive them as examples of 'testimonial frankness', the *impression* of testimony generated by the contextual and paratextual material is reinforced at text level.

If we allow *Suite française* to function as a textualization of its context, its *literarity* emerges clearly. This also involves resisting the reverse chronological reading of Némirovsky's *œuvre* which results from the fact that it is her last novel which has made her famous in our own time. As I have demonstrated elsewhere,[26] when read as the culmination of a literary career rather than as the starting point of a new phase of popularity, *Suite française* is very obviously in a continuum with the novels which directly preceded it, particularly the posthumously published *Les Biens de ce monde* (1947) and *Les Feux de l'automne* (1957).[27] *Suite française* was not an unprecedented and instantaneous literary response to contemporary events, but a literary experiment in which Némirovsky was perfecting a novelistic technique she had been trying out for some years already – the integration of a fictional narrative with historical fact. Némirovsky's textualization of the beginnings of the Occupation is *fictional* before it is *testimonial*. In her notes, she wrote: 'Pourquoi suivre servilement la vérité? Pourquoi ne pas imaginer?'[28] *Suite*

---

[26] See Angela Kershaw, *Before Auschwitz: Irène Némirovsky and the Cultural Landscape of Inter-war France* (New York and London: Routledge, 2010), especially pp. 172–179.

[27] *Les Biens de ce monde* was serialized in *Gringoire* in 1941 but did not appear as a book until after the war.

[28] IMEC NMR 15.2 Nouvelles 1940, projets.

française is a deliberate and complex engagement with the fuzzy boundary between truth and imagination. As such, it should be evaluated not against the criteria which define testimony, but against those which define literature. As Young remarks, 'By mixing actual events with completely fictional characters, a writer simultaneously relieves himself of an obligation to historical accuracy (invoking poetic license), even as he imbues his fiction with the historical authority of real events.'[29] *Suite française* does benefit from the authority of real events, but its author was under no obligation to respect either truth or completeness.

Nonetheless, *Suite française* has been accused of a lack of historical accuracy.[30] According to some American critics, Némirovsky sinned by omission: *Suite française* fails to give a complete picture of the Occupation, they say, because it does not deal with the persecution of the Jews under Vichy. The absence of Jewish characters from the novel has been taken as evidence that Némirovsky failed to convey the specificity of her situation as a foreign Jew in the Occupied zone. This 'omission' has been said to demonstrate 'how little her particular situation seems to have influenced her story' and to prove that 'there is no sense of history' in the novel.[31] This sort of reading takes the contextualization of the novel according to twenty-first-century frames of reference to its extreme, and refuses to hear Némirovsky's textualization of her context. It refuses to accept that Némirovsky was quite within her rights to be Jewish in 1942 and not to write a novel about Jews. Furthermore, given that the text was written before the fate of the Jews was a dominant feature of public discourse on the Occupation in France, it is completely in accord with the historical and political imperatives of its moment of production. The American, and to some extent the British, reception of *Suite française* has demonstrated the truth of Young's proposition that if narrative is required to fulfil a documentary function, the writer is left open to criticism:

> For by emphasising the putative documentary function of Holocaust narrative over its valuable interpretive achievement, the critic might even be leaving this narrative vulnerable to undeserved – and ultimately irrelevant – criticism regarding historical points of fact.[32]

---

[29] Young, *Writing and Rewriting the Holocaust*, p. 52.

[30] See Kershaw, *Before Auschwitz*, pp. 179–181.

[31] Alice Kaplan, 'Love in the Ruins', *The Nation*, 29 May 2006; Edward Rothstein, 'Ambivalence as Part of Author's Legacy', *The New York Times*, 21 October 2008.

[32] Young, *Writing and Rewriting the Holocaust*, p. 18.

Reading *Suite française* as testimony can lead to berating the author for not having produced the 'correct' testimony. This sort of response to Némirovsky can be explained in relation to the dominance of a certain cultural and historical model in the USA, which Young identifies, according to which Jewish history and culture must always be filtered through the Holocaust:

> While the Holocaust is studied and taught in Israel as one event – even of watershed proportions – among others in a long Jewish history, it has already begun to dominate all Jewish past and present in America. Instead of learning about the Holocaust through a study of Jewish history, too many students in America are learning the whole of Jewish history through the lens of the Holocaust ... Holocaust museums in America tend to organize Jewish culture and identity around this one event alone, rather than representing events as part of a greater Jewish continuum.[33]

This is not, of course, to contest, in Elie Wiesel's words, the 'centrality in our lives and in history' of the Holocaust.[34] It is to contest a partial and anachronistic reading of *Suite française*. To object to the absence of Jewish characters from *Suite française* is to seek to 'organize' the novel around the Holocaust. It is to refuse to understand it as part of the 'greater continuum' of Némirovsky's *œuvre*. That continuum has, of course, its disruptions and its contradictions. As Omer Bartov says, '[t]he memory of the past will always project itself into the future, always threaten to monopolise our hopes and aspirations. And so we mould it to fit our needs, and in the process distort it, and project that distortion into our future, making it too into a distorted mirror of imagined, fabricated recollections'.[35] Némirovsky is inevitably caught up in these 'distortions'; they constitute what Felman and Laub describe as reinscriptions, as translations, as a rethinking of biography and history. We cannot view Némirovsky from some neutral standpoint outside of our own cultural moment. But we must respect the ways in which she chose to textualize the history of the Occupation, if we are to engage in the important process of revision of the frames of reference via which we seek to apprehend the Occupation in the twenty-first century.

If, as Felman and Laub argue, Holocaust literature testifies to the impossibility of testimony, *Suite française* seems to be a different sort of

---

[33] Young, *Writing and Rewriting the Holocaust*, p. 187.

[34] Wiesel, 'The Holocaust as Literary Imagination', p. 6.

[35] Omer Bartov, 'Trauma and Absence', in Peitsch, Burdett and Gorrara (eds), *European Memories of the Second World War*, pp. 258–271 (p. 263).

testimony, one that is not impossible. Némirovsky believed in the value of writing in the face of death. Two days before her arrest, she wrote to Albin Michel: 'Cher Ami . . . pensez à moi. J'ai beaucoup écrit. Je suppose que ce seront des œuvres posthumes, mais ça fait passer le temps.'[36] *Suite française* is not 'about' the Holocaust, it is not a testimony of the Holocaust, but, because of Némirovsky's fate, it must be read in this discursive context. And it is this context which has made *Suite française* available and interesting to a new generation of readers. The Holocaust is an absent presence in *Suite française*, and in this respect the novel actualizes Dori Laub's idea of the Holocaust as an event without a witness.[37] By 'virtue' of that which makes it into 'Holocaust writing', *Suite française* is not afflicted by post-Holocaust doubts about the possibility of writing, and is therefore more accessible than much fiction which falls into this category. But for this very reason, we must approach it carefully. Colin Davis asks whether it is ultimately possible to distinguish between testimony and literature.[38] Certainly, Derrida's image of 'the meshes of the net formed by the limits *between* fiction and testimony, which are also *interior* each to the other' is compelling.[39] But in Némirovsky's case, it is important to make such a distinction. To fail to do so is to fail to recognize and to celebrate her literary project in its own terms, and to expose her to inappropriate ethical criticism.

---

[36] Némirovsky, *Suite française*, p. 22.
[37] Felman and Laub, *Testimony*, p. 80.
[38] Davis, 'Rewriting Memory: Wiesel, Testimony and Self-reading', pp. 123–124.
[39] Derrida, *Demeure*, p. 56.

Chapter 11

Hoaxes and the memory of the Second World War: from *Un Héros très discret* to Misha Defonseca

Virginie Sansico

The way in which so many key witnesses of the Second World War have acquired the status of media icons,[1] and the way in which so many themes relating to that period[2] have come to occupy such a major role in France's literary and cinematographic output, are two of the most obvious signs of the massive presence of the memory of the Occupation and the Vichy regime within French public space. Both these ways in which the last world war is remembered are closely related to a significant dual phenomenon of the 1990s, namely the publication of the memoirs of self-styled Holocaust survivors which, after having enjoyed considerable success even though they were in some cases improbable, proved to be complete fakes; and the emergence in fiction of characters who, at the end of the war, used lies and deceptions to pass themselves off as brave Resistance fighters when they in fact behaved in distinctly unheroic fashion and either did nothing during the Occupation or became collaborators.

These hoaxes, both real and fictional, affect the two major emblematic figures of the 'age of witnessing'[3] that French society has been living

[1] See, in particular, the intense media coverage of the death of the Resistance veteran Lucie Aubrac on 14 March 2007.

[2] The scale of the war's literary presence in France can be gauged by the winners of literary prizes, and especially the Goncourt, which is the most prestigious of all of them and which was won by Jonathan Littell for *Les Bienveillantes* (Paris: Gallimard, 2006). Soazig Aaron's *Le Non de Klara* (Paris: Editions Maurice Nadeau, 2002) won the Goncourt du Premier roman (2002), as did Frédéric Brun, *Perla* (Paris: Stock, 2007) and Laurent Binet, *HHhH* (Paris: Grasset, 2010). The film *La Rafle* was released in 2010.

[3] The expression is borrowed from Annette Wieviorka's *L'Ere du témoin*.

through in recent decades: the Jewish Holocaust survivor and the *résistant*. Although both figures have been the object of various studies (of varying quality) in recent years,[4] such studies have rarely adopted a comparative approach.[5] Yet far from being a mere coincidence, the simultaneity of the two phenomena reveals the existence of two parallel but quite distinct memorial constructs. It also tells us something about the current state of French representations of this period. On the one hand, the fake memoirs produced by contemporaries of the Holocaust almost fifty years after the event demonstrate how central the Holocaust has become to the memory of the Second World War, as well as revealing the increasingly obvious tendency to identify with its victims. On the other hand, the fictional appropriation of the figure of the '*faux résistant*' shows how the authors of these works have distanced themselves and almost become suspicious of the Resistance episode, still widely seen as one of the most glorious episodes in the history of France even though its memory appears to be losing something of its centrality.

The figure of the '*faux résistant*' in fiction

Jean-François Deniau's novel *Un Héros très discret* was published in 1989.[6] It tells the story of a young man with no particular claim to fame who in the post-war years briefly achieves unwarranted success when he passes himself off as a former member of the Resistance. The film of the same name was directed a few years later by Jacques Audiard; it was a box office success on its release in 1996 and won the 'best screenplay' award at the Cannes Film Festival that same year.

[4] On *Un Héros très discret* and Binjamin Wilkomirski, see, for example, K.M. Lauten, 'Dusting off Dehousse: *Un Héros très discret*', in P. Powrie (ed.), *French Cinema in the 1990s: Continuity and Difference: Essays* (Oxford: Oxford University Press, 1999), pp. 58–68; H. Seal, 'Screening the Past: Representing Resistance in *Un Héros très discret*', in L. Mazdon (ed.), *France on Film: Reflections on Popular French Cinema* (London: Wallflower, 2001), pp. 107–117; B. Eskin, *Life in Pieces: The Making and Unmaking of Binjamin Wilkomirski* (New York and London: Norton, 2002); S. Maechler, *The Wilkomirski Affair: A Study in Biographical Truth* (New York: Schocken Books, 2001).

[5] Mention should, however, be made of a major article by Christopher Lloyd which, while it is devoted to the Resistance, also discusses the case of Binjamin Wilkomirski's false claim to have survived the Shoah: Christopher Lloyd, 'Inventing the French Resistance: Heroes, Traitors and Fakes in the Resistance Novel and Memoir', in P. Knight and J. Long (eds), *Fakes and Forgeries* (Buckingham: Cambridge Scholars, 2004), pp. 107–117.

[6] Jean-François Deniau, *Un Héros très discret* (Paris: Editions Olivier Orban, 1989).

Albert Dehousse, who is the main character, has nothing in common with the heroic figures who had until then been the staple of the vast majority of epic novels and films about the Resistance. Although it demonstrates the important role played by networks of former Free French agents in shaping the post-war elites in France, the narrative undermines their prestige in that the ease with which Dehousse insinuates himself into their ranks without any legitimacy raises certain questions for the viewer. This effect is heightened by the way in which the film cleverly mingles fiction with fact in a deliberate bid to sow doubts in the viewer's mind. That ambiguity was already present in the book. In the film, some characters are genuine *résistants* who are playing themselves, and the line between what is real and what is pure fiction is so blurred that no one who has just watched the film can be sure which is which.

The film's success and the publicity surrounding it make it a special case, but it is not the only one to deal with the question of imposture among former members of the Resistance. Both made-for-TV movies and novels have tackled the same theme, and have usually done so in portentous ways that cannot reproduce the relatively detached atmosphere created by Jacques Audiard. *Le Lien*, directed by Denis Malleval and shown on the state-owned France 3 TV channel in 2007, is one example. The *milicien* responsible for the arrest and deportation of a Jewish family takes in its only survivor. She is a little girl only a few weeks old, and he and his wife adopt her as they do not have children of their own, even though the adoption is completely illegal. Sixteen years later, when she is a *lycéenne*, the girl happens to get to know her real grandmother, now a French teacher and the only witness to the arrest of her family, who died in Auschwitz. She tells the girl her real story and reveals that her father was not, as he has always boasted, in the Resistance: he was a *milicien*, and he is to blame for the death of her real family.

Sorj Chalandon also adopts a family framework in his novel *La Légende de nos pères*, which was published in 2009.[7] In this novel a 'family biographer' is asked by the daughter of an old *résistant* to record the memories of a man who has said very little about what he did during the Occupation and who has always refused to accept any of the honours for which he has been recommended. The old man is at first reluctant to cooperate, but eventually agrees. The biographer gradually realizes,

[7] Sorj Chalandon, *La Légende de nos pères* (Paris: Grasset, 2009).

however, that the man he is interviewing has spent his life lying about his involvement with the Resistance: he pretended to have been in the Resistance purely to impress his daughter who, as a child, had been captivated by René Clément's film *Le Père tranquille*.

These books and films all feature characters who make up stories about their involvement in the Resistance even though, like most of the French population, they either did nothing and survived the war without mishap, or chose to collaborate. There are also works of fiction that question the unfailing heroism of a number of genuine *résistants*. *La Vérité en face*, which was shown on a state TV channel in 1983, is one example.[8] For many years, the hero, who is a provincial *notable*, has been seen as an irreproachable *résistant*. Long after the war, a ceremony is held to honour the memory of the five members of his network who were executed by the Germans; he admits that, when arrested, he talked under torture and the information he gave led to the death of the five men. The film does not, however, portray him as a 'traitor' – which is how French fiction usually describes *résistants* who 'talked' – but as an ordinary and fallible human being. In this case, it is a myth that has long been sustained by historiography that is being undermined: the myth of the *résistant* who never betrays his comrade, even under torture – anyone who 'talks' no longer enjoys the status of *résistant* – and who would rather die than save his own skin by betraying them.

A major change in the way the Resistance is remembered

These examples illustrate the process of the fictional appropriation of the figure of the fake *résistant* – and of the *résistant* who is more fallible than he seems – and it probably represents a turning point in the gradual shift in the way the Resistance is remembered.[9] And yet this question is not a memorial construct that emerged *ex nihilo*, not least because it is based upon a reality that goes back to the Occupation period itself and to the conflicts that emerged between different tendencies within the Resistance. These sometimes took the form of a violent settling of scores. Some of the FTP who made up the armed wing of the

---

[8] The film was made by the Belgian director Etienne Périer.

[9] It should, however, be noted that even at the time of Liberation, the novel was an important vector for challenges to orthodox Gaullist and communist memories of the Resistance.

Communist Party were accused of ignoring the national chains of command and were regarded as quasi-outlaws by some of the leaders of the united Resistance and especially the Armée secrète, whose members included many devout anti-communists.

These quarrels were consubstantial with the history of the Resistance, and they were compounded by the issue of the *résistants de l'été 1944*, or of those individuals who are known to have joined the Resistance only after the Allied landings in Normandy, in other words when German defeat was only a matter of time. Although many of these last-minute *résistants* paid with their lives during the most violent weeks of the Liberation (most of the *résistants* who were killed during the war were killed during this period), those who survived were still suspect in the eyes of the *résistants de la première heure*, who tended to regard late-comers as opportunists.

The period of the *épuration* did nothing to reduce these tensions.[10] The debates sparked by the true/fake *résistant* issue that took place during and after the war could be heated, and there are examples of hoaxes that were inspired by the codes governing the social representations of the day: for many French people, putting on the uniform of a fighter who had helped to liberate the country was a sure-fire way of demonstrating one's worthiness in a country that was busily reconstructing its identity.

It was the renewed interest in historiography that allowed the memory of the Resistance to undergo a significant change from the 1970s. It was at this point that a number of historians began to challenge what they called *le mythe résistancialiste*, which was, in their view, a joint creation of former Gaullist and communist *résistants* that had produced an overly hagiographic, and therefore distorted, image of the Resistance.[11] The polemics surrounding the figure of François Mitterrand – a Vichy *fonctionnaire* until he joined the Resistance – and, more generally, historiography's attempts to come to terms with the complex issue of *vichysto-résistants* – made the historiography and memory of the Resistance even more problematic.[12] It was mainly in this context that eye-witness accounts came under increasing challenge from some

---

[10] On the legal purge and the political issues involved, see Simonin, *Le Déshonneur dans la République: une histoire de l'indignité, 1791–1958* (Paris: Grasset, 2008).

[11] Henry Rousso, *Le Syndrome de Vichy*.

[12] On this point, see J. Barasz's recent doctoral history thesis, *Les Vichysto-résistants, 1940–1944* (IEP, Paris, 2010).

historians on the grounds that they had not been read critically.[13] The controversies surrounding the Aubracs or the René Hardy affair, which received more attention when Klaus Barbie went on trial in 1987, should be seen in this context.[14]

The appropriation by the authors of works of fiction of the *faux résistant* is another product of these different stages in the historiography and memory of the Resistance. While hoaxes were a very real phenomenon in the immediate post-war period, the historiographical turn that began forty years ago has had a much greater impact upon French society: the country's literary and filmic output now seems to be on a collision course with the long-dominant Gaullist view of the Resistance. Both novels and films have viewed the period in terms that are both more distant and more critical.

A recent phenomenon: the testimony of fake Holocaust survivors

Hoaxes of a new kind began to appear in the 1990s and 2000s, and they are far removed from the fake *résistants* stories of the post-war years. The Wilkomirski and Defonseca affairs had a particular impact in France, even though their origins lay in Switzerland and Belgium respectively.

Bruchstücke by the unknown Binjamin Wilkomirski, a clarinettist and musical-instrument maker living in Switzerland, was published in Germany in 1995.[15] It was very quickly translated into nine languages, including English and French.[16] The author describes his birth (probably in Lithuania), the war, the murder of his family, the time he spent in the camps in Maïdanek and Auschwitz, the ill-treatment and medical experiments to which he was subjected and his survival against all the odds.

---

[13] This tendency is not restricted to French historiography. See, for example, N. West, *Counterfeit Spies. Genuine or Bogus? An Astonishing Investigation into Secret Agents of the Second World War* (London: St. Ermin's Press, 1999).

[14] On the Aubrac affair, see *inter alia*, L. Douzou, *La Résistance française: une histoire périlleuse* (Paris: Points Seuil, 2005), pp. 262–271; Susan Rubin Suleiman, *Crises of Memory and the Second World War* (Cambridge and London: Harvard University Press, 2006), pp. 36–61. On Hardy, see Lloyd, *Collaboration and Resistance in Occupied France*, pp. 140–148.

[15] Binjamin Wilkomirski, *Bruchstücke; aus einer Kindheit* (Frankfurt: Jüdischer Verlag, 1995).

[16] *Fragments: Memory of a Childhood, 1939–1948* (New York: Schocken Books, 1996); *Fragments: Une Enfance, 1939–1948* (Paris: Calmann-Lévy, 1997).

This autobiographical narrative was very quickly hailed as a major work to be ranked alongside Primo Levi and Anne Frank, especially in the United States and France. It was awarded many prizes, beginning with the National Jewish Book Award in France and the French Prix Mémoire de la Shoah, which is awarded by the Fondation du Judaïsme Français. Three years after its publication, the book was denounced as a fake by, among others, Raul Hilberg, one of the greatest historians of the 'Final Solution'. Shortly afterwards, the author himself admitted that it was a hoax and identified himself as Bruno Grosjean. He is not Jewish, and was never in either Maïdanek or Auschwitz.

The Wilkomirski affair reveals the new phenomenon of identification with the victims of the Holocaust, whereas the 1960s and 1970s tended to be characterized by the reappropriation of stories of armed resistance by a generation that had not experienced it.[17] This was not the last hoax. Misha Defonseca's fake memoir and its reception in France is a striking example.

Defonseca, a Belgian woman living in the United States, published her *Misha: A Memoir of the Holocaust Years* in 1997.[18] Translated into eighteen languages, it appeared in French as *Survivre avec les loups* that same year.[19] In a totally improbable narrative, the author described how her parents were arrested and 'deported to the East' when she was a girl living in Brussels, and how she crossed Europe in search of them with the help of a compass and a pack of wolves. The book, which was privately distributed in the United States, was a best-seller in France. To make matters worse, the French director Véra Belmont adapted it as a film that was released and heavily promoted in the press and on television in 2007.

It was only at that point that the criticisms, which had so far received little media attention, became more widespread. The story was quickly challenged and then completely discredited, even before any historians had assessed its value. The author, whose real name is Monique De Wael, had no option but to admit that the book was a hoax in an interview

---

[17] See, for example, Pierre Goldmann, *Souvenirs obscurs d'un Juif polonais né en France* (Paris: Seuil, 1975). The author, who was the son of Jewish *résistants*, explained on several occasions how he regretted the fact that he had been unable to take part in the same fight as his parents and how the burden of his family history influenced his own political trajectory.

[18] Boston: Mount Ivy Press, 1997.

[19] Paris: Robert Laffont, 1997.

given to the Belgian daily *Le Soir* on 28 February 2008. The daughter of *résistants* who died in the Sonnenburg and Ravensbrück camps, she was especially affected by the fate of her father, who, after being arrested by the Nazis, was turned under interrogation and who was therefore partly responsible for the way the Resistance network to which he belonged was rolled up. Misha Defonseca was undeniably a victim of the war – having lost both her parents and then having had to live with the consequences of her father's betrayal once the war was over[20] – but she admits to having deliberately invented a different story that was more likely to attract sympathy in the late 1990s, and to having reinvented herself as a Holocaust survivor.

A specifically French phenomenon?

While these books illustrate the process of identification with the victim, they also raise questions about the media and popular credulity that turned them into best-sellers. What is more important, they reveal the discrepancies between the way such memoirs were received by the general public and the reception they were given in scholarly circles. And in France, there is the important precedent of Martin Gray.

Written in collaboration with the popular historian Max Gallo, Gray's *Au Nom de tous les miens*[21] was the work of a genuine Holocaust survivor whose Polish family was wiped out by the Nazis. It enjoyed huge success in France, especially after the release of Robert Enrico's film of the same title in 1983. And yet, more and more criticisms were made of it throughout the 1980s. Its critics included the French historian Pierre Vidal-Naquet and Gitta Sereny, an expert on Treblinka.[22] They identified a number of errors and approximations and concluded that, whatever horrors he may have experienced, Martin Gray had never set foot in Treblinka, despite the claims advanced in his book.

Although Max Gallo and Martin Gray quietly accepted these criticisms, the fact that they had little impact outside professional historical circles indicates how difficult it is for researchers to resist the steamroller effect of films. That is still the case today. Forty years after its publication,

---

[20] M. Metdepenningen, 'Le Sombre Passé du père de Misha', *Le Soir*, 2 March 2008.

[21] Paris: Robert Laffont, 1971.

[22] See in particular her *Into That Darkness: From Mercy Killing to Mass Murder. A Study of Frantz Stangl, the Commandant of Treblinka* (London: André Deutsch Ltd, 1974).

historians do not regard Martin Gray's memoir as a reliable source,[23] but
its accuracy is rarely questioned by the general public. The *Wikipedia*
pages devoted to it in French and English, for instance, make no mention
of the doubts expressed by researchers,[24] and the author, who now chairs
philanthropic organizations, regularly gives public lectures all over France.

Is there something specifically French about the way the Holocaust
is remembered? Whatever the truth of the matter, the fact is that the
positive reception given to these new hoaxes is testimony to the way the
Jewish genocide has become central to the national memory of the Second
World War. The repercussions of this phenomenon within the public
space are all the greater in that it comes after a long period in which
the facts were almost completely covered up, largely because of the Vichy
regime's role in implementing the 'Final Solution' in France. The work
of Robert Paxton and Michael Marrus,[25] and the research undertaken by
Serge Klarsfeld, definitely allowed Holocaust survivors to speak more
openly from the 1970s onwards. Voices that had long been inaudible
were now in demand, and the accounts they provided gradually came
to be regarded as sacred and virtually immune to historical criticism.

The tendency to regard the words of Holocaust survivors as 'sacred'
is, moreover, not unrelated to the development of a strong negationist
current in France in response to the way historiography changed in
the 1970s. One of its methods is to claim that all memoirs written by
survivors of the 'Final Solution' are fakes. This goes some way to explaining why criticisms of the stories of Martin Gray and Misha Defonseca
were slow to emerge and why they have to some extent gone unheard:
expressing doubts about their veracity may look to the general public
and the media like the methods used by the negationists. And yet many
historians have tried to counter these arguments: Pierre Vidal-Naquet,
Gitta Sereny and Raul Hilberg never fail to point out that inaccurate
memories help, on the contrary, to promote negationist theories. The
same point has been made by Véra Belmont, who directed *Survivre
avec les loups* and who was a victim – albeit a willing one – of Misha
Defonseca's hoax.

---

[23] Even though there are few direct eye-witness accounts of Aktion Reinhard, Gray's
book is not cited in Y. Arad's *Belzec, Sobibor, Treblinka: The Operation Reinhard Death
Camps* (Bloomington: Indiana University Press, 1987).

[24] http://en.wikipedia.org/wiki/Martin_Gray (Holocaust survivor); http://.fr.wikipedia.
org/wiki/Martin_Gray (accessed April 2010).

[25] R.O. Paxton, *La France de Vichy, 1940–1944* (Paris: Seuil, 1973); R.O. Paxton and
M.R. Marrus, *Vichy et les Juifs* (Paris: Calmann-Lévy, 1981).

We cannot, however, ignore the other explanation for the reception given to fake Holocaust memoirs: the influence of the Gaullist memory of the Resistance, which for a very long time denied that the period 1940–44 could be remembered in any way that might undermine the need for a new national cohesion. To that extent, the extraordinarily credulous reception given to Wilkomirski and Defonseca's stories, and the failure to publicize the historians' criticisms of Gray's story, cannot be divorced from the way the figure of the French *résistant* has come under attack in works of fiction in recent years, as in Deniau's book and the film it inspired. Midway between history and memory, a study of the hoaxes born of the Second World War and of their reception in France teaches us a great deal about how national historical figures are constructed and about how changes in the way we view a given period constantly give rise to debates and polemics.

Chapter 12

Framing the past: illustrating the Second World War in French children's fiction

Penny Brown

> Children are central to the Shoah ... their experience is the heart of that horror and evil laid bare of rationalizations and stereotyped conventions.[1]

Discussions of fictional representations of the Second World War and the Holocaust rarely touch on children's books, and then generally focus on texts written in English, with scarcely any reference to books produced for young French readers. Yet, as Susan Zuccotti has written, 'the story of the children is the most horrifying, heartrending episode of the Holocaust in France, and the most shameful'.[2] In the *grande rafle* of 16 and 17 July 1942, in which nearly 13,000 Jewish men, women and children were arrested in Paris by French police, 6900 people, including 4051 children, were kept in appalling, inhumane conditions in the Vélodrome d'Hiver (the Vél d'Hiv, a glass-roofed cycling stadium) for a week of starvation and humiliation before being deported to the death camps, mainly to Auschwitz.[3] The Vichy government had actually amended and extended the German operation to include children under the age of sixteen. It is estimated that of the 72,000 Jewish children living in France in 1939, approximately 12,000 died in the course of the war. In French children's books about the Occupation, the round-ups feature repeatedly, as do the experiences of those Jewish children who survived

---

[1] Deborah Dwork, *Children with a Star: Jewish Youth in Nazi Europe* (New Haven and London: Yale University Press, 1991), p. 256.

[2] Susan Zuccotti, *The Holocaust, the French and the Jews* (New York: Harper Collins, 1993), p. 113.

[3] See Zuccotti, *The Holocaust*, pp. 110–112.

by being hidden, and one of the more infamous events: the massacre of the forty-four Jewish children living at the *Maison d'Izieu*, a children's home near Lyon, on the morning of 6 April 1944, on the orders of Klaus Barbie (the Butcher of Lyon). In 1995, President Chirac spoke of 'des moments qui blessent la mémoire' and stated that 'La France, patrie des lumières et des Droits de l'Homme, terre d'accueil et d'asile, la France, ce jour-là, accomplissait l'irréparable.'[4] The specific sensitivities about this period inevitably affect the way in which events are mediated in fiction, especially to young readers, and make them different from novels about the Holocaust written for an English-speaking audience. There is, inherently, a different relationship between text and reader, as the family background of many French child readers may include victims, survivors, collaborators or members of the Resistance. The lingering effects of these sensitivities became evident once again in February 2008, in the reactions to President Sarkozy's plan to twin every French school child with a victim of the Holocaust.

In her book on the difficulties of writing about the Holocaust for children, Lydia Kokkola first raises the issue of whether such a project is ethically responsible, in that it is at odds with the widely held view that children should be sheltered from the more frightening or horrific elements of reality.[5] The events of this period are potentially too traumatic for a child reader and therefore problematic to write within the conventions of children's literature. The opposing view is that it is imperative to inform and instruct younger generations about the horrors of which human beings are capable, especially since they are exposed to them on a daily basis on television and in newspapers. Many French writers of books for young readers, themselves the children and grandchildren of both survivors and those who perished, make it clear in their prefatory material, dedications or author profiles that they have felt a personal need to understand what happened and to communicate this to their own children and, through the publication of their writing, to young readers in general. The origin of such texts is therefore an attempt to

---

[4] Jacques Chirac's speech can be found on a number of Internet sites.

[5] Lydia Kokkola, *Representing the Holocaust in Children's Literature* (New York and London: Routledge, 2003), p. 13. Other useful works on the Holocaust in children's literature include Hamida Bosmajian, *Sparing the Child: Grief and the Unspeakable in Youth Literature about Nazism and the Holocaust* (New York: Routledge, 2002); and Adrienne Kertzer, *My Mother's Voice: Children, Literature and the Holocaust* (Peterborough, Ontario: Broadview Press, 2002).

recapture and transmit 'memories', not those of the readers themselves, but memories that are part of their heritage.

The next question, then, is *how* to mediate information, how to sensitize impressionable young readers to the events of the Holocaust without traumatizing them. In effect, a range of strategies of reassurance are commonly employed in children's books, with varying degrees of success. Writers of books for any age wrestle with the concern about whether it is legitimate, decent or moral to exploit the horrors of the Holocaust in *fiction*, and, moreover, fiction that is enjoyable. While fiction undoubtedly helps to bring history to life, books for young readers who may lack background knowledge of the Second World War have to be able to communicate that the Holocaust is historical fact and not itself a fictional construct. An uninformed reader may be unable to judge the veracity of a historical tale in which fictional characters are embedded or fully appreciate the implications of the narrative, resulting in a distorted view of history, a concern currently voiced in the press about the use of historical films in school curricula. There is also, of course, the question of the legitimacy of creating a consolatory and optimistic happy ending, even if this contradicts historical fact.[6] Many children's books about the Second World War, in French as in English, do in fact provide some form of closure that offers a message of hope to characters and readers alike. The theme of survival, return, reunion and restoration of family life is one such common reassuring strategy.

These questions are in many respects more critical in respect of picture books, especially those for younger readers. Arguably, picture books have more potential than a novel to impart to the reader a sense of the time and space of a particular period through easily recognized visual markers that make an immediate impact, and thus may engender anxiety and distress.[7] Of course, the choice of markers will reflect the aims and ideological ethos of the author and illustrator, and the relationship between text and image must therefore be carefully scrutinized. Images may simply reflect the text, but may also expand upon it, drawing attention to what is suppressed in the text, or even offer a counterpoint or contradictory narrative. At the simplest level lies the dilemma of how much to show young readers. Picture books for young readers are likely to offer a sanitized picture of horrific events that may undermine the

---

[6] See Louise Sylvester, 'A Knock at the Door: Reading Judith Kerr's Picture Books in the Context of her Holocaust Fiction', *The Lion and the Unicorn*, 26:1 (2002), 16–30.

[7] Kokkola, *Representing the Holocaust*, p. 69.

implications of the narrative itself as well as historical truth. Different types of illustrations raise a number of issues in terms of appropriateness and effectiveness. Photographs or mimetically accurate illustrations may initially be seen as more effective in communicating historical fact than cartoon or symbolic images, but are equally open to selectiveness and manipulation. Moreover, inexperienced readers may be unable to decide whether images should be interpreted as realistic or symbolic without prior historical knowledge or familiarity with pictorial conventions.[8] The five picture books considered here, aimed for the most part at readers aged seven and above, approach these issues in different ways.

Both Yaël Hassan's *A Paris, sous l'occupation*[9] and *Il faut désobéir! La France sous Vichy* by Didier Daeninckx and Pef[10] tackle the sensitive issue of the actions of the French police while offering reassurance about the forces of law and order, and, indeed, human nature, to the present-day reader by focusing on individual characters who disobey orders and help Jews (a strategy that calls to mind Henry Rousso's 'myth of Resistance'). The former, marketed at age seven and upwards, blends fact and fiction in the story of the close friendship between two children, Julien and Clara, who is Jewish. The narration is in the past tense, thus firmly embedding the story in the context of history. Julien's father is a policeman who is reluctantly involved in the round-ups but also helps to warn Clara's mother of the impending operation and hides the child herself in his home when her mother, betrayed by a neighbour, is arrested. Although present at the Vél d'Hiv, he tells how he tried to help people escape while his colleagues obeyed orders without a qualm. The disillusionment that Julien initially feels about his father's involvement, and the destruction of his belief that the police are there to protect people, effectively impart, at the level of the child's consciousness, the betrayal of Vichy, while subsequently providing reassurance to character and reader alike that not all were equally to blame. Each brief chapter, with a full-page, loosely realistic colour illustration on every page, is followed by a brief explanation of historical events in clear, straightforward language, which makes no attempt to exculpate the French

---

[8] Kokkola, *Representing the Holocaust*, p. 66. See also Adrienne Kertzer, 'Saving the Picture: Holocaust Photographs in Children's Books', *The Lion and the Unicorn*, 24:3 (2000), 402–431.

[9] Des enfants dans l'Histoire series with illustrations by Ginette Hoffmann (Paris: Casterman, 2000).

[10] Paris: Rue du Monde, 2002.

government and the police for their actions at the time. The flat, bright, clean colours of the illustrations and the happy ending in which Clara and her mother, a camp survivor, are reunited, might be said to modify the horror of the situation for the reader, while the abrupt leap in the narrative from the Vél d'Hiv to liberation by the Allies tends to elide the implications of the intervening period for all concerned. However, overall, Hassan's strategy successfully integrates the two levels of fact and fiction.

Daeninckx's *Il faut désobéir! La France sous Vichy*, a 'lucky escape' – type narrative with comic illustrations by Pef (the title of which, in its very subversiveness, is designed to appeal to young readers), is based on a true story of the resistance of one individual, Pierre Marie, an Inspecteur de Police who, with seven of his colleagues from Nancy, saved the lives of 300 Jews by disobeying Vichy orders. The story is narrated by an elderly Jewish survivor, to his grand-daughter, Alexandra, thus linking past and present, a narrative strategy that both informs and reassures, and one that echoes the traditional structure in children's books of the passing on of wisdom from generation to generation, while also foregrounding the themes of testimony and memory. On the eve of a reunion of war veterans, the unnamed grandfather describes how he and his friend Sarah were disobedient children, often catching the eye of Monsieur Pierre, the local policeman, by stealing apples and sneaking into the cinema through a back door. Ironically, the narrator's favourite films are cowboy films and he longs to be a sheriff with a large star on his chest, until he is forced to wear a star of his own. When the Occupation situation worsens, Monsieur Pierre, although ostensibly carrying out orders, saves the lives of the narrator's family and Sarah by tipping them off about the impending round-up. Sixty years on, at the reunion, the narrator, his wife (Sarah) and Alexandra meet Monsieur Pierre again and ask the former policeman about his actions. His reply, that 'il faut parfois désobéir pour rester un homme', suggests the elements of humanity that persisted in the midst of madness, while his assertion that 'mon métier, c'était d'arrêter les voleurs de pommes, pas d'éteindre les étoiles' is a lyrical, but, for young readers, perhaps an unnecessarily opaque and euphemistic explanation of his motivation (*Il faut désobéir*, pp. 32–33). At the top or bottom of each page is a parallel historical narrative depicting the major stages of the war in brief but explicit italicized paragraphs with photographs which emphasize both the culpability of Vichy and collaborators, and the actions of the Resistance. The fictional story offers a far more reassuring picture than the documentary material, however, focusing as it does on friendship and altruism. Pef's cartoon-like illustrations distance the story from reality, although the dark colours and distorted shapes of figures and buildings surrounding the child in his red jersey (a gesture towards the archetypal victim, le Petit chaperon rouge, perhaps) create a sense of foreboding and lurking terror beneath the humour.

A common narrative strategy is a first-person narrative of a child or adolescent protagonist's involvement in events which the reader thus experiences vicariously. In such texts, the focus on the quotidian in text and image allows the child reader to identify more readily with the characters' incomprehension of the progressive and insidious changes that affect the fabric of their daily lives and destroy their faith in a safe and stable world.[11] The 2005 *Journal d'un enfant pendant la Seconde Guerre mondiale: Léonore 1939–1945*, by Yaël Hassan,[12] presents the text as a diary written by a fictional young girl, Léonore, living in Paris between 1939 and 1945, with a cardboard clasp, lined paper and hand-written date headings. This format offers an effective structure for tracing the developments of the situation and the progress of the war and the everyday effects of the Occupation. She writes energetically of the daily privations and shortages of food, clothing and heating as well as of her absent mobilized father, the furious outbursts of her vehemently anti-Vichy brother Henri, who goes to join the Resistance, and the loss of her best friend Léa in the *rafle* of 16 July 1942. The ending offers a qualified note of hope for the future: although Léa never returns, Léonore's father and brother do, and she herself resolves to become a doctor after she learns about the concentration camps. Juxtaposed and intertwined with the fictional narrative is a factual narrative that com-plements, explains and expands upon Léonore's story. A wide range of verbal and visual material charting the stages of the war and the main protagonists is clearly and simply presented throughout on side panels or under flaps so that the reader can choose whether or not to explore those sections as they read or at a later date. The more extreme horrors of the war are recounted but not illustrated in graphic detail, although there is a double-page-spread illustration (beneath pp. 30–31) of the arrival of a train-load of prisoners at the camp at Auschwitz-Birkenau which readers can open or keep hidden as they wish. The illustrations reflect and support the two-fold structure of the text: the images in the

---

[11] Dwork, *Children with a Star*, p. xxxiv.
[12] Illustrations by Olivier Tallec and Nicolas Wintz (Paris: Gallimard, 2005).

diary itself are child-like drawings while the factual sections have clearer, mimetic images. The image on the front cover encapsulates the strategy of presenting a fictional testimony as a typical experience. Objects that matter in Léonore's daily life (a biscuit, a ration book, a yellow star) are overlaid on some pages as though she had just left them there. There is a huge amount to look at in this book and it is thus potentially rather overwhelming, but it is very informative on all levels and Léonore's narrative is lively and convincing.

Titles and cover images of children's books often signal the subject matter by foregrounding the iconic image of the yellow Star of David to aid the reader grasp the concepts of difference, alienation, racism and genocide.[13] *Le Petit garçon étoile* by Rachel Hausfater-Douïeb, dedicated to her father, a hidden child survivor, is a book for very young readers that takes a symbolic approach.[14] The story, mediated through large, full-page, childlike images in bright primary colours that take precedence over the brief accompanying text, works on different levels for readers with or without prior knowledge of the Holocaust by manipulating an intriguing text/image dynamic. The text itself is devoid of any specific reference to time or place, while the illustrations suggest a specific level of interpretation by drawing on images familiar to the informed or adult reader: the six-pointed yellow star, the swastika, the sealed train and the concentration camp. The dehumanizing experience inherent in the persecution of the Jews is hinted at as the individuality of the unnamed protagonist, whose dress recalls Le Petit Prince, becomes totally subsumed in the star he wears. The central themes of confusion, isolation and fear are powerfully communicated in two illustrations, one the sinister red and black negative of the other, of the vulnerable figure of the child standing alone and separated by a broad strand of colour from the dwellings in the background. In the frightening illustration that follows, small fleeing human figures are seen to be pursued by giant soldiers like eyeless automata, the 'chasseurs d'étoiles', coloured red and black echoing the nightmare scenario on the preceding page. The swastika on the arm of the nearest soldier stands out, with the intention perhaps of prompting the more curious reader to ask questions that will clarify the specific narrative behind the text. The Final Solution, an element often only dealt with obliquely in children's books, is depicted symbolically

---

[13] See Dwork *Children with a Star*, p. xvi. See also Jane Marks, *The Hidden Children: The Secret Survivors of the Holocaust* (London: Piatkus, 1994).

[14] Illustrations by Olivier Latyk (Paris: Casterman, 2001).

in the double page spread that depicts a train travelling across the pages to an isolated building, clearly recognizable as a death camp, from the chimney of which issues a great cloud of smoke filled with stars. The boy sees them 'partir vers la nuit. Et s'éteindre.' (n. p.) The image is ambiguous, however, as the cloud of smoke in the black night sky resembles a wedge of blue with clouds, suggesting a less threatening image of daylight when stars are not visible. Ultimately, this book too offers a hopeful ending depicting survival and recuperation from trauma. The 'adoption' of Jewish children, rescued and hidden in the open with French families in the countryside, is a common plot in French children's books, perhaps not surprisingly, because it was a widespread experience, but also because it removes the child protagonists from the worst scenarios of the war and offers the possibility of a happy ending. This plot type also emphasizes the reassuring fact that there were 'good' French people, Jews and Christians, who were willing to risk their lives for others in spontaneous or long-term acts of humanity, and hence acts as a reassuring counterbalance in some measure to the actions of the Vichy government.

Elisabeth Brami's *Sauve-toi Elie!*, with illustrations by Bernard Jeunet,[15] is an enigmatic text that captures the young child's incomprehension of what is happening to him when he is sent to live with an old couple on a farm in the country. Throughout this book, dedicated in an afterword to 'tous les enfants cachés, et ceux qui n'ont pas eu la chance de l'être' (*Sauve-toi Elie!*, p. 51), the viewpoint is entirely that of eight-year-old Elie, with no authorial exposition or explanation. The text begins simply, 'On est parti sans fermer à clef. Maman pleurait', opposite an image of a large key and a sad teddy bear (pp. 8–9). The reader is invited to collaborate in revealing the meaning of the text by recognizing clues in both text and illustrations; therefore some degree of prior knowledge seems to be essential to a full appreciation of the book. In some respects, however, a young reader's ignorance of the war renders the story more surreal and chilling. Bernard Jeunet's illustrations, full-page paper collages of figures and objects against the background of pages from a missal, are strange, sombre and menacing images evoking violence, pain and fear juxtaposed with attractive vignettes of photographs of paper sculptures of animals, birds, insects and everyday objects.[16] The images of domestic objects, the

---

[15] Paris: Seuil, 2003.

[16] Jeunet's collages actually pre-date the text, as they were created in 1998 for an exhibition and Brami subsequently built the story around them.

farmyard and church, the thorns, poppies and barbed wile, have a literal reference but are also imbued with specificity through often minute details. The illustration depicting the boy in a pair of striped pyjamas wearing a dunce's cap and carrying a bucket ostensibly refers to his farm work and his difficulties at school, but the border of tiny letters spelling out the words 'ramasse merde' is an allusion to work carried out by children in concentration camps and thus alters our view of the image (p. 23). Elie's perplexity and alarm at the reaction of his playmate and her mother's threats when he urinates in front of her and thus gives away his Jewish identity are foregrounded by a full frontal illustration of a urinating figure within a circle of thorns bearing the words 'pisse pieuse' (p. 39). A link between fiction and fact is effected when, on trying to run away, Elie witnesses the arrest of children from a children's home nearby. The little girl who urges him to escape while he can ('Sauve-toi, Elie') is named subsequently as one of the children taken away from the Maison d'Izieu on convoy 71, who all disappeared, as Elie claims he now understands, into 'le grand ventre de la guerre', an image accompanied by a chilling illustration of a group of anguished faces peering out from behind barbed wire under a woman's skirts, thus playing on connotations of birth and death (p. 47). As far as Elie is concerned, Brami opts for an open ending, as the boy continues to wait and wonder whether his mother will return, thus refusing an artificially comfortable form of closure.

Of course, while aiming to assess the effectiveness of these very different texts, one has to be aware that the views of an adult commentator, well aware of the context and implications of these narratives, cannot presume to be an authoritative statement about the way in which any given young reader may react. This is the perennial problem that faces commentators on children's books and is the subject of another, different kind of study. A didactic agenda clearly informs *A Paris, sous l'occupation*, *Il faut désobéir!* and *Journal d'un enfant pendant la Seconde Guerre mondiale*. In these texts, the illustrations complementing the primary narrative both depict aspects of reality, evoking a sense of 'being there' with different degrees of historical specificity, and act as distancing devices to some extent, filtering the full horror through modified and sanitized versions of reality, or humorous and cartoon-like images. *Le Petit garçon étoile*, conversely, avoids explicit and direct instruction by employing a fairy tale-type narrative, the pursuit of a vulnerable and abandoned child by monsters, that evokes a young child's most intimate fears through bright, stylized and symbolic images that dominate the minimal text and open up a space for further elucidation by an adult. The alarming symbolic illustrations that accompany the innocent and uncomprehending first-person narrative in *Sauve-toi Elie!* provoke a sense of horror that suggests what the narrative cannot articulate, disturbing the reader in ways that demand further exploration and questioning. In their very different ways, then, these texts do offer young and his- torically uninformed readers both education and enjoyment, albeit a complex and uneasy kind, within the context of what is referred to in the epilogue of *Un journal d'un enfant pendant la Seconde Guerre mondiale* as the need to create 'lieux de souvenir et de recueillement' for future generations (p. 61).

Chapter 13

The traumatized national community in Anna Langfus's *Les Bagages de sable*[1]

Angela O'Flaherty

In 1962, Anna Langfus won the Prix Goncourt for the novel, *Les Bagages de sable* (LB), in which she describes the difficult relationship between a survivor of the Second World War, Maria, and her much older suitor, Michel Caron. Lauded for its accurate portrayal of the psychological condition of the survivor, this text also rewarded the attentive contemporaneous reader with a subtle interrogation of the collective memory of the Second World War in France and the underlying communal trauma which continued to shape it.

Before embarking on a discussion of Langfus's treatment of the traumatized national community in this novel, a number of preliminary remarks are necessary. First, although Langfus had written about her experiences as a Polish Jew during the Second World War in her first novel, *Le Sel et le soufre*, in her second novel, *Les Bagages de sable*, she turns her attention to her adopted country, France, and in doing so hints at the particular difficulties the French faced when dealing with the war and its legacy. Olivier Wieviorka notes that in the face of a memory of the war years which was 'fragmentée, conflictuelle et politisée',[2] the national policy, carried out by state institutions, municipalities and associations from the Liberation onwards, 'visait tant à panser les plaies qu'à offrir une interprétation sensée et admissible des années sombres'.[3] During the Fourth Republic and the early years of the Fifth Republic,

---

[1] Anna Langfus, Les Bagages de sable (Paris: Gallimard, 1981). Research carried out for this chapter was funded by the Carnegie Trust for the Universities of Scotland.
[2] *La Mémoire désunie: le souvenir politique des années sombres de la Libération à nos jours* (Paris: Seuil, 2010), p. 23.
[3] Wieviorka, *La Mémoire désunie*, p. 18.

this was achieved by the repeated national rejection of an unflattering collective memory of the war, in particular with regard to the extent of collaboration, as well as by the bolstering of the *résistancialiste* myth, in order to create a memory of the war which was at once 'résistante' and 'patriotique'.[4] In his now seminal *Le Syndrome de Vichy*, Henry Rousso describes the progressive stages of French memory of the war years.[5] Although *Les Bagages de sable* dates from the period of 'refoulements', in her writing Langfus draws attention to the collective malaise contributing to and resulting from the enforced denial of the wartime past.

Secondly, although collective memory of the war in 1962 was dominated by the desire for repression and denial, paradoxically the figure of 'the survivor' was beginning to gain a place in public awareness. Annette Wieviorka attributes this development directly to the 1961 Eichmann trial where 'le survivant acquiert son identité sociale de survivant, parce que la société la lui reconnaît'.[6] Given *Les Bagages de sable*'s subject matter and publication date, this novel can reasonably be considered to feed into and play off this nascent but difficult public recognition of the survivor. During a round table organized by the contributors to *Réalités*, Jean-Louis Clément suggested that the Prix Goncourt was awarded to this novel precisely because it was 'une œuvre qui correspond à la sensibilité actuelle et qui rejoint quelques-unes des expériences les plus profondes de notre époque'.[7] Nonetheless, while the survivor may have begun to garner public recognition from 1961 onwards, the emergence of the survivor in France did not quash hostility towards a full reckoning with the past, particularly with regards to the question of French involvement in the persecution of Jews during the Occupation.[8] In *Les Bagages de sable*, Langfus plays on the precarious and contradictory situation created by this coupling of the increasing contemporaneous visibility of the survivor with the continuing repressive attitude towards the past. Superficially, the novel's protagonist, Maria, appears simply as the embodiment of the 'survivor'. However, readers already familiar

---

[4] Wieviorka, *La Mémoire désunie*, p. 277.

[5] Rousso, *Le Syndrome de Vichy*, pp. 18–19.

[6] Wieviorka, *L'Ere du témoin*, p. 117.

[7] M. de la Rochenfoucauld, 'Débat sur le Goncourt', *Réalités*, No. 204 (1963) 9–10 (p. 10).

[8] M. Rothberg, *Multidirectional memory*, p. 196. Rousso notes that in the same year that Eichmann was hanged (1962), the architects of the Shoah in France, Karl Oberg and Helmut Knochen, were granted early release from prison by de Gaulle. Rousso, *Le Syndrome de Vichy*, p. 339.

with Langfus's first novel will recognize in her the figure of the Jewish survivor.[9] As will be discussed in greater detail in a later section, Langfus remains deliberately vague about Maria's past for various reasons. However, when it was pointed out to her in a 1963 interview that she did not specify that Maria was Jewish, she responded 'offusquée': 'Mais tout le monde le sait!'[10] Such an affirmation suggests that with this novel, Langfus not only intended to introduce a questioning of the general repression of the past, but also to gently move towards a more specific reckoning with the difficult history of the persecution of Jews during the war and French involvement in these events.

Inevitably, the subject matter of this text placed Langfus in a tricky position. In publishing her work, she knew that she had to confront the reality of contemporaneous French society. The very people she implicates in *Les Bagages de sable*, that is, predominantly the French middle class, were her natural (and expected) readers. However, she allows, even encourages this overlap. She presents the stark reality of society's attitudes towards the survivor, and by extension the past, in the hope of forcing contemporaneous readers to question their own relationship to the war. In this manner, *Les Bagages de sable* becomes at once a response and a challenge to the collective traumatic repression of wartime memories.

Impossible reception: communal trauma and the testimonial blockade

Although *Les Bagages de sable* is primarily a study of the traumatized survivor, within this novel Langfus also points to an underlying communal trauma which results in the difficult assimilation of wartime survivors into 'normal' post-war society. Typically, trauma refers to an individual survivor/victim; however, Kai Erikson suggests that one can also speak of a traumatized community whereby, in certain circumstances, community is created by a shared experience of trauma. This shared trauma results in 'the creation of social climates, communal moods that come to dominate a group's spirit'.[11] In *Les Bagages de sable*, the communal 'traumatisme' 'engendré par l'occupation' manifests itself in

---

[9] Although *Les Bagages de sable* can be read as a stand-alone text, it is widely considered an unofficial sequel to Langfus's 1960 text, *Le Sel et le soufre*.

[10] C. Cerf and M. Cohen-Musnik, 'Interview d'Anna Langfus', *Kadimah*, 31 January 1963, 3–4 (p. 4).

[11] K. Erikson, 'Notes on Trauma and Community', in C. Caruth (ed.), *Trauma: Explorations in Memory* (Baltimore: The Johns Hopkins University Press, 1995), p. 190.

a group spirit dominated by the desire to obliterate wartime memories from collective consciousness.[12] However, as the traumatized individual's efforts to repress traumatic experiences result in the 'delayed, uncontrolled repetitive appearances of hallucinations and other intrusive phenomena', so too do the traumatized community's efforts at the neat repression of the past meet with failure.[13] For the national community, the figure of the survivor acts as a physical embodiment of the traumatic flashback, a stark reminder of the suffering, wrongdoing and shame of the war.

From the opening pages of *Les Bagages de sable*, the intrusive presence of the survivor in post-war society is highlighted by the use of spectral imagery. Throughout this novel, Langfus blurs the lines between the living and the dead. Maria is haunted by the ghosts of her dead family members. Furthermore, she has been rendered ghost-like by her proximity to death. She wanders through the streets of Paris, inaudible and virtually invisible. Her ghostly quality reinforces the sense of unease she generates in the community. A trace of that which the national community has worked and continues to work so hard to repress, she haunts post-war society. If, as Des Pres notes, 'the survivor is both sought and shunned' with 'the desire to hear his truth . . . countered by the need to ignore him', then, in her writing, Langfus reacts to and circumnavigates these paradoxical desires.[14] In particular, Langfus uses her depiction of Maria's interaction with her extended family and with Michel Caron to emphasize the discomfort of 'normal', that is, non-surviving, society when confronted with the survivor.

Maria's interaction with her Uncle Charles and Aunt Simone provides readers with an initial impression of society's traumatic repression of the survivor. Upon meeting his niece, Charles 'ne pose aucune question' (LB, p. 22), deciding that it is best not to dwell on Maria's past. Aunt Simone's reaction to Maria is even more telling. Although she acknowledges Maria's experiences, she downplays their severity. She sympathizes with Maria by thrice repeating a variation of the sentence 'cela a dû être si terrible pour toi' (LB, p. 24). In 1963, the year following the publication of *Les Bagages de sable*, Georges Perec commented on the easy application of the term 'terrible' as a popular response to descriptions of

[12] Rousso, *Le Syndrome*, p. 18.
[13] C. Caruth, *Unclaimed Experience: Trauma, Narrative and History* (Baltimore: The Johns Hopkins University Press, 1996), p. 11.
[14] T. Des Pres, *The Survivor: An Anatomy of Life in the Death Camps* (Oxford: Oxford University Press, 1976), p. 41.

the concentrationary universe and the war, noting 'nous croyons connaître ce qui est terrible. C'est un événement «terrible»; une histoire terrible. Il y a un début, un point culminant, une fin. Mais nous ne comprenons rien.'[15] As if to pre-emptively demonstrate Perec's argument, Simone scandalously uses the adjective 'terrible' (LB, p. 27) not only to describe Maria's experiences but also to describe her own (brief) encounter with German soldiers. In this case, the soldiers' terrible behaviour consisted of a visit to her home during which they opened all her cupboards and removed her 'plus beau service de table' (LB, p. 27). Through this 'adjectival' sharing, Simone aligns her wartime experiences with Maria's. Although one must be wary of a schematization of suffering, it is safe to assume that Simone's brief visit by the German soldiers cannot compare with the years of deprivation, ghettoization, violence and suffering to which Maria alludes. By showing herself to be concerned only with her own wartime suffering, Simone adds credence to the narrator's later musings that 'toute souffrance' is 'unique, inhérente à un seul être et incompréhensible à tous les autres' (LB, p. 77).

In particular, it is the difficult relationship between Maria and Michel Caron which serves as a microcosm of the tense interaction between the survivor and the larger community. Their relationship is built on 'refoulements', 'non-dits' and even outright lies: Maria hides her real identity from Michel, Michel hides his married status from Maria and they both hide the truth of their relationship from the people in the village in the South of France where they holiday. More importantly, the relationship between Maria and Michel flounders due to a lack of communication, or more precisely as a result of Michel's refusal to receive Maria's testimony. Langfus emphasizes the vacuous nature of the exchanges between the pair. Words are a 'dérisoire barricade' (LB, p. 78) between them. She also highlights Michel's strained relationship to language and his difficulty engaging in conversation with Maria: 'Il cherche les mots avec maladresse, trébuche et bafouille un peu' (LB, p. 37). For Michel, Maria represents a problem to be dealt with, a threat to be nullified. While Uncles Charles tried to marry her off to a fellow survivor, Michel takes it upon himself to return Maria to life: 'je ferais n'importe quoi pour vous rendre la joie de vivre' (LB, p. 66). Ironically, he fails to provide her with the one thing she truly needs: a listener. When Maria does finally try to open up to Michel, he greets

---

[15] G. Perec, 'Robert Antelme ou la vérité de la littérature', in R. Antelme, *Textes inédites sur L'Espèce humaine: essais et témoignages* (Paris: Gallimard, 1996), pp. 176–177.

her with patronizing sympathy: 'tu es jeune, tu as encore toute ta vie devant toi' (LB, p. 76).

Michel, Charles and Simone blame the presence of the survivor as the source of their malaise. They fail to ask themselves why they so desperately want to contain her. The possible reason for their discomfort, and associated 'testimonial blockade', becomes clearer at the close of the novel. Michel admits that he turned to Maria because he believed her youth would help him flee old age and death; paradoxically, the lazarean quality of her existence meant that with her, death was 'plus présent que jamais' (LB, p. 214). The combination of Michel's refusal to receive Maria's testimony and his subsequent abandonment of her merely underlines his difficulty in incorporating the brutal revelation of (inappropriate) death revealed during war. Maria must be rejected because her proximity to death renders all those close to her vulnerable.

Towards the close of the novel, Maria melodramatically declares 'tout le monde est contre moi' (LB, p. 186), and an inventory of the other characters' behaviour would appear to confirm this impression. Society does not accept Maria nor does it want to deal with the reality that she as a survivor represents.

Textual manifestations of the traumatized community

Langfus is not content simply to allude to the unease of the external community when confronted with the figure of the survivor and memories of war; she also builds this malaise into her writing. She re-creates this discomfort for and in readers through her textual organization and layout and through her use of gaps. Although a chapter structure would have been possible, Langfus opts instead for a block text which closes in around readers, creating a textual claustrophobia.

Langfus also manipulates the gaps in her narrative to increase readers' sense of discomfort. Much of the narrative arc of *Les Bagages de sable* is constructed around past-orientated delays concerning Maria's wartime experiences. Langfus remains deliberately vague about the details of her narrator-protagonist's past. Hints are given, such as her fear of train stations, her nightmares and the flashbacks she experiences, but fundamental gaps remain. Readers are left to ask: what exactly happened to Maria during the war? How did her parents die? How did she survive? The enigmatic quality of this character is reiterated by Langfus's use of the first-person narrative. Although this technique may afford readers privileged access to the workings of the narrator's mind, it also ensures that basic information about the narrator, such as her real name, can logically be kept a secret.

Langfus's reliance on gaps is significant. If, as Iser asserts, the 'unwritten' part of the text stimulates readers' creative participation, then in the case of this novel, Langfus's withholding of information encourages readers to fill in the historical gaps themselves (and thus inform themselves about the war or at the very least acknowledge that which they already know).[16] While she may have been willing to admit that people only wanted easily swallowed facts about the war and the Holocaust, she also recognizes that this scrambling for facts results in what Anny Dayan Rosenmann calls 'un savoir sans savoir où la multiplication des chiffres et des données concrètes risque de faire écran à une prise de conscience réelle'.[17] *Les Bagages de sable* is underscored with the reality of this thwarted 'prise de conscience réelle'. Notably, Langfus describes a dream Maria has where she is back in school, being tested on her knowledge of concentration camps. Her teacher screams, 'vous êtes incapable de me citer un seul camp de concentration' (LB, p. 60). Although Maria knows 'tous les détails', she is greeted by the teacher's disgust: 'les détails n'intéressent personne . . . des noms et des chiffres, c'est tout ce que je demande' (LB, 60). Through this nightmare, Langfus alludes to the external tendency to reduce the war to sanitized dates and figures, a tendency which she rages against in her writing. Instead, she highlights the vacuum in which these war-related 'noms' and 'chiffres' have existed. Specifically, she presents a text which is built entirely on the absence of a 'nom' (i.e. Maria's real name) and, in doing so, unsettles readers and encourages them to question their supposed 'savoir'.

Responsible readers?

Although Langfus acknowledges and incorporates societal reticence before memories of war into her writing, the act of writing itself can be seen as an attempt to circumnavigate such tendencies. By its very existence, this novel serves to undermine the trend towards 'refoulement' which dominated French society in the early 1960s. Speaking in 1963, Langfus declared that as a writer she had 'une responsabilité non seulement vis-à-vis de ceux qui l'avaient vécue avec moi, mais aussi de tous

---

[16] W. Iser, *The Implied Reader: Patterns of Communication in Prose Fiction from Bunyan to Beckett* (Baltimore and London: The Johns Hopkins University Press, 1974), p. 275.

[17] *Les Alphabets de la Shoah: survivre. témoigner. écrire* (Paris: CNRS éditions, 2007), p. 152.

ceux qui, plus tard, en prendraient connaissance'.[18] For her, writing ought to contribute to the creation of responsible readers, that is, ones capable of confronting and dealing with the traumatic past.

Langfus was conscious of the obstacles and resistance which war writing, and particularly Holocaust texts such as hers, faced. Recognizing that 'si la réalité nous frappe comme une masse, par sa violence même elle nous étourdit, nous anesthésie, avant de pouvoir atteindre notre sensibilité. Et de ce fait elle échappe à notre compréhension',[19] she proceeded cautiously, adopting an approach reminiscent of that championed by survivor-writers Robert Antelme and Jorge Semprun.[20] Her decision to opt for a fictional format complete with an element of 'l'artifice de l'œuvre d'art' rather than a purely testimonial account of the war was part of a calculated move to appeal to the traumatized national community and, more importantly, to override their reticence and reluctance before such accounts. She maintained that 'plus une situation est horrible, plus une situation est anormale, plus doit être grande la distance qui permet de la comprendre dans sa vérité'.[21] In *Les Bagages de sable*, Langfus indicates that her interpretation of 'distance' does not equate with ignorance or denial but rather with a willingness to move beyond the 'document brut' towards an appreciation of the realities of the war.

Significantly, although Langfus is quick to criticize the response of outside society throughout this novel, she recognizes the universality of the desire to shun tales and memories of the many years of suffering. No one can escape this inherent self-centredness, not even her narrator-protagonist, Maria. Maria may criticize Michel Caron for failing to listen to her but she is guilty of the same fault, lamenting, 'je ne vois pas pourquoi on me chargerait des histoires des autres' (LB, p. 133). In recognizing such a viewpoint, Langfus shows herself to be realistic and pragmatic. In this novel, she distinguishes between the possibility of 'écouter' and 'se charger' 'des histoires'. She asks only that her readers

---

[18] 'Un cri ne s'imprime pas (Discours prononcé devant la WIZO en mars 1963)', *Les Nouveaux Cahiers*, 115 (1993–94), p. 42.

[19] Langfus, 'Un cri ne s'imprime pas', p. 48.

[20] In a much-cited passage from *L'Espèce Humaine*, Antelme affirms that 'il faut beaucoup d'artifice pour faire passer une parcelle de la vérité' and in an equally well-known passage from *L'Ecriture ou la vie*, Semprun declares, 'la vérité essentielle de l'expérience n'est pas transmissible ou plutôt elle ne l'est que par l'écriture littéraire, par l'artifice de l'œuvre d'art, bien sûr.' R. Antelme, *L'Espèce humaine*, revised edition (Paris: Gallimard, 1957), pp. 317–318; J. Semprun, *L'Ecriture ou la vie* (Paris: Gallimard/Folio, 1994), p. 167.

[21] 'Les écrivains devant le fait concentrationnaire', *L'Arche*, No. 50 (1961), 32–33 (p. 33).

listen to, and not be burdened by, her war narrative and recognizes that
readers can receive and engage with survivors' accounts, as long as they
are presented in an unthreatening fictional package. Furthermore, she
primes them to experience a version of LaCapra's 'empathetic unsettle-
ment'.[22] It is the resulting balance of identification and estrangement
which allows her writing to act as a kind of watershed, preparing readers
to better deal with new testimonial accounts of the Holocaust and the
war in general.

Her efforts to create a responsible reader and the associated softly-
softly approach may seem to contradict Langfus's aforementioned
rejection of the sanitization of war memories. However, by adopting such
an approach she accepts that tackling communal trauma is about incremental steps. As she proclaimed in 1963, all that she could hope for was
that in the case of 'cet homme qui n'a pas connu la guerre directement
. . . une fois sa lecture terminée . . . les mots: guerre, persécution raciale,
camps de concentration, chaque fois qu'il les lira ou les entendra pro-
noncer, ont désormais quelque chance d'évoquer en lui des images plus
précises' and that subsequently, 'peut-être, son comportement, dans
certains circonstances, s'en trouvera-t-il légèrement infléchi, peut-être
sera-t-il amené à prendre telle position, à agir de telle manière nouvelle'.[23]
For Langfus, this 'imperceptible modification' alone is enough to justify
conferring the 'étrange entreprise' that is writing with the responsibility
of transmitting experience.[24]

In *Les Bagages de sable*, Langfus proves herself adept at understanding
not only the psyche of the survivor but also the *esprit* of the community
in which the survivor finds herself. Superficially, this narrative is driven
by Maria's desire to discover, even to construct, a post-war identity; in
reality, Maria's efforts are guided almost exclusively by her dealings with
the outside community. Ultimately, Langfus does not explicitly destroy
the many 'refoulements' upon which her contemporaries constructed
post-war society but she does begin to subtly undermine them. Langfus's
tactics may not seem radical or innovative by today's standards; nonetheless, they provide an important foundation for the move towards
a questioning and rethinking of the collective memory of the war and
its legacy in subsequent decades.

[22] D. LaCapra, 'Trauma, Absence, Loss', *Critical Inquiry*, 25:4 (1999), p. 699.
[23] Langfus, 'Un cri ne s'imprime pas', p. 47.
[24] Langfus, 'Un cri ne s'imprime pas', p. 43.

Chapter 14

When the SS man says I: on Robert Merle, Michel Rachline and Jonathan Littell

Luc Rasson

Much of the scandal surrounding *Les Bienveillantes* has to do with its use of the first person. A Nazi, a member of the SS who is one of the functionaries of genocide, or in other words a monster, is allowed to speak in the first person. This enunciative fact explains why so many readers who are asked how they react to the novel say that they are 'confused'. One commentator says that reading the novel left him 'hagard et pantelant',[1] while others say they were 'sidérés'.[2] The latter image is often used by critics, and that, presumably, is no accident. *Sidération* is in fact a medical term meaning 'anéantissement soudain des fonctions vitales' (*Robert*), but its etymology goes back to the Latin *siderari* – 'to come under the baleful influence of the stars' – and it is also related in part to the verb *désirer*. This adequately captures the reader's experience of destabilization: the reader is plunged into a state midway between (figurative) exhaustion and the desire to go on reading all the same.

Having said that, Jonathan Littell is not the first novelist to have given a 'monstre politique' a monopoly on speech. One thinks of Latin-American writers such as Augusto Roa Bastos, Mario Vargas Llosa and Gabriel Garcia Marquez, who allow dictators to speak in their respective novels. In the European context, one thinks of the Spanish writer Manuel

---

[1] Alexandre Fillon in *Lire*, September 2006, consulted at www.lire.fr (accessed April 2010).

[2] Fillon speaks of the novel's 'souffle sidérant'. Pierre Assouline, for his part, entitles his review 'Un premier roman sidérant', and then adds that the look leaves the reader in a state of 'sidération'. See www.passouline.blog.lemonde.fr/2006/08/25/2006_08_un_premier_roma (accessed April 2010).

Vazquez Montalban, whose excellent *Autobiografía del General Franco* was published in 1993, or of the British historian Richard Lourie's *Autobiography of Joseph Stalin*, which appeared in 2001. And speaking of Stalin, one thinks of Alexander Solzhenitsyn and Anatoly Rybakov, who allowed the Soviet dictator to speak at length in, respectively, *The First Circle* and *Children of the Arbat*. Stalin was in fact given a platform as long ago as 1949 in *The Case of Comrade Tulayev*, a great novel about the political purges by the unjustly forgotten Victor Serge.[3]

Allowing a Nazi, rather than a communist, to speak appears to be a more delicate matter. While Stalin does have a discursive presence, there are almost no texts that allow Adolf Hitler to speak, the notable exception being the final chapter of George Steiner's novel *The Portage to San Cristobal of A.H.* (1981), in which the reader has to come to terms with the leader of the Third Reich's attempts to justify his actions – and they are not stupid, as it happens. The taboo on allowing Hitler to speak – for the moment – does not really apply to more minor figures such as Max Aue or, going further back, to Rudolf Lang, who is Rudolf Höss's fictional alter ego in Robert Merle's *La Mort est mon métier*. Mention might also be made of how, in 1972, Michel Rachline gave the impenitent Nazi Frédéric Marelle a discursive monopoly in his *Le Bonheur nazi* – a novel which fell into oblivion and which was rediscovered when *Les Bienveillantes* had such success.

I would like to compare Jonathan Littell's novel with his two predecessors in the French domain. I will look on the one hand to the *ethos* of their respective narrators – what self-image they project – and, on the other, at the figure of their implied readers. That should make it possible to demonstrate the cleverness of *Les Bienveillantes*, as compared with Merle and Rachline's novels, and to point out that the three novels have a similar effect on the reader, who has to come to terms with the dialectical space that the texts open up between the poles of alterity and proximity.

Nazi monsters?

The one thing that the three novels have in common is that a homo-diegetic narrator describes his involvement in National Socialism. In the case of Merle, the narrator is based upon the historical figure of Rudolf

---

[3] On Victor Serge, see the first two chapters of my *L'Ecrivain et le dictateur. Ecrire l'expérience concentrationnaire* (Paris: Imago, 2008).

Höss, the Commandant of Auschwitz. In his preface, the author states that his novel was largely inspired by the book by G.M. Gilbert, who was one of the American psychologists present at the Nuremberg trials and who devotes a few pages of his *Nuremberg Diary* to Höss.[4] *Le Bonheur nazi* is described as a fictional memoir of a fictional French Nazi who is writing twenty-six years after the end of the Second World War. In formal terms, the novel therefore has much in common with *Les Bienveillantes*, as Max Aue also begins to speak long after the war. The perspective is retrospective: the narrators write with hindsight and have internalized some of the models that were elaborated to explain Nazism after the war – this is especially true of Max Aue and we will come back to this point. In contrast, Rudolf Lang, who is the narrator and protagonist of *La Mort est mon métier*, tells his story from a viewpoint contemporary with the events he is describing, and uses the diary form.[5] Robert Merle chooses to abandon the retrospective perspective of Höss's historical autobiography, perhaps because this does more to convey the process of Nazification to the readers, and thus makes it easier to observe the genesis of the 'monster'.

This elementary formal difference between, on the one hand, the novels by Rachline and Littell and that by Merle, on the other, has its effects at the level of meaning, and especially on the way the narrators describe themselves or their ethos. Let us begin with Rudolf Lang, the protagonist of *La Mort est mon métier*. The first thing about him that strikes the reader is his unconditional respect for authority, which was inculcated into him by his father. It comes as no surprise to see that, when his father dies, Rudolf Lang internalizes the way he used to behave and becomes a real dictator when he is at home with his family. Lang-Höss is a vertical personality who sees human relationships solely in terms of a top–down (command–obedience) axis. He is fascinated with authority and emotionally insensitive: the death of his mother leaves him indifferent, as does that of his friend Schrader, and this attitude will make it easier for him to do his duty in Auschwitz. His other

---

[4] See G.M. Gilbert, *Nuremberg Diary* (New York: Da Capo Press, 1995 [1947]). Merle did not base his account on Höss's autobiography, which was not published until 1958. See Martin Broszat (ed.), *Kommandant in Auschwitz. Autobiographische Aufzeichnungen des Rudolf Höss* (München: Deutscher Taschenbuchverlag, 2008 [1958]). English translation: *Commandant of Auschwitz* (London: Phoenix Press, 2000).

[5] The fact that the chapter titles indicate the year suggests the text belongs to the 'diary' genre.

characteristic is his taste for violence. When he joins the Freikorps, he states that, 'Les choses étaient bien réelles, puisque je pouvais les détruire.'[6]

It will be recalled that Merle's novel dates from 1952. The character traits described fit perfectly with the profile of the authoritarian personality that Adorno and his team had recently drawn up in *The Authoritarian Personality* (1950), with the possible exception of the pronounced interest in sexuality; there is no sign of that in *La Mort est mon métier*.[7] It can be assumed that Robert Merle, whose background was in English studies, was familiar with Adorno's work and that he incorporated it into his portrait of Rudolf Lang-Höss. The Nazi described in the 1952 novel is a character marked by an otherness that nothing can overcome. Rudolf Lang and the reader have nothing in common: this is the 'Nazi monster' hypothesis.

Can the same be said of *Le Bonheur nazi*? The title itself is oxymoronic and evokes a feeling that tends to exclude the post-war reader: how can Nazism be a source of happiness? And it is obvious from the novel's first sentences that the reader is not concerned. The narrator begins by rejecting two stances: he refuses to apportion blame (to Nazism) and does not attempt to justify himself. That is why he states, quite openly and in contradictory fashion, 'J'ai décidé de publier ce livre à la gloire du national-socialisme.'[8] What follows is the story of Frédéric Marelle, who was born on 20 April 1911. The date is worthy of note. While Littell made a point of giving Max Aue his own birthday, Rachline goes one step further: 20 April is the *Geburtstag des Führers*. Frédéric is French, a doctor by training and a National Socialist by conviction, as the end of the exordium makes quite clear: 'je me bats: contre la Liberté, contre la Démocratie, contre les Juifs, les Nègres, les Jaunes, les rouges . . . j'appartiens à la race de bourreaux' (*Le Bonheur nazi*, p. 18).

This sets the tone for the four hundred pages that follow. We see the young German-speaking Frenchman settle in Germany in the late 1920s. He moves in Nazi circles, gets to know Horst Wessel, Himmler, Hitler and *tutti quanti*, and above all becomes imbued with the values, ways of thinking and practices that are associated with Nazism. Michel

---

[6] Robert Merle, *La Mort est mon métier* (Paris: Gallimard, 1952), Folio no. 789, p. 140.

[7] Rudolf Höss's historical autobiography, on the other hand, does express a horrified fascination with homosexuality.

[8] Michel Rachline, *Le Bonheur nazi* (Paris: Guy Authier, 1972); Livre de poche no. 4117, p. 17.

Rachline is not afraid of being caricatural: his character's rabid racism is no more than a very slim ideological excuse that allows him to give free rein to his intrinsic sadism. The novel abounds in scenes in which defenceless individuals are handed over to killers who assume that they have the right to humiliate, torture and eliminate those who do not match up to their racial ideal.

Michel Rachline actually makes even more use of the Nazi monster stereotype than Robert Merle. This is a novel that dismisses its reader and prevents all empathy with the protagonist. There are no allusions to the 'ordinary man' thesis, which is quite understandable given that Christopher Browning's pioneering study was not published until 1992.[9] It is, on the other hand, surprising that the novel's bibliography should contain no reference to Hannah Arendt's seminal essay on the banality of evil, which was published over ten years before the novel appeared. Ultimately, and despite the gratuitous violence the novel indulges in, its effect is *reassuring*: the main message is that the Nazi is the absolute other, and that we post-war readers share moral and political values that are the complete antithesis of Nazi ideology: the politico-sadistic delusions of a man like Frédéric Marelle are nothing to do with us.

Before going on to discuss *Les Bienveillantes*, it is worth pointing out that many analogies can be found between Littell's novel and Rachline's, rather as though the former had, to some extent, been inspired by the latter. Both protagonists – Max Aue and Frédéric Marelle – are of dual French-German heritage. Both are drawn to National Socialism, join the SS and have similar jobs: both go to Auschwitz as inspectors. Both are homosexual, and both have active sex lives that are not without their perverse aspects: Max Aue is fascinated by incest while Frédéric Marelle is a sadist. By chance, they come into contact with the Nazi elite and meet Himmler and Hitler, among others. Both narrators like to dwell upon the same ideological themes, and happily hold forth about the similarities between Jews and National Socialists,[10] basing their arguments on their readings of the Bible. And it should be noted in passing that both these impenitent Nazis are circumcised: Mau Aue for hygienic reasons, and Frédéric Marelle as a result of a clash between the SA and the SS. Both, finally, become traitors. As we know, Max Aue murders

---

[9] Christopher Browning, *Ordinary Men: Reserve Police Battalion 101 and the Final Solution in Poland* (New York: Harper Collins, 1992).

[10] This is one of *Les Bienveillantes*'s leitmotifs. Cf. *Le Bonheur nazi* (p. 128): 'Le nazisme n'a fait qu'appliquer les principes révérés par les juifs.'

his best friend Thomas in order to steal his identity, while Frédéric Marelle works for Simon Wiesenthal's organization and tracks down 'Dr M' in Latin America (he once worked with this fictional alter ego of Dr Mengele).

Does Jonathan Littell's character Max Aue reinforce the 'Nazi monster' stereotype? The character's commitment is not in doubt. At no point does he challenge the rationale for the National Socialist *Weltanschauung*, and he sometimes – albeit rarely – becomes a spokesman for its most repugnant racist ideas. Having said that, Max Aue is also a man who claims not to be a blind follower of the ideology of Nazi Germany; he is, as he himself puts it, 'un intellectuel un peu compliqué'[11] who prides himself on his critical reflexes and who does not subscribe to the dogma of blind obedience[12] that became the cornerstone of the defence of so many Nazis – including Rudolf Höss and Franz Stangl – after 1945. His doubts are, of course, limited to minor aspects of extermination, the methodical way in which it is implemented and the sadism of some of his colleagues. Max Aue is offended by marginal aspects of genocide but never questions its goals, the one exception being the conversation with his friend Thomas in which he states that 'le meurtre des juifs, au fond, ne sert à rien' (p. 209). We do not find such statements in either *La Mort est mon métier* or *Le Bonheur nazi*: it is clear that, unlike Rudolf Lang or Frédéric Marelle, Max Aue is not a *flat character*, and that is probably one of the reasons why some readers find the novel so offensive.

Les Bienveillantes's protagonist seems to avoid stereotypes in one other respect. Too little attention has been paid to the character's *passivity* – which is difficult to reconcile with the spirit of initiative that is usually associated with members of the SS. This Nazi is not in control of anything. Things happen to him. He is, for instance, blackmailed into joining the *Sicherheitsdienst* after being caught with a male prostitute (Littell, pp. 106–113). He is unaware of what is going on when he is decorated by Hitler after having escaped from the hell of Stalingrad (pp. 621–623). His posting to Himmler's personal staff is something else that simply happens to him and frustrates his own plan to get himself posted to France (pp. 767–768). The passive nature of his character is, in other

[11] Jonathan Littell, *Les Bienveillantes* (Paris: Gallimard, Folio, 2008), p. 344.
[12] 'Mais il était quand-même vital de comprendre *en soi-même* la nécessité des ordres du Führer: si l'on s'y pliait par simple esprit prussien d'obéissance, par esprit de *Knecht*, ... alors on n'était qu'un veau, un esclave et pas un homme' (pp. 153–154).

words, made obvious, and it is not unrelated to his sex life. As he puts it at the end of his exordium: 'J'aurais sans doute préféré être une femme.' By 'femme', he means not a wife and mother but, 'une femme nue, sur le dos, les jambes écartées, écrasée sous le poids d'un homme' (p. 40).

It should also be noted that the character's passivity is also bound up with his claim to be a spectator throughout. Max Aue is basically some-one who watches. And he watches with great attention, as the first scene in which he appears suggests. The narrator attends an orgy, but refuses to join in and is happy to watch, 'comme si mes yeux étaient un appareil de Roentgen: sous la chair, je percevais clairement les squelettes' (p. 134). The demystifying power of his gaze becomes even more pronounced when he is wounded at Stalingrad: it is his 'pineal eye' that allows him to see 'the naked face of death' behind every face. Once again, Max Aue – and perhaps we should call him Max *Auge* – is a passive spectator rather than an actor, and has little to do with the commonplaces we have observed in the novels of Robert Merle and Michel Rachline.

Given that Max Aue is not a monster in the sense that Rudolf Lang or Frédéric Marelle are monsters, are we to conclude that he comes into the 'ordinary men' category described by Christopher Browning? The one thing we can be sure about is that the protagonist has indeed inter-nalized a reading of *Ordinary Men*. We can at least infer that much from the opening chapter, which is entitled 'Toccata'. The initial apostrophe attempts, as we know, to force the reader into a fraternal relationship with the narrator. The rest of the chapter simply develops the idea that, given the right circumstances, anyone can become a cog in the genocidal machine: 'les hommes ordinaires dont est constitué l'Etat . . . voilà le vrai danger' (p. 39). Having said that, can we argue that the novel sets out to defend and illustrate the 'ordinary man' thesis, as though it were a sort of fictional counterpart to Christopher Browning's study? Nothing could be less certain.

Max Aue's crimes are not in fact restricted to the context of the extermination of the Jews. He is a killer in his private life too. We can overlook the murders of his mother and stepfather, as it is never explicitly stated that he killed them, even though all the evidence points that way. The SS officer is trigger-happy when he is off duty too. He impulsively kills an old man who, as the Soviet troops approach, insists on playing *The Art of Fugue* on a church organ. He kills his Romanian lover Mikhail when he comes on to him too openly. The final, and perhaps most shocking, murder is that of his friend Thomas on the penultimate page of the novel. This is the murder that allows him to make his escape in time. These murders, which are either gratuitous or motivated by personal interest, invalidate the narrator's claim to any 'ordinary man' status. Even the ordinary members of the *Einsatzgruppen* studied by Christopher Browning were not in the habit of killing their best friends. Is Jonathan Littell recuperating *in extremis* the 'Nazi monster' stereotype? *Les Bienveillantes*, as compared with the novels of Merle and Rachline, is 'clever' in that its relationship with the stereotypical image of the genocidal Nazi is so ambiguous. Max Aue is neither a monster nor an ordinary man. Or perhaps he is both. He is a complex character and cannot be seen as the product of any one determinant.

Alterity/proximity

I said, perhaps somewhat hastily, that the reader is irremediably excluded from the world of *La Mort est mon métier* and *Le Bonheur nazi*. Their protagonists are such political and human monsters that the reader is disgusted by them and, as Michel Rachline suggests, is eventually *sickened* by both the novels and their protagonists.[13] And yet these novels also suggest that the reader is, despite everything, concerned. These monsters move in societies that are not unfamiliar to us – far from it. One only has to look at the way the Nazis in *La Mort est mon métier* talk about how genocide is organized. Their discourse is, to cut a long argument short, bureaucratic and technocratic: they speak of 'chiffres d'arrivages', of 'unités', 'traitement spécial' and 'rendement de pointe'. More worrying still, Merle does not fail to suggest that the discourse of Reason itself is involved, that there is a link between mass murder and our rational faculties. We see this when, for example, Rudolf Lang discovers the advantages of using Zyklon B; the discovery is a cause for intellectual jubilation. The protagonist takes the view that there is 'quelque chose de satisfaisant pour l'esprit' about the fact that, once the Jews have been locked in the changing room, everything happens 'dans un même lieu', as though it was a classical tragedy (*La Mort*, p. 298).

We have, of course, known since Horkheimer and Adorno published their *Dialectic of Enlightenment* in 1947 that 'the dark horizon of myth is illumined by the sun of calculating reason, beneath whose cold rays the seed of the new barbarism grows to fruition', and Merle probably

---

[13] See the author's *Avertissement*: 'A moins que mon livre et l'idée seule d'une résurrection nazie ne produisent sur vous les mêmes effets que sur moi! Qu'ils ne fassent vomir!', *Le Bonheur nazi*, p. 14.

took his inspiration from them.[14] That Zygmunt Bauman puts forward a more nuanced version of the same analysis[15] only goes to demonstrate that, even though Rudolf Lang is a repulsively insensitive, cold and violent man, the society in which he lives is not unfamiliar: it is a society based upon values that we still recognize today: rationality, efficiency and profitability.

Despite all the horror that his protagonist inspires in us, Michel Rachline makes a similar suggestion. It is clear from the author's foreword – which supposedly warns the reader that Frédéric Marelle's story is being told by a madman – that fascism (or Nazism; no clear distinction is made between the two) is not a political reality that belongs to a specific time and place. This is Michel Rachline's proposed definition of fascism: 'C'est une maladie du corps social, un désordre des forces et des parties nécessaires à l'exercice de ses fonctions' (*Le Bonheur nazi*, p. 8). From that point of view – which is medical rather than historical – fascism becomes a timeless phenomenon that has little to do with the situation in Italy or Germany between the wars. The author concludes that fascism (or Nazism) did not die in 1945:

> Nous sommes tous des Nazis. A la lueur d'un événement, le nazi qui dormait se réveille: la guerre d'Algérie, celle du Vietnam, la guerre d'Irelande, que sais-je? Dès que l'homme affronte l'homme, tout devient possible . . . Nous sommes des brutes. (p. 9)

In the author's view, fascism represents nothing but the violent, sadistic depths of human nature. This way of depoliticizing the notion and extending its semantic field allows the novelist to implicate the reader. If fascism is just another name for the violence we see throughout history, no one can ever be safe: neither you nor I, nor even the Jews. While Michel Rachline does not deny that he is Jewish, he still attacks 'Israël, que le fanatisme et la religion d'Etat dévorent comme d'autres fascismes' (p. 12).

The reader undecided

Narratives that are recounted by 'political monsters' – Nazis, in this case – establish a space of readings that unfolds between the twin poles

---

[14] Max Horkheimer and Theodor W. Adorno, *Dialectic of Enlightenment*, trans. John Cumming (London: Allen Lane, 1973), p. 32.

[15] See his *Modernity and the Holocaust* (Ithaca: Cornell University Press, 1989).

of alterity and proximity. The reader feels uncomfortable as he is torn between these two poles. At times, he is confronted with the irreducible but reassuring otherness of the narrator, and at other times with his worrying familiarity. This is not a comfortable position by any means; no sooner has he reached the reassuring conclusion that the narrator is a monster, than he is expelled by Merle, and realizes that the society in which he lives is not, basically, any different; Rachline tells him that the defeat of Nazism did not signal the end of violence in history, while Littell tells him that the genocidal SS man can claim the status of the ordinary man.

Despite all the differences between the three novels under discussion, and despite the apparent lucidity of *Les Bienveillantes*, we have to conclude that they reach the same impasse. And they are not in fact convincing: even if Rudolf Lang's way of thinking is the same as ours, his character is too one-dimensional to be credible. For similar reasons, Rachline's novel cannot escape the contradiction between the contention that fascism is a permanent feature of history and the individuality of a character who seems to have more to do with teratology. Ultimately, *Les Bienveillantes* presents us with an undecidable question: the 'ordinary man' rhetoric of the opening sentence is undermined, at the narrative level, by a criminal narrator whose sex life – and this is an aspect that I have not discussed – can scarcely be described as ordinary. The enigma, in other words, remains intact. None of these novels gives a convincing answer to the question: how can one say 'I' *and* be a member of the SS?

Part 3

Trajectories

Introduction

The theoretical and methodological importance of the return to the past, the importance of bringing historical awareness to narratives of history and memory: these are issues that have not surprisingly been raised in the course of the earlier sections, but 'Trajectories' focuses particularly on the structural and thematic consequences of historicization for narrative and for critical approaches. Here, we ask how this historical subject matter is itself historicized in relation to its moment of enunciation.

The periodization of the Vichy syndrome, the stages through which, according to Rousso, French attitudes evolved over the decades, is an important point of reference in a section which traces the dynamics of historical and cultural changes in narratives about the Occupation and war. Leah Hewitt takes Rousso's image of the broken mirror to follow through a number of films over four decades depicting Jewish experiences under the Occupation, tracking the shifting nature of Jewish and national identity. Hilary Footitt presents a historiographical mapping of French views of their Anglo-American allies from the 1940s to the present, the many tensions to be seen in the representation of foreign liberators in narratives of French national identity, and the questioning in recent years of the liberators' behaviour, which has been illuminated by the critiques of Orientalism. Danièle Sabbah discusses the diary of Hélène Berr, written in occupied Paris and interrupted by her arrest and subsequent deportation to Auschwitz, but only published in 2004. Sabbah delineates her use of the genre and how it changed over the three years of its writing, tracing its double journey; rooted in the precise temporality of anti-Semitic persecution, it undergoes a double evolution from diary, with the associated rhetoric of immediacy of living, to historical record, both for its author, as she registers the scale of the atrocity taking place around her and the imperative to counter its invisibility, and for the contemporary readership sixty years later.

David Uhrig's subject is Blanchot's avant-garde novel of 1943, *Aminadab*. Contextualizing Blanchot's views on authoritarianism, France and his anti-Nazism, and elucidating the politics and its memorial structure of the text, he establishes the importance of its precise temporality against later readings taking it into a more general critique of society, and its use of Halbwachs's pre-war study on collective memory, in order to present the interplay of dynamic movement and stasis, of individual and plurality, quite incompatible with the direction being taken by Vichy. The final two chapters consider canonical authors in Occupation studies whose work has been very influential. Marie Chaix and Patrick Modiano are exemplars of a younger generation, the children who returned time and again to the Occupation years in their quest to recover and understand the figure of the parent. Katherine Cardin compares Chaix's early and more recent fiction on the Occupation, revealing the evolution in her attitude to her father and his legacy within the broader context of the 'paysage familial' involving her own children, while Alan Morris explores the language of Modiano's more recent novels, apparently less focused on the Occupation, and demonstrates the intricate linguistic and stylistic work through which the incidents, themes and motifs characteristic of his approach to the Occupation continue to shape the narrative.

Through these analyses of both individual and collective trajectories, we can see that texts and their readers (or spectators) are enmeshed in, and contribute to, the evolving historiographical debates which have shaped post-war cultural approaches to the war and Occupation, as well as those already in play in the ideological confrontations under Vichy. Opening up texts profoundly anchored in their own, sometimes individual, often multiple temporalities, these readings reveal the importance of paying critical attention to the processes of individual and collective history.

Chapter 15

Distorted mirrors: Jewish identity in French post-war films on the Occupation

Leah D. Hewitt

In keeping with the theme of *Framing Narratives*, I would like to offer some frames of reference in which to place the cinematic mirrors I am considering. My interest lies in the construction of a problematic French national identity, one in crisis that has obsessively manifested itself through the cinematic fictions of the Occupation.[1] Given that France was the first country in Europe to give Jews full citizenship and that the intersection of ethnic and national identities has remained a vexed issue in France, I would agree with Jonathan Judaken that 'the battle over national identity throughout the twentieth century (and continuing today) has depended in crucial ways on the image of "the Jew" and on the perception of Judaism in the French cultural imagination'.[2]

Jean-Paul Sartre's remarkable, if highly flawed *Réflexions sur la question juive*, offers just such a mix of conflicted identities for Jews that in turn impact Sartre's reading of the nation-state and his own role as an intellectual. Written at the end of the war when most remained silent about 'the Jewish question', this work was instrumental in defining the terms in which Jewish identity would be articulated in the post-war era. Implicit within its title and throughout its analysis is the trope of the mirror and its *réflexions*, thoughts on, and mirrors of, Jewish identity. Sartre presents Jewish identity as an impossible or reversed reflection: either as the Other characterized by the anti-Semite (who needs the Jew

---

[1] See my *Remembering the Occupation in French Film: National Identity in Post-War Europe* (New York: Palgrave Macmillan, 2008).

[2] Jonathan Judaken, *Jean-Paul Sartre and the Jewish Question* (Lincoln: University of Nebraska Press, 2006), p. 18.

in order to establish his own identity), or as the mythic abstract citizen of democracy who becomes invisible. This latter is, of course, part of the republican discourse that has dominated national identity issues in the contemporary period. Sartre makes of Jewish identity the prototype of alterity. According to Sartre's model, within the nation-state the Jew becomes a French citizen at the price of losing his Jewish identity through assimilation. His analysis is noteworthy in the ways it counters both the particularist terms of anti-Semitic discourse and the universalist vision of 'human nature' in the French Enlightenment model. Sartre must, however, turn to a future revolution and a post-historical, classless society to envisage Jewish identity in terms other than those of the anti-Semite or the 'inauthentic' assimilated Jew. Even as he takes issue with the stereotypes initiated by the anti-Semite, Sartre often ends up using them despite himself. Later, Sartre would alter his transhistorical characterization of Jewish identity in order to acknowledge Jewish history, culture and the Shoah which he had neglected in the *Réflexions*. It is to his credit that even in the early work of the *Réflexions*, he ends on a note of solidarity: 'Not one French man will be secure so long as a single Jew – in France or *in the world at large* – can fear for his life.'[3]

Sartre's use of the rhetoric of Same and Other, coupled with his discourse on the inauthentic versus the authentic Jew, has created a type of argument that French film-makers representing the Occupation have continually felt compelled to address. In 2002, Joel Rosenberg and Stephen Whitfield described the contemporary cinematic situation as a transcendence of these dialectics: 'It is presently less a matter . . . of how authentic or inauthentic, how favorable or unfavorable, is the representation of the Jew (or of any other ethnic figure or group) on screen. It has come to be more important to consider what the ethnic screen image says about the civil society from which the film emanates.'[4] Now while I think that Rosenberg and Whitfield are absolutely right that the question of ethnic portrayal has much to tell us about social values and concerns of the period when a film is made, nevertheless, questions of definitions, of authenticity and of the relationship between public and private memory have naggingly remained in the post-war period, even

---

[3] Jean-Paul Sartre, *Anti-Semite and Jew*, trans. George J. Becker (New York: Schocken Books, 1948), p. 53.

[4] Joel Rosenberg and Stephen J. Whitfield (eds), *Prooftexts: a Journal of Jewish Literary History*, special issue: 'The Cinema of Jewish Experience: Introduction', 22:1/2 (winter/spring 2002), 1.

in recent years. The issue is how one historically constructs Jewish identity, makes it visible, while remaining within France's tradition of *laïcité*.

My second frame involves Henry Rousso's famous broken mirror stage in *The Vichy Syndrome* located in the early 1970s when the myth of generalized French resistance was shattered. Structurally, Jewish identity arises as a question of memory and erasure at the same time that the memory of Vichy´s complicity, on individual and collective levels, resurfaces. Although I am considering the mirror as a trope for the question of Jewish identity in the post-Holocaust era of French film, whereas Rousso's broken mirror concentrates equally if not more on the revelations of French collaboration and a crisis of French identity, it is crucial to note that the opening of discussion on collaboration coincides with breaking the silence on Jewish experiences of the war and the Shoah.

Before focusing on a recent film, I'd like to provide a third frame, this one cinematic, through a review of some of the ways mirrors have represented the *questioning* of Jewish identity in post-war films. I emphasize the question over a definition, the mirror as distortion or trickery rather than faithful reflection, for the film-makers do this themselves, believing perhaps, as Alain Finkielkraut has maintained, that 'Judaism's very lack of definition is precious; it shows that political categories of class and nation have only a relative truth, and stand as a sign of their inability to encompass the world in its totality. The Jewish people don't know who they are, only that they exist, and that their disconcerting existence blurs the boundary, inaugurated by modern reason, between the public and the private.'[5] In *Les Tabous de l'histoire*, Marc Ferro also reminds us that 'la race juive' is actually a mosaic of cultures, languages and religious rites, and that a monolithic identification served both the Shoah *and* the establishment of Israel.[6] In a different twist, Jean-François Lyotard used the 'Jew' as the prototypical figure of the outsider for European culture.[7] Identity is indeed a tricky, slippery concept, susceptible to all shapes of manipulation.

One of the earliest films to set in motion the questioning of Jewish identity is Claude Berri's autobiographical film, *Le Vieil Homme et l'enfant*

[5] Alain Finkielkraut, *The Imaginary Jew*, trans. Kevin O'Neill (Lincoln: University of Nebraska Press, 1994), p. 169. Quoted in Stuart Z. Charmé, 'Varieties of Authenticity of Contemporary Jewish Identity,' *Jewish Social Studies*, 6:2 (2000), 148.

[6] Paris: NiL Editions, 2002, pp. 105–124.

[7] *Heidegger et les juifs* (Paris: Galilée, 1988), p. 45. Quoted in Simon P. Sibelman, 'The Imaginary Jew: Alain Finkielkraut and Contemporary Jewish Identity in France,' *European Studies Journal*, 13:2 (1996), 1–2.

from 1966, about a young Jewish boy taking refuge during the war at the farm of a pro-Vichy, pro-Pétain elderly peasant couple who don't know the little boy is Jewish. *Le Vieil Homme et l'enfant* offers an effective portrayal of a young Jew facing anti-Semitic bigotry as embodied in the old farmer played by Michel Simon. Adopting a light touch, Berri's film uses the visual metaphor of the mirror to stage the issue of Jewish identity. Berri's film comically deconstructs the image of the 'Jew' found in the anti-Semitic propaganda swallowed by the old farmer who clearly loves the little boy. In a key scene, as the boy and the old man look into a mirror together (the spectator is looking at their reflection), the boy pretends to be worried he might be Jewish (given the wholly negative image of the Jew that the old man has painted for him), and then the boy slyly accuses the old man of being Jewish because he supposedly possesses 'Jewish traits'. There is something immensely satisfying in these amusing scenes in which a child, using reason and logic, deconstructs the irrational, ignorant and wrongheaded arguments of anti-Semitism. In this instance, rather than a broken mirror, we find a distorted or deceptive mirror as the reigning metaphor of identity.

Throughout the 1970s and early 1980s, questions of the representability and identity of Jews were continually thematized in critical discussions of French films on the Occupation. Critics of Louis Malle's *Lacombe Lucien* (1974) were often troubled by the untypical appearance of the characters Albert Horn and his blonde daughter, France, who didn't look or act Jewish enough to suit them. The controversies touched off by *Lacombe Lucien* had to do both with the emphasis on French collabora-tion and on how Jews were portrayed both psychologically and physically. Could one portray a Jew as a blonde beauty, *authentically*, as Annette Insdorf uncomfortably put it when speaking of Aurore Clément playing the young Jewish protagonist?[8] Mona Ozouf complained that Malle created wandering Jews with accents, who were unattached to the Resist-ance and were passively involved with a collaborator.[9] The portrayal of who/what is Jewish has sparked controversy in such films, especially when the portrayal was not expressly positive. This question of the 'authentic' Jew persists throughout these two decades in films such as *Les Violons du bal* (1973, Michel Drach), *Monsieur Klein* (1976, Joseph

---

[8] See Annette Insdorf, *Indelible Shadows: Film and the Holocaust* (New York: Cambridge University Press, 1989), p. 126.

[9] Mona Ozouf, 'Sans chagrin et sans pitié', *Le Nouvel Observateur*, 489 (March 1974), 56.

Losey), *Le Dernier Métro* (1980, François Truffaut) and *Au revoir les enfants* (1986, Louis Malle).

Michel Drach's autobiographical film *Les Violons du bal* makes especially effective use of the mirror: it is a self-reflexive film emphasizing that the construction of the past is articulated through *memory* in the present rather than through an 'objective' past. The film weaves Drach's passion for the techniques of his craft into his obsession with a Jewish childhood lived under the threat of deportation, and a political attention to the relationship between past and present (including the 'May '68 generation'). Just as in *Le Vieil Homme et l'enfant*, secrets and lies abound: the little boy Michel (played by Drach's own son) does not learn from his family that he is Jewish until one of his classmates accuses him of being Jewish. We are again reminded of Sartre's *Anti-Semite and Jew*. As in Berri's film, Drach uses the mirror to question what constitutes Jewish identity and to emphasize the construction of memory through film. As a trope to explore the production of visual 'facts', the mirror makes us aware of lies and fictions. There is almost a pedagogical feel to the way Drach repeatedly uses mirrors to remind us that we must retain a critical distance, that this is not the real but an artistic creation of memory. We are also made aware of the profoundly alienating effects of the rhetorical mirror: in a mirrored scene where Michel is told by mother and grandmother about what it means to be Jewish, their explanation is based entirely on Judaism's relation to Christianity – there is nothing specific about Judaism, its customs, tradition or culture, in their description. This linguistic excision is prepared through a visual metaphor just beforehand: after the mother violently chops off the wing of a dead chicken on the kitchen table with a large cleaver, the grandmother picks up the discarded feathers and holds them to her head like a hat ornament as she smiles at herself in an old mirror. The sequence seems to imply that Judaism has become incidental, a mere adornment, after having been brutally silenced. Drach self-consciously thematizes the messy complications about representation and typicality that had made *Lacombe Lucien*'s portrait of Jews questionable for critics. He also suggests, albeit indirectly, that the French republican model of identity, implicitly rooted in a Christian tradition, maintains difficult negotiations with the particularities of a Jewish heritage.

In the last ten years, there have been several French films that focus on Jewish dilemmas during the Occupation. There are three in particular that offer portrayals of Jewish identity in the French context, weaving these portrayals more tightly into the twists of their French narratives:

Monsieur Batignole (2002, Gérard Jugnot), *Le Promeneur du Champ de Mars* (2005, Robert Guédiguian) and *Un secret* (2007, Claude Miller). The latter is most distinctive in that it is one of the rare fictional works on the Occupation to focus on a discussion of Jewish identity *from the inside*, with Jewish characters asking themselves what it means to be Jewish, to be a French Jew under the Occupation and in the contemporary period. Inspired by Philippe Grimbert's 2004 fictionalized autobiography of the same name, *Un secret* is reminiscent of Patrick Modiano's obsessive novelistic theme of a hidden (and guilty) Jewish identity.[10] Grimbert's story features an adolescent boy's discovery of his parents' past, his Jewish origins and a half-brother whom he never knew. At several turns, it questions Jewish stereotypes and is a romantic tale of passion and betrayal, with the Shoah playing a key role in the drama. Similar to *Le Vieil Homme et l'enfant*, *Les Violons du bal* and *Monsieur Batignole*, Miller's film centres on the development of identity in a child, and it relies on autobiographical data to structure its story; like *Les Violons du bal*, it shows the memory of the war *and its telling* as a key to understanding – and living in – the present. This telling, however, is intimately bound to the creative act of the imagination even more than in Drach's work, since it consists of a narrator from a new generation *imagining* what the wartime memories would be. *Un secret*, both film and novel, stages the creative act *as* memory. In many ways, *Un secret* represents a coming to terms with the interplay between ethnic identity and national identity through fiction; it showcases the sacrifices that the modern Jew undergoes in aspiring to the French model of citizenship and, as such, offers one of the few critical renderings of the model, as well as a more complex understanding of it.

Many of the works of the post-war generation are troubled *and* inspired by their parents' secrets. One is reminded of Alain Finkielkraut's lament that post-war Jewish children became 'imaginary Jews' deprived of their heritage and culture, because of the Shoah but also because of their parents' silence about Judaism. In Grimbert's case, the unveiling of the parents' secrets, akin to a primal scene structuring traumatic symptoms, is designed as a liberating narrative both for the parents and the children. Grimbert, a Lacanian psychoanalyst by profession, has written a multi-layered autofiction with an intricate web of metaphorical connections between the living and the dead. His story is composed of

[10] Both Grimbert and Modiano were born after the war and Miller, born in 1942, was too young to remember it.

a complicated chronology concerning four generations of French Jews (grandparent emigrés from Eastern Europe, assimilated parents, and the adolescent child of the 1950s who becomes the adult narrator and therapist with a daughter of his own). Its associative network links adolescent sexual fantasy, parental love, infidelity, the Shoah and national identity. Like Rousso, who uses a psychoanalytic model for the Vichy syndrome, Grimbert dramatizes the individual Jew's family scenario and concurrently suggests a French collective malaise.

Grimbert's account first imagines an idyllic parental past during the war as fantasized by the post-war child he was, before revealing an entirely different version of what happened, one that would point to a guilty, painful, parental past from the war, a secret that was kept from the narrator throughout his adolescence. The film opens with a visual metaphor for this process of discovery: spectators think they are seeing a half-naked boy walking through a gauzy curtain (perhaps a mouldy shower curtain) towards the camera, only to discover that they are looking at the boy's reflection in an old, cloudy mirror. Director Miller uses the mirror as a trope to frame the versions of the Grimbert past and to suggest the identity quest theme. Like Michel Drach's *Les Violons du bal*, Miller's film uses colour film to portray the past, and black and white for the present, as if to suggest that the (created, imagined) past was more vibrant or intense than the present.[11] Both films self-consciously include their stories' authors on screen: Drach appears in his own film at the beginning as film-maker; Philippe Grimbert plays the small role of a *passeur* taking fleeing Jews to the safety of the countryside.

For those unfamiliar with Grimbert's story, here are the broad lines of some of the secrets the film narrates (there are, in fact, many): in the film, François Grimbert (Mathieu Amalric),[12] a middle-aged therapist of troubled children, recounts his sickly, post-war childhood and adolescence in the 1950s and 1960s, emphasizing how he always felt inadequate with his parents, Maxime (Patrick Bruel) and Tania (Cécile de France), who were superb athletes. The young François invents a strong, athletic brother to keep him company; he also imagines an idyllic romance about his parents getting together during the war. He discovers through

---

[11] In *Un secret*, a certain reconciliation of past and present is suggested at the film's final scene when the present is filmed in colour.

[12] Valentin Vigourt and Quentin Dubois play François as a child and adolescent. Contrary to the novel, which does not provide a first name for the boy, the film gives him a fictional name distinct from the author's.

a family friend, however, the family's guilty secret, that his parents had in fact been married before to a brother and sister, Hannah and Robert, who died during the war (Robert of typhus as a soldier and Hannah at Auschwitz). The adolescent François also discovers that his father Maxime and his first wife, Hannah (Ludivine Sagnier), actually had a son, Simon, born in the mid-1930s, who was deported to Auschwitz with his mother and died there. Thus François's imagined brother turns out to have existed. Maxime's passion for his sister-in-law Tania and their subsequent marriage are forever tainted with the guilt of Hannah and Simon's deaths. The family's silence surrounding the death of François's half-brother Simon ironically reproduces the Nazi's erasure of his life. Silence becomes the obstacle to healing and understanding, even when it is maintained as a form of protection or respect.

As I noted, many other secrets and lies populate this tale that jumps back and forth between time frames. First, the fact that the Grimbert family is Jewish is hidden, depriving the boy of his origins. Maxime had the family name's spelling officially changed (from Grinberg to Grimbert) to make the name less recognizably Jewish, more 'typically' French. The narrator compares this patronymic 'scar' to his family's attitude about his circumcision, casually referring to it as a simple surgical procedure, with no rituals or religious connotations involved. François is never told he is Jewish and is baptized Catholic as an adolescent, although the boy intuits his Jewish origins. This erasure of Jewish identity in turn recalls the family's generational disputes of the past, with grandparents, aunts and uncles proudly partaking in Jewish practices. During the war, some wear the yellow star with pride, some with fear, but both groups acknowledge ethnic identity. On the other hand, François's father Maxime, the prototype of the French *républicain*, staunchly refuses the star and proclaims his modernity and French citizenship at the price of forsaking his ties to Jewish rituals, culture and language (Sartre's inauthentic Jew). Maxime and Tania's intense athleticism and physical prowess appear as ways to counter negative stereotypes of Jews – to imagine them as powerful as the Nazis – but this distances them from their son François. Parenthetically, I would add that the casting is such that the physical appearance of the Jewish characters is varied so that there is no one model. Marriage celebrations and Shabbat are represented as part of the pre-war Jewish culture, and the language of the families of Maxime and Hannah is peppered with Yiddish while the older members of the family speak French with a foreign accent. The post-war scenes of François's parents neglect such ethnic markers. In the documentary made during the filming of *Un secret*, Claude Miller explains that he paid a personal homage to his own Jewish relatives through the inclusion of Yiddish in the dialogue.

François in turn, keeps his own secret, as he does not tell his parents that he has learned about Hannah and Simon until much later, when he is an adult, after the accidental death of a pet dog revealingly named Echo whom a now aged Maxime seems to mourn beyond measure. François consoles his father telling him that even if Maxime was responsible for the dog's death, he is not to blame for those of Hannah and Simon. Because François has researched their deaths, the son is also able to tell his father that Hannah and Simon died right after arriving in Auschwitz, so their suffering was not prolonged.

Both book and film are constructed to highlight the importance of setting the record straight, of finding ways to put the past in its place in a historic web work, with all its connections to other places and times. The text is studded with questions, as if to underscore the fictive, tentative nature of the memory being constructed. Imagining the parental stories gives these 'memories' a resting place, a proper burial, a memorial. If learning about his parents' past, and thus his own, is liberating for François, paradoxically he in turn is able to release his parents from their guilt and responsibility, so the process goes in both directions. One of the adult narrator's own acts of commemorative burial lies in providing a photo of his dead half-brother to Serge Klarsfeld for a book on deported children. Grimbert's book ends with the declaration: 'Ce livre serait sa tombe.' The narrator leaves open the possibility that 'ce livre' refers to the book we have just read by Grimbert as well as to Klarsfeld's. The film's visual equivalent is a tracking shot of the memorial wall displaying the names of Shoah victims. The shot occurs just after the narrator and his daughter have explored a dog and cat cemetery at the abandoned chateau of Pierre Laval's daughter, Josée de Chambrun. This pet cemetery of a collaborating family provides the impetus, says the first-person voiceover, for bringing the tale of Hannah and Simon out of the silence. Thus perpetrators and victims are linked in unexpected ways. Pet dogs are just one of the numerous metaphorical connections that bridge the gap between them and between the Occupation past and the narrator's present.[13]

---

[13] The pet dog first appears in the guise of a stuffed toy previously owned by the dead Simon. François discovers the toy in the family attic and, to his parents' dismay, stubbornly holds on to it.

The dispassionate tone of the narrative (in novel and film) provides the critical distance necessary to tell this story effectively, avoiding the temptation of melodrama and placing it in the context of other stories and other times. History is made less academic by describing people and events without necessarily naming them. Hitler is never named although he is alluded to and is seen in old newsreel clips in the film; in the book, circumcision is described but not identified by the term. But naming is also important for incorporating the past into one's life: once Grimbert knows his parents' secret about Hannah and Simon, a weight is lifted from him. With the ghosts named, the pain of the hidden past becomes an enabling tool for the adult psychoanalyst. In accordance with a psycho-analytic model (perhaps an idealized one), bringing the past to language, written or visual, is a creative act of liberation that leads to healing, not just of one's self but of others. Grimbert's book and Miller's film are both exorcisms and acts of mourning. In a sort of homage to, and dialogue with, the dead, 'mourning', to quote Judith Butler on Derrida, becomes 'a continued way of "speaking to" the other who is gone, even though the other is gone, in spite of the fact that the other is gone, precisely because that other is gone'.[14]

I would like to focus briefly on an exemplary scene of *Un secret* whose emotional force highlights a profound ambivalence about Jewish identity. It is a flashback to the war, as Hannah (Maxime's first wife) and her son Simon flee Paris and are accosted at a café rest stop by a policeman who asks Hannah for her identity papers. Here, to identify by ethnicity, to acknowledge being Jewish, is tantamount to suicide. Hannah carries it one step further. Not only does she identify herself as a Jew, but she also identifies Simon as her son, effectively signing his death warrant too. Hannah's motivation is relatively clear: she is painfully aware that Maxime is in love with Tania, his sister-in-law. What I find particularly intriguing about the moment of crisis for Hannah is the interpretative spin that Grimbert has placed on the scene. He fully admits in an interview that it is not known why Hannah gave the wrong identity card to the policeman (one conjecture was that she forgot to get rid of her Jewish card). As a psychoanalyst and perhaps as the son of Maxime, Grimbert cannot accept that Hannah's action might have been accidental. The film-maker Miller follows Grimbert's version of a wilful, sacrificial act on Hannah's part. It seems significant to me that the *passeur* played

<hr />

[14] Judith Butler, 'Jacques Derrida', *London Review of Books*, 4 November 2004.

by Philippe Grimbert is a spectator to this scene of Hannah's 'suicide', thus providing a diegetic and extradiegetic frame. Grimbert's close involvement with the adaptation of his novel and his witnessing of imagined scenes from his family's past during the filming (such as the marriage ceremony of Hannah and Maxime or the arrest of Hannah) are indicative of the dual nature of the fictive creation for the author. The performative side of the film allows both a pleasurable recovery of a Jewish past, including its traditions and dramas, and a connecting of his concerns to a more general phenomenon of growing up in an adult world full of secrets.

Thanks to the fictive scene of Hannah's arrest, the real-life son is able to become a spectator (like us) to the dramatic moment of ethnic revelation that disculpates his father: it is Hannah's choice of identifying herself as Jewish, not Maxime's actions, that causes her death. The narrator re-creates the scene in order to bear witness to this interpretation, perhaps to justify his own lineage. At the same time, no doubt, Grimbert is providing a history of Hannah and Simon's disappearance, making it visible, legible. It seems significant that Hannah does not *say* she is Jewish, does not identify herself in this direct, unambiguous way; the policeman must read it on the identification card that the Vichy government has issued. Both Grimbert and Miller frequently identify people and things in a similarly indirect way: there is a circuitousness that avoids the name, even as it alludes to it, that seems not only to repeat Hannah's gesture, but also Maxime's avoidance of being labelled Jewish. Grimbert's narrative frequently imagines what the various protagonists were thinking at each turn of the story. Slipping into Maxime's mentality, for example, the text speaks of the Jewish wedding celebration of Hannah and Maxime as 'manifestations traditionnelles' without identifying them as Jewish. Naming is like revealing a potentially culpable secret. The act of showing or describing Jewish custom without calling it that is rather like a game of hide-and-seek: it allows for the representation of Jewish culture but cannot call it that in the context of the French republican tradition of the anonymous *citoyen*.[15] This is the impasse that *Un secret* so effectively unveils.

But there is another side of naming that novel and film emphasize in significant ways. Although Jewish lore is not always identified as

---

[15] The cinematic version of the story has merely to *show* the wedding ceremony, so the act of naming is relatively easy to avoid.

such, and historical perpetrators like Hitler are not named,[16] there *are* historical figures whose names are woven into the story and they are specifically guilty *Frenchmen*. Robert Brasillach, editor of the fascist newspaper *Je suis partout* who was executed at the war's end, is identified with his most damning sentence: 'Débarrassez-nous des juifs en bloc, et surtout n'oubliez pas les petits.' This ties him to the individual fate of Simon. Also mentioned is Pierre Laval, two-time prime minister to Pétain, who becomes integral to the metaphorical nexus: Laval's name enters the cinematic narrative in the epilogue when the adult François and his daughter stumble upon the pet cemetery of Josée Laval. The commemoration of dead pets becomes linked to Laval's name, to the death of the Grimbert family dog, and to the deaths of Hannah and Simon. Historical responsibility, caring and loss are thus bound to personal suffering and remembering in the present. The naming of Laval and Brasillach is an act of conjuration, even if in Laval's case his name is indirectly associated with mourning the dead (via his daughter's pet cemetery).[17] In *Un secret*, there are virtually no acts or actors that don't carry a double, contradictory meaning. This is the identity lesson that the French Jewish characters so compellingly embody. *Un secret* is also a powerful reflection about *adolescent* identity in the French context, one in which being Jewish is just one identity marker that a young person must negotiate. It should not come as a surprise that Grimbert's work was awarded the Prix Goncourt des lycéens in 2004: it offers a suspenseful mystery about family secrets as viewed by the son. Both text and film offer themselves up to many kinds of reading, both sophisticated and popular, and their pedagogical dimension can be witnessed in the enthusiasm of teachers to include these works in their offerings.

Has French film arrived, then, at a mainstreaming of Jewish issues? Clearly, the exploration of Jewish identity in the French national context is still very much in the public eye. Although I have concentrated on feature *fictional* films that dramatize the ethnic/national rapport through distorting/distorted mirrors of the Occupation and the Shoah, the issue has also recently appeared in non-fictional cinema: the documentary of Yves Jeuland, *Comme un juif en France* (2007), traces the knotty complexities of the situation of Jews in France from the Dreyfus affair to the

---

[16] I should mention too that the names of the dead victims are changed: Hannah is listed as Anna on the memorial wall and Simon's name was actually Michel.

[17] Even Brasillach's opprobrious utterance can be twisted enough to say he didn't want the children separated from their parents.

present through interviews, photos and archival film footage.[18] Jeuland emphasizes the multiplicity of ways one can be a Jew in France rather than closing the issue to debate. His film confirms our sense that French Jewish history has in many ways traced the history of France's struggles to define itself. Although Henry Rousso has effectively argued that the obsessive phase of the 'Vichy syndrome' has wrongly reduced Vichy to its anti-Semitic dimensions, I would contend that it is also true that sustained imaginings of French Jewish identity under the Occupation, in a French cinematic context, have been long in coming.

[18] French documentaries such as Alain Resnais' *Nuit et brouillard* (1955) and Claude Lanzmann's *Shoah* (1986) do not thematize the intersection of French and Jewish identities. *Le Chagrin et la pitié* (1969, Marcel Ophuls) does bring in this identity theme through interviews with Pierre Mendès-France, French statesman and resister of Sephardic background. Mendès-France's eloquent remarks in *Le Chagrin* on the desire to prove his patriotism (when arrested under Vichy) are profoundly moving.

Chapter 16

The liberal way of war? French representations of the allies, 1944–2008[1]

Hilary Footitt

For any state that has been liberated by another state, building a narrative of national identity which includes the liberators is problematic. As Pieter Lagrou has remarked, 'being liberated' is a passive mode, which relates uneasily to the recovery of national independence.[2] This chapter examines the ways in which the Anglo-American allies have appeared in French post-war narratives, with particular reference to historiography and memorialization. In the record of these representations there is, to borrow Henry Rousso's classic formulation, a sort of 'Syndrome des anglo-saxons'. Like the 'syndrome de Vichy', the role of the allies in the war, absent or present, has acted as a screen on which later generations in France have played out arguments about national identity. This 'syndrome' has three broad stages: first, the immediate post war until the end of Gaullism (1945 to the late 1970s); secondly, the decades of post-Gaullism (the 1980s and 1990s); and finally, the new millennium. If this 'syndrome des anglo-saxons' is neither as obsessional nor as internally divisive in France as 'le syndrome de Vichy', it is one which has now gone beyond the boundary of French national narratives, in order to discomfort and question its avowed object of study, namely the British and Americans, and the long-held Anglo-American consensus that what was done in our name in 1944 and beyond was unimpeachably good and just.

---

[1] The research for this contribution was supported by the Leverhulme Trust through the University of Reading's Liberal Way of War Programme.
[2] P. Lagrou, *The Legacy of Nazi Occupation: Patriotic Memory and National Recovery in Western Europe* (Cambridge: Cambridge University Press, 2000), p. 26.

Immediate post war until the end of Gaullism, 1945 to late 1970s

In the early years of the Fourth Republic, French historiography of the war was an officially sanctioned activity. A Commission d'Histoire de l'Occupation et de la Libération was created in 1946, succeeded in 1950 by the Comité Français de la Deuxième Guerre Mondiale. These were organized as formal government bodies, attached to the Prime Minister's Office, and had a membership of senior *fonctionnaires* from all ministries and a nation-wide network of departmental correspondents who fed material back into its subcommittees. The ambition was to constitute an *objet de mémoire* of the Resistance, to produce a complete picture of all Resistance activity – every Resistance attack all over France/all Resistance victims – and to map this in a vast card-filing system with hundreds of thousands of cards. Large standardized questionnaires were established and huge collections of written local witness statements were amassed. The focus was entirely French, with the underlying historical rationale that the country had functioned in war, not through its so-called legitimate government, but rather through its native Resistance movement. The historical monographs which came from the Comité, and its influential director, Henri Michel, in the 1960s,[3] reflected this French internal perspective, focusing on the history and political philosophies of the Resistance movements, and of Free France.

Internal debates between French historians at this period were largely centred either on the detail of particular Resistance movements, or on the polemic around the *passation des pouvoirs* at the Liberation, and in par-ticular on the role which the French Communist Party had or had not played in effecting or not effecting a revolution.[4] When, post-1968, there was a more rigorous challenge to the hegemonic resistance narrative, the allies still remained absent. In the twenty-five years from 1949 to 1975, the Comité's official journal, the *Revue d'histoire de la Deuxième Guerre mondiale*, carried only five articles which explored the position of the allies. The key official conference on the Liberation, held in October 1974, had only one paper, out of nineteen, which focused on the Anglo-American role.[5]

---

[3] H. Michel, *Les Courants de pensée de la Résistance* (Paris: Presses universitaires de France, 1962); *Histoire de la France Libre* (Paris: Presses universitaires de France, 1963); *Jean Moulin, L'Unificateur* (Paris: Hachette, 1964).

[4] See, for example, G. Madjarian, *Conflits, pouvoirs et société à la Libération* (Paris: Union générale d'Editions, 1968).

[5] Comité d'Histoire de la Deuxième Guerre Mondiale, *Actes du Colloque international sur la Libération de la France* (Paris: CNRs, 1976).

The French historiographical narrative, fixated on establishing the credibility and national importance of the Resistance, left whatever the Americans and British had been doing as something entirely separate which should rightfully be discussed by their own, largely military, historians. The cultural division between what were properly French and properly allied concerns was illustrated physically in the landscape of remembrance of Normandy where a ring of separate allied *lieux de mémoire* – twenty-one cemeteries for war dead, two allied-focused museums (Arromanches and Cherbourg) – bordered the Normandy coast, and where early D-Day memorial events were largely allied-directed veterans' experiences, essentially private ceremonies in which, judging from national and regional media coverage, French public interest was relatively low, and in which official French government representation was limited to quite junior ministers.

What the French had done in the war, and what the allies had done, were seen both historiographically and in remembrance terms as totally separate, and of primary interest only to the nations concerned. The only major crossing of this historiographical divide was by the American historian, Robert Paxton, whose book on Vichy France was translated into French in 1973.[6] However, this devastating study mainly contributed to the French internal debate on resistance and responsibility, rather than to a positioning of the allies as part of a shared historiographical discourse.

With the advent of the Fifth Republic, de Gaulle and Gaullism represented this very invisibility of the allies in the national story as in itself a vindication of France's post-war recovery. The General's monumental war memoirs, published in 1954, 1956 and 1959,[7] accorded the Anglo-Americans a relatively slight role, but crucially one which had often been hostile to French interests (the nightmare of a Roosevelt-inspired AMGOT, Allied Military Government of Occupied Territory), and which had had to be defeated by de Gaulle himself.

Beside this discourse of allied invisibility as national vindication went a Gaullist recuperation of that part of the war story, namely the Liberation and 6 June, from which it was difficult totally to exclude the Anglo-American presence. The Normandy coastline, with its ring of allied war cemeteries, gradually became the site of an alternative

---

[6]   R.O. Paxton, *La France de Vichy*, trans. C. Bertrand (Paris: Seuil, 1973).
[7]   C. de Gaulle, *Mémoires de Guerre*, Vol. 1: *l'Appel, 1940–42* (Paris: Plon, 1954); Vol. 2: *L'Unité, 1942–44* (Paris: Plon, 1956); Vol. 3: *Le Salut, 1944–46* (Paris: Plon, 1959).

memorialization exercise which sought to question both the immediate and longer-term chronology of the allied D-Day. In immediate terms, rather than 6 June 1944, the key date in this Gaullist recuperation was 14 June, the day on which de Gaulle himself had landed in France and made his first speech on French soil at Bayeux. In 1952, a vast fresco by Lamourdedieu was erected in Bayeux, showing, over twenty-one blocks of granite, the landings of 6 June 1944, next to the events of the return of de Gaulle on 14 June. In the mid-1960s, as the French relationship with the Americans and British became more problematic, the General absented himself from joint 6 June commemorations on the beaches, and successive Gaullist governments tended to send a higher level of ministerial representation to memorial events outside Normandy, to sites in Brittany for example (Plumelec and Saint-Marcel) where some 430 French parachutists had landed on 5 June.

Within a questioning of longer-term chronology, the French government represented D-Day as less related to the Second World War than to a thirty-year war fought by France since 1914. Thus the tenth anniversary of D-Day had been described as, '40e anniversaire de la Marne, 10e anniversaire de la libération, deux combats, une seule cause: la liberté de la patrie'.[8] This thirty-year theme was incidentally taken up in a film sponsored by the Anciens Combattants' Ministry, and directed by the Comité's historian director, Henri Michel. Over seven and a half hours, the film depicted a war which had started in August 1914, and had ended only with the liberation of Strasbourg and Alsace, by the French themselves, in November/December 1944.

Post-Gaullism: the decades of the 1980s and 1990s

The deofficializing of 1940–44 historiography in this later period provided French historians with broader, non-national analytical frameworks. Symbolically, the Comité, which had been attached to the Prime Minister's Office, was first made into a Centre National de la Recherche Scientifique laboratory, and then, in 1978, with Henri Michel's retirement, renamed the Institut d'Histoire du Temps Présent, with the former review of the history of the Second World War becoming a wider-ranging journal, *Guerres mondiales et conflits contemporains*. In this sense, French experience in the Second World War was positioned nominally at least

[8]   C. Barcellini, 'Deux Mémoires en parallèle', *Stratégie dans l'Histoire*, www.stratisc.org/partenaires/ihcc/ihcc_44prov_Barcelli.html (accessed 23 July 2007).

as less national, less exceptional and more as an integrated part of
an internationally shared war experience. Thus, the fortieth D-Day
anniversary conference led by the new Director of the institute, René
Bédarida, himself an *angliciste*, sought to provide a perspective on
the strategies of all the major participants in liberation – Anglo-
American, Soviet, German and Gaullist – and included papers by four
English-speakers.[9]

This same international perspective was evident in official D-Day
commemoration ceremonies in 1984 and 1994. Whereas the immediate
post-war and Gaullist period had seen French participation in these
events limited, or deliberately self-excluded in favour of alternative French
commemorations, both President Mitterrand and President Chirac
choreographed the fortieth and fiftieth anniversary programmes in order
to serve the exigencies of contemporary French international diplomacy
– such as the inclusion or otherwise in the ceremonies of the USSR or
of Germany, or the tepidity of relationships with the USA.

The opening of a new museum in Caen in 1988 continued this inter-
nationalization of the French war narrative by arguing that the museum
would aspire to give its visitors a history of twentieth-century peace and
human rights. The Gaullist thirty-year war perspective was replaced by
a much longer time frame, a 'failure of peace' journey which conducted
visitors physically from the beginning of the century to the cold war.
Anglo-American participation in the liberation of France was subsumed
in a presentation which maintained that the conflict had anyway been
an international one: symbolically thirteen memorial stones were erected
in the museum to recognize the contribution of all the nations involved.
The allies thus entered French official narratives as one of an assembly
of nations which had failed to keep the peace, but which had ultimately
won the war.

Stimulated at least partly by these developments in Caen, there was also
at this period a growing French historiographical interest in how the French
themselves had perceived the Normandy landings and Liberation. In a
sense, by internationalizing the context, it seemed to be more politically
acceptable to examine what many states caught up in war had suffered,
namely victimhood at the hands of their allies as well as their enemies.
In the early 1990s, Michel Boivin, an academic at the University of Caen,
produced two detailed studies of the French experience of allied bombing

---

[9] F. Bédarida (ed.), *Normandie 44: du Débarquement à la Libération* (Paris: Albin
Michel, 1987).

in Normandy.[10] Although both books eschewed overt moral condemnation of the allies, their abundant statistics, and the use of first-hand testimony from survivors, provided a perspective, from the French point of view, of the suffering which had been caused, a perspective which incidentally had not thus far figured much in Anglo-American accounts of the landings.

The Caen museum itself recorded interviews with Normandy survivors remembering what is termed *L'Autre Mémoire*,[11] in which participants talked candidly about the apparent failure of allied officers to appreciate the damage they were doing – one French woman for example recalled that when she asked the British commander why his forces had continued to shell Caen when it was clear that the Germans had left, his reply was: 'Mademoiselle, the life of one single English soldier is worth more than the lives of thousands of French civilians.'

New millennium: 2000 and beyond

The events of 9/11, and the subsequent coalition invasions of Iraq and Afghanistan brought a new interest in allied concepts of a 'just war', and hence of the just war waged in 1944. After being invisible or subsidiary, and then being represented as one of several international participants, the allies now found that their own actions in the course of the Liberation were subjected to minute examination, and held up against the mirror of their professed liberal values. Waging war, in the name of bringing peace and freedom to an occupied country, inevitably brings challenges for liberal states aspiring to act militarily in a manner consistent with their liberalism. Michael Howard had raised some of these complications in 1978 in his seminal, *War and the Liberal Conscience*, and the nature of liberal war-making has subsequently been taken up and examined by later scholars, most recently by Michael Dillon and Julian Reid in their 2009, *The Liberal Way of War*, and in the current Leverhulme project researching this topic.[12] After 2000, commentators turned increasingly

[10] M. Boivin, *Villes normandes sous les bombes: juin 1944* (Caen: Presses universitaires de Caen, 1994); *Les Victimes civiles de la Manche dans la bataille de Normandie: 1er avril–30 septembre 1944* (Caen: Editions du Lys, 1994).
[11] D. Maestrali, (dir.) *Caen 1994: L'Autre Mémoire*, video production (Zorilla Productions, 1994).
[12] See M. Howard, *War and the Liberal Conscience* (Oxford: Oxford University Press, 1978); M. Dillon and J. Reid, *The Liberal Way of War: Killing to Make Life Live* (London and New York: Routledge, 2009); 'The Liberal Way of War', www.reading.ac.uk/spirs/research/spirs-leverhulme.aspx (accessed April 2010).

to an examination of the allies' behaviour during the liberation of France, exploring the extent to which the British and Americans might have regarded the zone of conflict in which they were engaged as a privileged space in which the usual rules and laws of their own liberal society did not necessarily apply. Two areas which came under particular scrutiny were first, the alleged immoral behaviour of allied liberators, and secondly the influence of racial segregation on the justice which was accorded to convicted allied criminals.

The major critique under these two headings, undertaken by American scholars, was rapidly published in French. Indeed, in the case of the American criminal historian, J. Robert Lilly, his study of GI rape cases in England, France and Germany could not originally find an English-language publisher, and actually appeared for the first time with a French publisher in 2003, with the title *La Face cachée des GI's*. The book was introduced by the respected CNRS historian Fabrice Virgili, who specifically noted links between the contemporary post-2000 political situation and what had occurred in 1944–45: 'Qu'une partie de la "face cachée des GI's" soit dévoilée alors que l'armée des États-Unis est intervenue en ce début de XXIe siècle en Afghanistan puis en Irak peut soulever des questions . . . l'engagement militaire américain rendait difficile . . . une telle publication aux États-Unis.'[13] While there had been references before by French commentators to the behaviour of GIs in Europe, Lilly's work, based on painstaking research in the Judge Advocate General's records of military crimes and trials, provided strong evidence that around 17,000 women and children had been raped by American soldiers in Britain, France and Germany. As Lilly himself suggested, his study placed an enormous question mark over what most Americans continued to regard as 'the greatest generation' of fighters, who had fought a fundamentally good war in 1944.

The second Anglophone contribution to this questioning of the allies' just war came via Alice Kaplan's study of the judicial aftermath of the murder of a French civilian in Brittany in November 1944. Her book, *The Interpreter*, published in English in 2005, was rapidly translated into French and published in 2007. Kaplan's thesis was that the racial segregation of the American army in 1944 had been the reason for the disparity shown by tribunals in sentencing GIs for crimes – the black soldier involved in this particular case was hanged, the white soldier

---

[13] J.R. Lilly, *La Face cachée des GI's* (Paris: Éditions Payot et Rivages, 2003), pp. 18, 19.

acquitted, and indeed given hero status. Kaplan argued that the French interpreter in the case, Louis Guilloux (whose novel, *OK, Joe* she had already translated into English) had seen this blatant racial discrimination as undermining allied pretensions to establish a just post-war society, an aim at the heart of any liberal war-making: 'What he wanted to convey . . . was the sense he had in 1944, at the moment of the allied landing, that the future promised a great new happiness, and to combine that expectation of happiness with his retrospective knowledge that the dream of a better society had not come to pass.'[14]

Another American historian at this time, Mary Louise Roberts, in an article appearing in French in the autumn 2007 edition of *Le Mouvement social*, deconstructed the long-accepted visual representation of the wartime GI in the American press, concluding that iconic photographs of American soldiers surrounded by grateful young French women in fact amounted to a gendered and orientalist depiction of a country which had been colonized and dominated by US force. Like the famous images of Iwo Jima, she suggested, the photographs of GIs in the war were designed to conceal the imperialism of the USA beneath the manufactured patina of a just war. Once more, the link between American activity in 1944 and in 2005–06 was overtly made, with the values of a liberal way of war brought under scrutiny: 'Cette tendance particulièrement américaine à s'embourber dans les mythes impériaux autoproduits cause d'ailleurs des ravages dans le monde actuel, comme en témoigne la déclaration de George Bush à propos de l'Irak: "Nous ne sommes pas une puissance impériale . . . nous sommes une puissance libératrice".'[15]

It was not only, however, Anglophone commentators, swiftly translated into French, who re-examined allied war actions in the light of liberal democratic intentions. For the first time, French historians started to reassess the allies within their own liberal terms, using British and American archives to do so. Régine Torrent[16] examined three controversial areas of allied engagement: bombing, the Franco-American relationship on the ground and the threat of AMGOT (concluding incidentally that

[14] A. Kaplan, *The Interpreter* (Chicago and London: University of Chicago Press, 2005), p. 145.
[15] M.L. Roberts, 'La Photo du GI viril: Genre et Photojournalisme à la Libération', *Le Mouvement Social*, 219–220 (April–September 2007), 56.
[16] R. Torrent, *La France américaine: Controverses à la Libération* (Brussels: Éditions Racine, 2004).

the threat had always been a Gaullist fiction). More substantially, Olivier Wieviorka crossed the former historiographical divide in his magisterial *Histoire du débarquement en Normandie: des origines à la Libération* (published in 2007, translated into English in 2008 and reviewed in the British daily press). The originality of Wiéviorka's work in French historiographical terms was that he showed no interest in what the French were doing. Rather, he sought, from Anglophone primary sources, to distil a different allied 6 June from the glittering Anglo-American legends which, he claimed, had surrounded it: the so-called inevitability of victory, the representation of allied troops as uniformly resolute and heroic. Wiéviorka's approach was deeply sympathetic to the plight of the ordinary soldier, and the psychological toll on him, and Wiéviorka's D-Day was an event in which the human cost of war was a good deal more crucial than any final military victory. His concluding chapter, suggestively entitled: 'Farewell to Crusades?', placed his enterprise firmly within the realm of contemporary Anglo-American military activity, and of the human cost it was exacting: 'Triumphalism no longer has a place in the telling of this great epic, for the stories of the soldiers themselves tinge it with the subtle but unmistakable shades of tragedy'.[17]

Conclusions

The evolution of French representations of the allies has moved from a national narrative which excluded the allies, or made their activity a subsidiary one in a French national history, through to an international perspective in which the Anglo-Americans occupied a role similar to that of other protagonists, including the French themselves, within a chronology which was broad and continuing, and in which issues of victimhood at the hands of ostensible friends could now be discussed. The final post-2000 chapter brings a new focus on to the allies themselves and the extent to which universalist values associated with the liberal way of war were evident in their actual behaviour. What is particularly interesting is that these narratives of cross-border relationships are themselves becoming a site of significant cultural exchange: Anglophone scholars are translated into French, French historians are translated into English; historians are crossing the former divide when national historians concentrated solely on the role of their own military and

---

[17] O. Wieviorka, *Normandy: the Landings to the Liberation of Paris*, trans. M.B. DeBevoise (Cambridge and London: Belknap Press, 2008), p. 361.

resistance. In this framework of transnational history, the nationality of the commentator may explain the departure point of the research (Paxton famously argued that he was originally motivated to look at Vichy by his disgust at US national conformism during the war in Vietnam), but the national point of departure of the writer is no necessary guide to the conclusions that will be advanced, nor to the destabilizing effects that these may have on all parties concerned, and on the consensus interpretations which have formerly been reached.

Chapter 17

'Avoir vingt ans dans cette effroyable tourmente': Second World War diaries in the light of Hélène Berr's *Journal*

Danièle Sabbah

The dates it covers (April 1942 to February 1944), the way it suddenly breaks off when the Berr family is arrested, the fate of the author (a French Jewish girl born in Paris in 1921; Hélène Berr was deported to Auschwitz in March 1944 and died in Bergen-Belsen in April 1945) and her personal qualities – she was an educated, bright young woman, a brilliant student and music-lover – mean that Hélène Berr's journal is especially representative of the period of the war and Occupation.[1] Quite apart from her courage, honesty and freedom of tone, the diarist's reflections lead her to comment on events and to refuse to fall back on the clichéd racist truisms of the day. Not the least of her virtues is that she displays a great talent for happiness, and an acute sensitivity to the harmony of the world, to the light and subtle poetry of colours and beings. The *Journal* (especially at the beginning) is a wonderful celebration of Paris, of the Latin Quarter, of walks along the rue Soufflot, the boulevard St Michel, in the Luxembourg Gardens or along the banks of the Seine. These were all so many strengths that allowed her to resist the presence of the occupying forces and to leave us some precious 'situated' notes on the period.[2]

---

[1] Hélène Berr, *Journal, 1942–1944* (Paris: Tallandier, 2008). Page references are given in brackets in the body of the text.

[2] Cf. Max Jacob, 'Elle [l'œuvre d'art] doit être située', *Les Cornet à dés* (Paris: Gallimard, 1967), p. 22.

Thanks to the tension that arises between, on the one hand, the descriptions of the beauty of the world, the desire to be happy, the affectionate camaraderie and, on the other, the Occupation, collaboration and the increasingly frightening persecutions, the *Journal* is more than a historical account. It bears witness to the 'tissu conjonctif'[3] of the atmosphere of the period, with its combination of a love for life and a failure to recognize the reality of the situation, the inversion of morality and the blind terror as the vice tightened on the population (and not just the Jewish population). This is more than a document. It is above all the diary of an intellectual and moral consciousness. It records the process that leads a happy young girl trying to ignore the ugliness of the enemy to realize before most people did so that an unprecedented massacre is taking place, and how, in the midst of a disaster that will destroy her too, she chooses to think rather than to weep.

From diary to reportage

The diary is an old genre: the practice of making a daily note or record of what we have said, done and spent is probably as old as writing itself. Defined in the narrowest sense of 'a first-person journal', it became much more popular in the eighteenth century, when women appropriated this scriptural space (together with the epistolary domain, it was almost the only space in which they were 'authorized' to write because it had been abandoned by men) and made it a place for subjective outpourings that paved the way for the immensely popular nineteenth-century literature of sense and sensibility. The genre has never died out, and still survives in more contemporary forms (Philippe Lejeune has studied the ways in which it has been transformed by the new means of communication).[4]

A special category has to be reserved for diaries written in times of war, and especially the Second World War, as their tragic context and significance for civilians mean that they are, almost despite themselves, invaded by the outside world. This has its effects on the genre itself: the subject is torn between his or her naturally selfish instincts, and history, or at least the way that history affects the subject, even in minor ways.

---

[3] 'C'est la description d'un tissu conjonctif, en quelque sorte, dans laquelle toute une génération peut se reconnaître', Georges Perec, *Je suis né* (Paris: Seuil, 1990), p. 92.

[4] Philippe Lejeune, *Cher écran. Journal personnel, ordinateur, internet* (Paris: Seuil, 2000).

Some choose to ignore it and deliberately turn a blind eye, while others record it. As David Boal has demonstrated, it is often a political choice that makes the difference.[5] Ernst Jünger, Marcel Jouhandeau, Pierre Drieu la Rochelle and Paul Léautaud write from a certain political perspective, but they also wrote with a view to publication (they were either writers or worked in the world of publishing). This gives their 'diaries' an unusual slant; when compared with Stendhal's *Souvenirs*, they are reduced to being what Léautaud calls a 'comptabilité de faits'[6] (and even so, we have to ask '*which* facts'? Are they historical facts, as Boal believes, citing the Vél d'Hiv round-up as an example, or are they strictly personal facts, as a stylistic comparison suggests?). Be that as it may, these diaries seem to be very different from Hélène Berr's *Journal*. It seems more appropriate to compare it with Anne Frank's diary: both diarists were young women who wrote truly private diaries that were not initially meant for publication or even to be read by anyone else. They share the same 'point of view' of the diarist. Both are Jewish, and both are witnesses to and victims of history. One writes in hiding with her family in Amsterdam while the other writes in the Paris she refuses to leave, even though the noose is tightening. Both were arrested and deported in accordance with a scenario that was as predictable as it was unavoidable. What is more surprising still, both reorientate their diaries at a given moment as they react to external events: their diaries cease to be records of private emotions and become historical documents written for future generations.

Philippe Lejeune has studied the genesis of Anne Frank's *Diary*.[7] After hearing a radio broadcast from the Dutch government in exile asking the population to produce eye-witness accounts of the Occupation, she reworked her diary in such a way as to make it fit for publication after the Liberation. When she was arrested in August 1944, she had managed to rewrite her diary up to the month of March; the rewriting was motivated mainly by a desire to 'socialize' her text, both by providing the reader with more information and by censoring passages that were too private (because they dealt with her sexuality, her views about her parents or her idyll with Peter). Hélène Berr's *Journal* underwent the

---

[5] David Boal, *Journaux intimes sous l'Occupation* (Paris: Armand Colin, 1993).

[6] Paul Léautaud, *Journal littéraire*, t. III, 9.1.1942 (Paris: Mercure de France, 1986), p. 494. Surprisingly, Boal describes what Léautaud calls a 'journal littéraire' as a *journal intime*.

[7] Philippe Lejeune, 'Comment Anne Frank a réécrit le Journal d'Anne Frank', in *Les Brouillons de soi* (Paris: Seuil, 1998), pp. 331–365.

same transformation: the violence of a pitiless history and a sequence of events that was incredible in the true sense of the word turn a girl's private diary into a form of reportage that dates, quantifies and records raw materials for future historians.

And yet both texts remain diaries, or in other words records of everyday life. Like seismographs, they record how private and collective events impacted upon a subjectivity. Hélène Berr, for instance, did not keep a diary on a regular basis: it breaks off from time to time, and devotes different amounts of space to the various days, periods and years that it covers. Just as the style and rhythm become more tense and the tone becomes more serious, her reasons for writing her diary change, and so does the content of her annotations. When her diary begins in 1942, she describes her life as a student (she is reading English literature at the Sorbonne) and the realization that she is falling in love (she has met Jean Morawiecki, a 'garçon aux yeux gris'), but events then speed up when her father is arrested and the police raids become more frequent. Her concern is now to preserve the memory of what is happening on a day-to-day basis. She reacts to the Vél d'Hiv round-ups of 16 and 17 July 1942 by writing 'Je note les faits, hâtivement, pour ne pas les oublier, parce qu'il ne *faut pas* oublier' (p. 106).[8]

As the repression becomes more severe in 1943, she writes because she is afraid that she will no longer be there to record what is happening. Writing becomes a form of personal resistance: 'chacun dans sa petite sphère peut faire quelque chose. Et s'il le peut, il le doit' (p. 171). She writes comments, tries to understand and to remain lucid and impartial, and strives to preserve something human in the midst of all the confusion. As she puts it, 'J'ai un devoir à accomplir en écrivant, car il faut que les autres sachent' (p. 169). She gathers this information because she realizes that, aside from the victims, other people do not know what is happening: no one suspects that a deliberate massacre is being perpetrated not only in France but all over continental Europe. And she realizes quite clearly that this ignorance is wilful: 'La marque atroce de ce régime, c'est son hypocrisie. Ils ne connaissent pas les horribles détails de ces persécutions' (p. 227). When a woman tries to justify the round-ups on the grounds that 'Mais on n'ennuie pas les Français [les juifs français], et puis on ne prend que ceux qui ont fait quelque chose', Hélène Berr comments: 'Le type de la rencontre qui fait tant souffrir. Et pourtant, je ne lui en veux pas, elle ne savait pas' (p. 199), and concludes with some

---

[8] Italics in the original.

bitterness, when the conservative Madame Agache is 'affolée' to discover that children are being deported too: 'Personne ne sait rien des gens qui souffrent' (p. 219).

When people do know, they know only in anecdotal fashion because, having ties of one kind or another with individual victims, they are upset about that person, but only about that person, as they have no idea that so many other people are suffering the same fate, and no understanding of the moral bankruptcy this represents. Their compassion is a narrowly defined pity for those they know, not any moral awareness of a disaster affecting an entire population, or a political understanding of the attempt to destroy a population on a continental scale.

Some are blind to what is going on. Others have become so morally perverse that they describe their blind obedience to the administration that is organizing the 'legal' destruction of a whole people as their 'duty':

> Les gendarmes qui ont obéi à des ordres leur enjoignant d'aller arrêter un bébé de deux ans, pour l'interner, mais c'est la preuve la plus navrante de l'état d'abrutissement, de la perte totale de conscience morale où nous sommes tombés. C'est cela qui est désespérant. N'est-ce pas désespérant de s'apercevoir que moi, avec ma réaction de révolte, je suis une exception, alors que ce devrait être ceux qui *peuvent* faire ces choses qui soient des personnes anormales'. (p. 217; italics in the original)

It is because basic moral principles are being flouted that Hélène Berr records the facts in the hope that, one day, humanity will come to its senses and will learn 'the evil tidings of what man's presumption [has] made of man'.[9]

The third part of the *Journal* was written in 1944, and there is no hope left. Hélène Berr was under direct threat, and her 'journées' are therefore a frantic record of the news she receives, and every piece of news is worse than the last. The sense of urgency is such, and there is so much catastrophic and unthinkable news, that she simply lists facts: 'Entre autres choses, j'ai appris les suivantes' (p. 259) . . . 'une simple collection de faits, entre des milliers' (p. 206; the reference is to the arrest of old people and children in the Hospice in Bordeaux) . . . 'il faut que je note quelques faits, de ceux qu'il ne faudra jamais oublier' (p. 165). Given that the journalists and columnists have abdicated their responsibilities, she accumulates raw material for historians: 'N'est-ce pas,

---

[9] Primo Levi, *If This is a Man/The Truce*, trans. Stuart Woolf (London: Abacus, 1987), p. 61.

tout cela a l'air d'un reportage? . . . Mais dans quel journal aujourd'hui lisons-nous des reportages sur ces choses-là? "Je reviens de Drancy". Qui en parlera?' (p. 278). She actually becomes an investigative journalist and asks an eye-witness about how life was organized in Drancy, and about the departures for the East (p. 274ff.). Hence the lucid comment: 'S'ils déportent pour faire travailler, à quoi servent les petits? . . . Ils ont un but, exterminer' (p. 276). Confirmation comes from a boy who unexpectedly witnessed the mass murder of a group of Polish Jews – men, women and children – who were thrown into a lake (p. 231).

The tone of the *Journal* changes very suddenly. Historical reality impinges upon the diarist, along with the unthinkable horrors she sees day by day (and not least the orphans she looks after at the UGIF), and the moral and intellectual bankruptcy of everyone around her. Her private *Journal* becomes a form of reportage: she is recording the facts for an implied reader who, after the great disaster, will try to understand.

Hélène Berr's method: thinking, not weeping

Is Hélène Berr a diarist, a journalist, a reporter or a journalist-philosopher? Not content with providing historians with raw materials, she tries to question the facts, and uses her acute awareness of the position of the individual to intellectualize the issue. Her 'method' might be characterized as calm reflection rather than pathos or hatred. Even when she speaks in the name of the children she is caring for – and some of them have lost even their names – she avoids sentimentality and respects their dignity: 'Combien y en a-t-il de ces petits enfants qui appellent leur mère et qui n'ont même pas de Neuilly [siège de l'UGIF]?' (p. 262).

She takes one example and uses it as the basis for generalization, and thus transcends the anecdotal nature of individual cases. To that extent, her approach is similar to that of Primo Levi who, having established the primacy of reason, can write an eye-witness account and draw upon his literary culture even though he is in a camp that is designed to crush all human points of reference (hence the '*Muselmänner*', who have lost even their survival instinct). In the midst of chaos, Primo Levi strives to give back their dignity to individuals in an attempt to resist the anonymity of mass murder, if only by naming the '*Häftlinge*' who have been tattooed with a number. In similar fashion, Hélène Berr's *Journal* represents an attempt to preserve individual values from mass destruction, to stimulate a moral understanding in the midst of a human disaster.

It is impossible to develop all the themes that are touched upon. For the record, we can note Berr's detachment from the trivial realities of the war (she says nothing about the German prisons, about weapons or about the hardships everyone is suffering), her thoughts about French identity, about her Jewish (non-) identity, her refusal to surrender to hatred, so as to preserve 'l'âme et la mémoire' (p. 197), her clear-sightedness (about whether or not to wear the yellow star, about whether to flee or stay in Paris, about Zionism, the role of the UGIF, and so on). One question occurs again and again throughout her journal, and it is the basic enigma of the period: what is the role of the ordinary people who, either actively or passively, collude with this evil?

The banality of evil?

Hélène Berr constantly comes back to the question of evil and, given that she rejects communitarianism,[10] she always associates the idea of crimes against Jews with the notion of 'crimes against humanity', which was actually invented at the Nuremberg trials: 'Concevez-vous que des hommes mauvais aient la faculté de faire périr une multitude d'hommes innocents par millions, comme cela c'est fait pour les juifs par exemple, autre part pour d'autres multitudes humaines' (p. 272). She then complicates the idea by noting that some people have taken in children: 'Dire qu'il y a une moitié de l'humanité qui *fabrique* du mal et un tout petit élément qui essaye de réparer' (p. 264, italics in original).

Particular examples become the starting point for moral meditations. She contrasts, for instance, the spirit and magnanimity of a pianist who has been arrested with 'la brutalité germanique': 'un garçon si artiste, capable de procurer au monde des joies si pures par son art, cet art qui ne connaît pas les méchancetés humaines, et en face la brutalité, la matière qui ignore l'esprit' (p. 271). She makes similar use of the case of Mme Samuel. She was deported in a cattle truck disguised as a hospital coach while both pregnant and ill, and illustrates 'la monstrueuse inanité de la politique nazie' (p. 199). The arrest of a two-and-a-half-year-old girl left in care after her parents were deported then triggers a denunciation of 'morality' and, more generally, civilization:

[10] Cf. her comments on the communitarianism and Zionism that she rejects: 'Pour moi, pareille distinction n'existe pas; je ne me sens pas différente des autres hommes, jamais je n'arriverai à me considérer come faisant partie d'un groupe humain séparé, peut-être est-ce pour cela que je souffre tellement, parce que je ne comprends pas' (p. 254).

C'est toujours la même histoire de l'inspecteur de police qui a répondu à Mme Cohen, lorsque, dans la nuit du 10 février, il est venu arrêter treize enfants à l'orphelinat, dont l'aîné avait 13 ans et le plus jeune 5 (des enfants dont les parents étaient déportés, mais il 'en' fallait pour compléter le convoi de mille du lendemain): 'Que voulez-vous, madame, je fais mon devoir!' Qu'on soit arrivé à concevoir le devoir comme une chose indépendante de la conscience, indépendante de la justice, de la bonté, de la charité, c'est là la preuve de l'inanité de notre prétendue civilisation. (p. 216)

Her comments on the sources of this evil have a lot in common with Hannah Arendt's analysis of the Eichmann case, and both women adopt the stance of the 'journalist-philosopher'.[11] Both contend that the subject is incapable of understanding his actions, or of thinking through their real meaning and consequences. Hence the blind obedience to orders: 'parce que ces gens ne savent pas ou plutôt, qu'ils ne *pensent* plus; ils sont pour l'acte immédiat qu'on leur commande . . . ils ignorent le principe de causalité', and, on the same page, 'Et puis ils ne pensent pas, j'en reviens toujours à cela, je crois que c'est la base du mal; et la force sur laquelle s'appuie ce régime. Annihiler la pensée personnelle, la réaction de la conscience individuelle, tel est le premier pas du nazisme' (p. 277, italics in the original).

Bureaucratic murder?

Her clear-sightedness leads her to note that there is a disconnection between the person who orders the killings and the person who carries them out: 'La chose terrible, c'est que dans tout cela, on voit très peu de gens sur le fait. Car le système est si bien organisé que les hommes responsables paraissent peu' (p. 217). The expression 'bureaucratic murder' is used to describe massacres that are ordered at the administrative level and organized 'according to regulations'. All that remains is for the minions to do what has to be done. The executioner does not see his victims and can therefore go on killing without any scruples. The victims do not know their executioner, and remain trapped between a nameless terror and a denial that they are in any danger.

There is one aspect of these crimes of which Hélène Berr has no real knowledge, but she does sense its absurdity. The evidence that mass

[11] Hanna Arendt, *Eichmann in Jerusalem: A Report on the Banality of Evil* (Harmondsworth: Penguin, 1994).

murder was taking place was long concealed by the incomprehensible and illogical fact that the victims were arrested all over Europe and taken (by train) to be annihilated somewhere in Upper Silesia.

The witness and her reception

Hélène Berr also has some important things to say about eye-witness accounts and their reception. As we have seen, she realized that there was no accurate information about the persecutions in circulation and, rather like a journalist, she therefore used her diary as a form of record and investigation. Even so, her sensitivity to the individual and to the singularity of every life meant that she was well aware that this collective history would distort the meaning of individual suffering: 'le seul reportage véridique, et digne d'être écrit, serait celui qui réunirait les récits complets de chaque individu déporté' (p. 278). Her sensitive approach to reality raises the basic question of how this pain can be represented. This is a contemporary theoretical issue if ever there was one. When it comes to the Holocaust, opinions are divided, with some arguing the case for eye-witness accounts while others argue for representation in, for instance, fictional form.[12] That Hélène Berr should raise this question is scarcely surprising. The combination of a moral conscience and a literary sensitivity means that she is interested in the singularity of individual stories but that she is also concerned about the 'receiver' who knows nothing about either the events she is describing or the suffering they caused: 'Ce qu'il y a eu, en dessous, de vie palpitante, de larmes, de sang, d'anxiété' (p. 181).

Besides, at the point when she is condemned to loneliness and concentrates on her pain, she enters into a dialogue with the literary works that she loves and uses them to sustain an ethical exchange for a time when all ethics have collapsed. Like a message in a bottle, these poetic texts speak to the wounded imagination of a girl who, in these times of distress, is trying to cling to a human presence, to sensitive words and to a book that can offer hospitality.

---

[12] Paul Ricoeur, for instance, contrasts the historical approach with the fictional approach; see *Temps et récit 3. Le Temps raconté* (Paris: Seuil, 1985), pp. 339 ff. One also thinks of the debate between Didi-Huberman, who has exhibited photographs of the gas chambers, and Claude Lanzmann, who completely rejects such 'realism'. See Georges Didi-Huberman, *Images malgré tout* (Paris: Minuit, 2003).

Hélène Berr was cruelly deprived of her right to speak, and it is our duty to give her the right to do so: 'beaucoup de gens se rendront compte de ce que cela aura été d'avoir vingt ans dans cette effroyable tourmente, l'âge où l'on est prêt à accueillir la beauté de la vie, où l'on est prêt à donner sa confiance aux hommes' (p. 200). Her *Journal* deals with war, suffering, deportation and death but it is also about the waste of a youth that was stolen from her. Hélène Berr obviously did not know that the 'garçon aux yeux gris' would not be her only reader. She met him 'au seuil du pire', and yet her book seems to be addressed to us and to speak to us. She addresses us because, day by day, her courage, her refusal to submit and her reflections speak directly to the readers and raise moral questions that are still of contemporary relevance. She speaks to us because she is one of the minority that refuses to be crushed. Although she was one of many victims, she continues to demand righteousness, and to require others to be righteous and to respect human beings. In the midst of the disaster, she stands tall and celebrates the beauty of the sky because she refuses to give in to death, to ideologies, political conformisms and sectarianism (even of the Jewish variety) and because she chooses to walk down the beautiful streets of Paris 'en territoire enchanté' (p. 29). Her Paris is a city of inner freedom, a place for an intelligent heart that the horrors of history could not destroy.

Chapter 18

Maurice Blanchot's *Aminadab*: a novel about collective memory under Vichy

David Uhrig

Given what he saw as the spinelessness of the Third Republic, Maurice Blanchot concluded that France required an authoritarian political solution; in 1933, like the other members of the 'jeunesse de droite', whose contradictory tendencies he had been trying to unite,[1] he thought that his country's political destiny was inescapable: 'périr ou . . . rencontrer quelque volonté de la sauver par une révolution'.[2] In 1937, he once more argued, for the same reasons, that France should have supported Franco in Spain in order to halt Hitler's Germany.[3] At the beginning of July 1940, Blanchot was encouraging parliamentarians to grant Maréchal Pétain full powers.[4]

The logic of this authoritarian line led Blanchot to take over as editorial director for the three issues of *Aux Écoutes* that were published

---

[1] In 1931–32, Blanchot tried, among other things, to bring about a rapprochement between Jean-Pierre Maxence's *Cahiers* and Jean de Fabrègues's *Réaction*. On 17 July 1931, he wrote to the latter: 'Les idées qui y sont exprimées me sont chères, comme à vous, et surtout ce mouvement franc sans faux détours, où l'on reconnaît d'abord le souci de l'essentiel.' On 7 January 1932, he wrote to him again: 'Je serais très heureux de savoir où en sont les *Cahiers-Réaction* et ce que je pourrais faire pour vous aider. Je forme pour eux les vœux les plus vifs.' N. Kessler, *Histoire politique de la Jeune Droite (1929–1942)* (Paris: L'Harmattan, 2001), p. 193.

[2] 'L'Histoire mélancolique de M. Daladier', *Le Rempart*, 73: 3 (July 1933), 3.

[3] 'Pour combattre L'Allemagne, il faut soutenir Franco', *L'Insurgé*, 26 July 1937, p. 4.

[4] 'Tout ce qu'on peut désirer dans une situation comme celle où nous nous trouvons, c'est la direction d'un chef énergique et respecté qui, avec des collaborateurs bien choisis, puisse faire face immédiatement et par une action décisive à toutes les difficultés. Il n'y a pas d'organisation plus simple.' M. Blanchot, 'Les Nécessités du gouvernement', *Journal des débats* (10 July 1940), 1.

in July 1940 while its founder Paul Lévy was seeking refuge in North Africa.[5] The three issues were entitled, respectively, 'De la défaite à la reconstruction . . .',[6] 'La Révolution nationale'[7] and 'D'abord rétablir l'ordre'.[8] Blanchot obviously hoped that a 'Révolution nationale' led by Maréchal Pétain would preserve something of his idea of what France was. He had begun to outline his idea of France as early as 1933 in *Le Rempart* – also edited by Lévy – which was one of the first papers for which he wrote. Even at that stage, he was insisting that there could be no question of any compromise with the things he was criticizing Germany for, namely 'les puissances instinctives, la frénésie des passions que la révolution a fait naître'.[9]

While 'les persécutions barbares contre les juifs . . . n'ont jamais eu de but politique determine',[10] the 'Révolution nationale' advocated by Blanchot would, he believed, at least preserve France from Nazism's anti-Semitic ideology; the work of Charles Maurras may well have helped to justify the *lois Alibert* by making a distinction between 'l'antisémitisme de peau and l'antisémitisme d'Etat',[11] but Blanchot was not prepared to allow an anti-Semitism *à la française* to pursue the policy of ethnic cleansing that had already been implemented in Germany, even if it did claim to be part of the counter-revolutionary tradition and took the form of 'un antisémitisme raisonnable'.

In January 1942, Blanchot sent Jean Paulhan a manuscript. In order to ensure that it was published in the NRF, Paulan had to sound out Drieu La Rochelle: 'Blanchot vient d'achever un second *Thomas*. A votre place, je lui demanderais un chapitre pour la *NRF*. Ce qu'il écrit est presque insoutenable en 400 pp et parfaitement beau en 10 pages. C'est le type d'écrivain qui s'impose pour la revue (il me semble)'.[12] This was clever thinking on Paulhan's part: he had found himself very much on his own when the *NRF* published Blanchot's first novel in September

---

[5] 'Je m'étais rendu en Afrique du Nord, le 18 juin 1940, dans l'espoir d'y trouver le gouvernement de la Résistance.' P. Levy, *Journal d'un exilé* (Paris: Grasset, 1949), 16.

[6] *Aux Ecoutes*, 1551 (15 June–13 July 1940).

[7] *Aux Ecoutes*, 1552 (20 July 1940).

[8] *Aux Ecoutes*, 1153 (27 July 1940).

[9] 'Des Violences antisémites à l'apothéose du travail', *Le Rempart*, 10 (1 May 1933), 3.

[10] 'Des Violences antisémites', 3.

[11] Charles Maurras, *La Seule France, chronique des jours d'épreuve* (Lyon: Lardanchet, 1941), p. 194.

[12] Jean Paulhan, *Choix de lettres 2, 1937–1945. Traité des jours sombres* (Paris: Gallimard, 1992), p. 263.

1941,[13] especially as *Je suis partout* had made a point of attacking a book that was 'aussi démodé que l'art juif dont il se réclame'.[14]

While Paulhan was still grateful (and indebted) to Blanchot for the articles he had published on *Les Fleurs de Tarbes*[15] in the *Journal des débats*,[16] he could easily have foreseen that Drieu La Rochelle would reject a novel whose Hebrew title – to say nothing of its content – would inevitably annoy a Vichy government that was eager to reach an accommodation with Nazi anti-Semitism. The possibility of publishing *Aminadab*[17] inspired Paulhan to begin plotting to regain editorial control of the *NRF* despite the embarrassing presence of Drieu la Rochelle who was, in the eyes of the occupying power, the only valid guarantor of its loyalty, and therefore the key to its survival.

Paulhan – who, for his part, stated that he would only 'rentrer à la NRF . . . quand les juifs y rentreront'[18] – was trying to find Blanchot a position that would allow their respective literary perspectives to have some influence: 'J'ai conseillé Blanchot, que l'on a pris. S'il me demande conseil à son tour de temps en temps, je ne puis mal agir en lui répondant, n'est-ce pas?' Paulhan's subtle outmanoeuvring of Drieu allowed Blanchot to play a central role at the *NRF* for a few weeks, and to publish one of the most heterodox novels to appear during the Occupation. The novel, which he may have begun before the debacle of 1940, and which was in any case greatly influenced by the political upheavals that occurred in France during this period, caricatures an organization of society whose workings have been mechanized to an excessive degree.

Michel Foucault has already underlined this essential aspect of the novel:[19] *Aminadab* describes a society in which individuals blindly obey a dogmatic logic that condemns them to reproducing simplistic identity

[13] On 19 November 1941, Jean Paulhan wrote to Monique de Saint-Hellier: 'Je passerai . . . vous remettre Blanchot (que tout le monde trouve décidément idiot. Je suis bien inquiet) mais vous êtes ma dernière (ou première) confiance.' Jean Paulhan, *Correspondance à Monique de Saint-Hellier, 1941–1955* (Paris: Gallimard, 1995), p. 47.

[14] *Je suis partout*, 534 (18 October 1941), 8. The article was signed 'R'. C. Bident (*Je suis partout*, p. 200) suggests that 'R' was [Lucien] Rebatet.

[15] Jean Paulhan, *Les Fleurs de Tarbes, ou La Terreur dans les lettres* (Paris: Gallimard, 1941).

[16] Maurice Blanchot, 'La Terreur dans les lettres', *Journal des débats* (21 October 1941), 3; 'Comment la littérature est-elle possible?', *Journal des débats* (25 November 1941); 'Comment la littérature est-elle possible?', *Journal des débats* (2 December 1941), 3.

[17] Paris: Gallimard, 1941. All in text references within this chapter refer to this title.

[18] Paulhan, *Correspondance*, p. 67.

[19] Michel Foucault, *La Pensée du dehors* (Paris: Fata Morgana, 1966).

schemata and encourages them to behave in a schizophrenic manner. But by relating *Aminadab* to the novels Blanchot published *after* the war, Foucault makes the novel part of a very general critique of what might be called contemporary societies' drift into a form of legalism.

To say that *Aminadab* describes the workings of power in contemporary politics may well be pertinent, but it obscures the specific context which, as we have seen, determined how the novel was written. There is therefore a danger that the unusual narrative construction of *Aminadab* might go completely unnoticed, when it seems to me that it reveals the maturation of Blanchot's views about society.

That is why I will begin by demonstrating that the path followed by anyone who reads *Aminadab* explores a space of memory where different individual and collective temporalities intersect. And without going into detail, we shall see that the main characters in the novel re-enact the roles that they play as individuals within society. This makes it possible to bring out the novel's narrative project more clearly: because the different individual discourses are interrelated synchronically, the collective schemata to which the characters think they belong are superimposed and promote an understanding of what the collective memory of the society in which they move should be.

It then becomes possible to understand the relevance of the historical context to the novel's message: the onomastic system around which it is organized makes frequent reference to Christianity, rather as though its purpose was to attack a society which, while it makes much of its Christian points of reference – if not its Christian aspirations – in fact excludes in authoritarian fashion elements that cannot, in its view, be assimilated. It is therefore not difficult to explore the various issues that made Blanchot wish to distance himself from the Vichy regime from July 1940 onwards.

The novel as memorial structure

From individual space to collective space

If we look at the overall construction of *Aminadab*, we find two tendencies. One is dominated by the protagonist Thomas's exclusive desire to reach the upper storeys of the house (pp. 166–167), which constantly propels him towards the future (p. 174); the other is a regressive movement that begins when Thomas meets Jérôme and then 'le vieil employé'. The former shows him the importance of the present (p. 83) to any would-be rational perspective, while the latter reveals to him the importance of the past (p. 137) in a memorial perspective.

If we restricted the discussion to Thomas's first encounter with Jérôme, *Aminadab* might look like a sort of apologia for totalitarianism, and there would be something disturbing about Jérôme's discourse, as it fully justifies the authoritarian workings of the house Thomas has entered (pp. 84–88) and, more importantly, rules out something that is essential to any organization of society: the possibility of challenging the way it works (pp. 89–90). Jérôme also attempts to get Thomas to take part in the judgement *and* sentencing of two men (pp. 111–131).

Fortunately, Thomas listens to the innocent men on whom he is supposed to be passing judgement and learns in extremis what they are really being accused of and what Jérôme fears above all else (p. 120). The two men are the embodiment of the precondition for any memory (pp. 137–144): they look to the past, and the only thing they can be criticized for is the failing identified by the sociologist Maurice Halbwachs in his *Les Cadres sociaux de la mémoire* (1925): 'le culte du passé, loin d'attacher les cœurs des hommes à la société, les en détache: il n'est rien de plus contraire à l'intérêt de la société.'[20]

Thomas, Jérôme and 'le vieil employé' represent three intersecting temporalities, and the reader realizes that the novel shows that 'la maison' describes a lack of social space: Thomas's obsession with the *upper* floors leads him to desire a *future* that blinds him to the reality of the present. And it is precisely because he denies its reality that Thomas finally colludes in the perverse workings of the house (pp. 150–151): he ends up thrashing the two men even though he refuses to pass judgement on them.

A sociological critique of collective memory

While the demonstration is to some extent encrypted, the allegorical nature of the figures of Thomas, Jérôme and 'le vieil employé' make what Blanchot is saying in *Aminadab* very clear: Thomas, who is *the* emblematic representative of Thomism, has come up against the urgency of the present imperatives of a Catholic Church personified by Jérôme (reputedly the author of the Vulgate, among other things),[21] who is *the* emblematic representative of the ecclesiastical institutionalization of the Church.

---

[20] Paris: Albin Michel, 1994, p. 11.

[21] It is impossible to discuss this onomastic interpretation in any detail here, still less to recall the importance of Neo-Thomism in the 1930s. It should, however, be noted that 'Dom', which is the name of Thomas's double, provides a further clue: it is well known that the Dominicans claim to be staunch Thomists.

When he was writing for *Le Rempart*, Blanchot criticized German Catholics for their 'abdication of responsibility' in the face of Hitlerism. *Aminadab* introduces a new note: because the problematic relationship between Catholicism and the totalitarian state is displaced into a literary framework, the contradictory temporalities of political and religious history in the West are juxtaposed in a contradictory and critical way. *Aminadab* therefore reveals an influence that probably goes back to 1927, when Blanchot was still a student in Strasbourg, where he had Maurice Halbwachs as one of his teachers.[22] In *Les Cadres sociaux de la mémoire*, the pioneering sociologist also wrote: 'tandis qu'à la vie terrestre le Chrétien en préfère une autre qui, pour lui, est au moins aussi réelle que celle-là et qu'il place dans l'avenir, homme sait bien que le passé n'existe plus, et il est bien obligé de s'adapter au seul monde réel, qui est celui où il vit maintenant' (p. 111).

Halbwachs then asks: 'Comment ne pas voir que si l'homme était, dans la société, comme un ressort toujours tendu . . . il pourrait bien s'incliner devant les lois sociales, mais il les subirait comme une dure et continue nécessité, et . . . aucun élan généreux et spontané ne le porterait vers elle? Il n'est donc pas mauvais que, lorsqu'il se repose et se retourne, à la manière d'un voyageur, pour reconnaître le chemin qu'il a parcouru, il y découvre tout ce que la fatigue, l'effort, la poussière soulevée, et le souci d'arriver à temps et au but, l'empêchait de contempler' (p. 111).

A challenge to Vichy's ideological framework

At a deeper level, it is the way Halbwachs conceives the role and workings of the collective memory that reveals what Blanchot's novel owes to him. Halbwachs writes: 'En un sens, la mémoire contemplative ou la mémoire-rêveries nous aide à sortir de la société: c'est un des rares moments où nous réussissons à nous isoler complètement . . . Toutefois, si nous nous dérobons ainsi à la société des hommes d'aujourd'hui, c'est pour nous retrouver au milieu d'autres êtres et dans un autre milieu humain, puisque notre passé est peuplé des figures de ceux que nous avons connus. En ce sens, on n'échappe à une société qu'à condition de lui en opposer une autre' (p. 109).

In similar fashion, the space of memory into which *Aminadab* introduces the readers forces him to extricate himself from present-day

[22] M.-A. Lescourret, *Emmanuel Levinas* (Paris: Flammarion, 1994), p. 57.

society in such a way that he has to contrast it with another society, with
a society that no longer exists even though memory preserves traces
of it. Now, within this house, it is figures representing Judaism who
are entrusted with the task of challenging the dominant representation
(a Catholicism that is being exploited for political purposes). We can
therefore understand why Jérôme prefers to keep 'Joseph' out of the way
when he entrusts the 'task' of the judge (and executioner) to Thomas:

> 'Quel est ce travail?' dit Thomas. Le jeune homme regarda Joseph qui
> n'avait cessé de l'écouter avec autant d'attention que s'il l'eût entendu pour
> la première fois parler de ces événements. Thomas se demanda si l'entretien
> n'était pas destiné à Joseph. Lequel après tout était plus capable que lui
> d'en comprendre le vrai sens. 'J'hésite à répondre à votre question,' dit le
> jeune homme. 'Mon ami est si délicat et le sujet est si grave qu'il pourrait
> ne pas supporter mes paroles.' (p. 111)

Thomas is charged by Jérôme with the 'task' of cleaning the building.
This will supposedly give the building he is visiting a structural unity it
has never actually had. When he reaches the top of the building, Thomas
looks in vain for a cornerstone: 'C'était à croire que les arceaux, en
arrivant au sommet, s'étaient rompus et que ce que l'on prenait pour la
clé de l'édifice n'était qu'une grande ouverture par laquelle pénétrait la
lumière du jour' (p. 186).

Thomas's 'task' consists, then, in concealing the truth about the social
edifice he has undertaken to explore so thoroughly and, above all, to
acknowledge, despite the irresistible dynamics of his upward movement,
the need for a 'religion statique' which, as Henri Bergson had emphasized
ten years earlier, 'attache l'homme à la vie, et par consequent l'individu
à la société, en lui racontant des histoires comparables à celles dont on
berce les enfants.'[23]

Blanchot's novel therefore centres upon the fact that faith is irreducible to religion. As Michael Holland rightly notes, the name 'Aminadab'
alludes to the mystical experience of St John of the Cross.[24] God does
not appear. God is not a historical figure. God is not made incarnate in
any form. There is no unifying vision of God.

---

[23] Henri Bergson, *Les Deux Sources de la morale et de la religion* (Paris: Quadrige,
2005), p. 223.
[24] Michael Holland, 'Qui est l'Aminadab de Blanchot?', *Revue des sciences humaines*,
253 (January–March 1999), 21–42.

There is no homogeneous collective space

If we now relate the meaning of the title to the contextual framework I have described, the primordial importance given to the Jewish theme of the unpronounceability of the name of God proves to have a critical function in the novel *Aminadab*. The novel questions the reader's ability to challenge a Catholicism whose spiritual function has been perverted and which has been made to serve institutional ends to which it cannot admit. It is up to the reader's conscience to put together the fragments of a shattered memory: a chronological reading of the novel may be of little interest, but if we look at the figures of Thomas, Jérôme and 'le vieil employé' in synchronic terms, we have a single memory structure that can dynamically 'integrate' a plurality of discourses.

The conception of memory that emerges from *Aminadab* is, moreover, not only collective but plural: identity is not a specific property of any one figure in the novel, and each figure is part of a fragment making up an overall structure, namely the 'maison', that the protagonist tries in vain to understand as a whole. The question of identity is of necessity a plural question addressed to a diversity of subjects: 'qui êtes-vous?' is a question that is asked of Thomas again and again, and the 'qui êtes-vous?' is at once a *polite* formula and a *plural* formula.[25]

What is the individual? A collective being whose *diversity* is a precondition for the existence of the *individual* being. Such appears to be *Aminadab*'s answer to the construction of real history. While he was working on *Aminadab*, Blanchot wrote in the *Journal des Débats* on 26–27 May 1941 – or a week before the publication of the second Statut des juifs: 'Toute notre diversité d'ambitions vient des sangs très disparates et des climats très variés qui, cependant, au lieu de nous diviser en des produits instables et composites ont fait de la France la personnalité européenne la plus nette, productrice d'une culture et d'un esprit caractéristique.'[26]

Such theoretical speculation was obviously of no relevance to the Vichy regime once its government had agreed to collaborate with the

---

[25] '«Qui êtes-vous donc?» dit-il à voix basse, mais l'écho se saisit immédiatement de sa question et ce fut comme s'il avait crié de toutes ses forces. Tout le monde se tourna vers lui; c'était très désagréable, mais maintenant il était trop tard, il ne pouvait plus reprendre des paroles. La réponse vint et elle n'était pas moins bruyante', p. 112.

[26] Maurice Blanchot, 'La France et la civilisation contemporaine', *Journal des débats* (26–27 May 1941), p. 3.

Nazi ethnic cleansing project. Vichy was now thinking purely in terms of a homogeneous society, and its sole concern was to make French society conform to the Nazi project. The theoretical stance adopted by Blanchot therefore raises the issue of how the idea of a social plurality fell into oblivion and of how Vichy came to deny its existence. As I have said, *Aminadab* was completed in January 1942[27] or, in other words, a few months before the French police, under the leadership of René Bousquet, agreed to take sole responsibility for rounding up the Jews (and therefore the big 'Vél d'Hiv' round-up of 16–17 July 1942).

While Blanchot had certainly hoped in 1940 that Marshal Pétain's Révolution nationale could preserve something of his very lofty and idealized idea of France, he also hoped that Pétain could help to spare France the racism for which he had been criticizing Germany since 1933; the last issue of *Aux Ecoutes* to be edited by Blanchot (27 July 1940) appeared in the week that Raphaël Alibert established a *commission de révision des naturalisations*. The first anti-Semitic Alibert laws (which were promulgated as early as 13 August 1940) quickly demonstrated to Blanchot that Vichy was ready to do more than make concessions to the Nazi Occupation forces.

Conclusion

Although it was delivered to Gallimard in January 1942, Blanchot's novel was not published until the autumn of 1942. Was *Aminadab* published too late, given that French society had already been swallowed up by the Nazi monster? Blanchot's novel at least contributes to the growing awareness of what was happening that would finally lead the Catholic bishops to protest, in September 1942, about the deportation of the Jews.

This is certainly an example of avant-garde art, and not only because its message is written in code to avoid being censored. But what is more important is that it places both the question of memory and the Jewish question in the centre of the literary field, to the embarrassment of those who would rather see them as a minor aspect of a collective history. Significantly, *Aminadab* claims to exist in some pre-historical space, but at the heart of the *dispositif* that forces us to reconstruct history, at the heart of a structure that mobilizes the reader's memory – as though memory were the best way to prevent all individual consciences

---

[27] Paulhan, *Choix de lettres*, p. 263.

from surrendering to a myth centred on the same fascinated vision of the present.

The novel's real target is the Vichy regime's lie. For Blanchot, the Jewish question became central not because Vichy had made it the central question, but because, on the contrary, Vichy wanted to deny the existence of the Jewish question. Hence the strength and contemporary relevance of Blanchot's analysis of the Vichy regime: *Aminadab* denounces, not the focus on the Jewish question, but the oblivion into which Vichy was attempting to plunge an essential part of France's collective memory.

Chapter 19

Life as an 'enfant de collabo': Marie Chaix's evolution, 1974–2005

Katherine Cardin

Nearly seven decades after the Second World War, the complex problems and startling choices of the *années noires* continue to captivate citizens and scholars alike. Numerous scholars have studied French collaboration with German occupying forces. Yet one aspect of collaboration has received little attention: its impact on children of French Second World War collaborators. Only a few scholars, such as Claire Gorrara, Alan Morris and Christopher Lloyd, have examined the literary confrontations of children of collaborators, notably Pascal Jardin, Marie Chaix and Evelyne Le Garrec, with their parents' legacies.[1] Moreover, existing studies address only works published by these three authors between 1970 and 1980.

Such temporal limitations are problematic in the case of Marie Chaix, daughter of PPF member Albert Beugras.[2] She has written about her father's wartime collaboration for three decades. Given this extended

---

[1] For an analysis of the interplay of myth and counter-myth in representations of the Occupation, consult Alan Morris' *Collaboration and Resistance Reviewed: Writers and the Mode Rétro in Post-Gaullist France* (New York: Berg, 1992). For a gendered approach to representations of the Occupation, see Claire Gorrara's *Women's Representations of the Occupation in Post-'68 France* (New York: St. Martin's Press, 1998). For a study of Pascal Jardin's Second World War-related works, refer to Christopher Lloyd's *Collaboration and Resistance in Occupied France: Representing Treason and Sacrifice* (Basingstoke: Palgrave Macmillan, 2003).

[2] The PPF was founded in 1936 by Jacques Doriot, who had been forced out of the Communist Party in 1934. Its creation was driven by anti-communist sentiment and a desire to restructure and reinvigorate France. After France's defeat in 1940, the PPF developed fascist tendencies. It became one of the most important pro-collaboration political parties in France during the Occupation. Doriot's 1942 bid to wrest power from Pierre Laval, head of government under Pétain, and to direct France's collaboration with Germany did not succeed, in part because of German opposition.

period of publishing, Chaix presents a fascinating case study in terms of the evolution of memory and narrative about the Second World War and collaboration. Restricting analysis of Chaix's works to those published in the 1970s unduly limits one's understanding of the transformation which occurs in Chaix's stance towards her father's collaboration. When one considers all six books in which Chaix addresses her father's collaboration, several trends emerge: a shift from a public to a private motivation for writing; a transformation in style; an expansion of identity; and the development of the possibility that Chaix will eventually come to terms with her father's legacy.

In writing *Les Lauriers du lac de Constance: Chronique d'une collaboration* (1974),[3] Chaix confronts her ignorance of the past and engages with her father's public persona as a collaborator and national traitor. What exactly *did* Albert do during the war? How did he end up imprisoned for collaboration? Moreover, did he merit society's condemnation? Rather than be stymied by gaps in her own memories and by her family's internal taboo on discussion of the war, Chaix rejects the constraints of personal, lived experience. She appropriates her father's voice and memories in *Les Lauriers* in order to reconstruct the defining experiences and decisions of Albert's trajectory, such as Albert's conversations with Jacques Doriot, the leader of the PPF. In each conversation, Albert attempts to break his ties with the PPF, and Doriot convinces him not only to remain an active member but also to take on additional duties. A meeting in 1940 reveals the importance of Albert's inability to resist the PPF leader. Disillusioned by France's defeat, Albert looks to Doriot for inspiration and guidance. After listening to Doriot extol the merits of collaboration, Albert asks a question that foreshadows his fate at the end of the war: 'Si l'Allemagne perd la guerre, ne serons-nous pas accusés de trahison?' (LL, p. 40). Unfortunately, he ignores this premonition and continues working for the PPF. Even towards the end of the war, after a trip to the war zone in Normandy, Albert does not heed his instincts. He asks the same question as in 1940, with predictable results. In spite of Doriot's admission that his fears are true, Albert is eventually convinced that his work for the PPF 'sera encore plus utile' (LL, p. 109). Albert seems to be a man of accurate instincts who is nevertheless politically hapless, due to his enthralment with Doriot. Moreover, he appears to be an ethical man who is devoted to his country. Diary-style entries in which Albert reflects on his political work present him as a man who is

[3] Paris: Seuil, 1998.

outraged to hear a politician declare that 'la France est foutue' and who 'ne se reconnaît pas' in the festive behaviour of his fellow PPF members living in exile in Germany (LL, pp. 43 and 107). Overall, Albert does not seem to be a villain. But whose opinion is this?

Because of the ambiguity in such scenes as to what is quotation or invention, it is difficult to take this account of Albert as a politician at face value as representing Chaix's assessment. In a brief note preceding the text, the publisher calls attention to this issue, stating: 'Marie Chaix s'est inspirée des carnets tenus par son père en prison. Elle met notamment à jour une version nouvelle de la mort de Doriot; mais la lecture des événements se fait à travers une trame romanesque' (LL, p. i). The reader thus begins *Les Lauriers* wondering which elements of the chronicle of Albert's collaboration are direct citations from his prison diary, which elements are modified and which elements are pure invention. This ambiguity is particularly troubling in passages directly presenting Albert's words and opinions, for these passages lack the narratorial commentary and punctuation marks that would clearly signal citation. The resulting ambivalence of Chaix's judgement of Albert as a politician is evident, for example, in the conversations in which Albert asks if PPF members will be accused of treason if Germany is defeated. On the one hand, Chaix could be seen as rejecting society's condemnation of Albert, arguing that he was a good man led astray. On the other hand, Chaix could be seen as accepting society's criticism of Albert. If Albert knew that his behaviour could be considered treasonous, why did he not end it? The combination of these provocative techniques – appropriation and uncertainty – places Chaix's stance in the grey zone somewhere between accusation and protestation.

However, Chaix's position concerning the identity imposed upon her by her father's identity is much clearer. She is troubled less by the fact of her father's collaboration than by what it meant for her life as a child during the war. Looking back, Chaix realizes that she was different from the moment she was born into a collaborator's family: 'Je suis née en 1942. D'autres sont les enfants de la guerre, on leur a fait absorber du calcium et des vitamines pour que leurs dents de lait ne tombent pas en petits morceaux. Moi, je suis un enfant de la collaboration, du maréchal, de Doriot, de la Wehrmacht et de l'antisémitisme' (LL, p. 53). The placement of Chaix's identification with collaboration at the start of a string of connotations linking collaboration to anti-Semitism suggests that there is more to her alienation than a difference in material comforts. It hints at the true source of her anguish: the difference between her fate and that of Jewish children. This is confirmed by a passage dealing with the infamous Vélodrome d'Hiver round-up in Paris in July 1942. Chaix again contemplates the difference that marked the 'enfant de la collaboration', but she no longer contrasts herself with the 'enfants de la guerre'. Now, it is Jewish children with whom she cannot identify: 'Je suis née en 1942. D'autres, enfants de la rafle, Vél' d'Hiv, wagons, Auschwitz. Moi, non. Moi, enfant rose, aimé, allaité, bercé. Enfant épargné. 1942' (LL, p. 59). Repeated use of juxtaposition underscores the dichotomy between experiences: Lyon versus Paris; the sanctuary of the Beugras's refreshing garden versus the heat and confusion of the stadium; the protected child versus the hunted child. Of the thousands of people caught in the round-up, only 'une petite poignée en reviendra' and '*pas un enfant*' (LL, p. 58). Chaix, the 'enfant épargné', is acutely aware of the dire fate she escaped, and the application of italics to the phrase 'pas un enfant' emphasizes this.

Even more overwhelming is the knowledge that her father's political group participated in persecuting the children whose fate especially troubles her: Jewish children. Once again, the use of italics hints at the significance of such knowledge for Chaix: 'A Paris, cette nuit-là, *trois à quatre cents jeunes gens chemise bleu marine, portant baudriers et brassards au signe PPF, sont venus prêter main-forte au service d'ordre*' (LL, pp. 58–59). Even though Albert is not identified as one of the PPF members at the round-up, Chaix is clearly troubled by the party's involvement. If the PPF facilitated the Holocaust, then her father's active membership in the PPF links Chaix herself indirectly to a crime against humanity. Chaix's observation about PPF participation in the round-up both indirectly criticizes Albert as a politician and, through Chaix's intensely personal reaction, directly attests to Chaix's acceptance of society's identification and condemnation of Albert as a collaborator.

Unlike *Les Lauriers*, which is predicated on Albert's legacy, Chaix's subsequent books take other people and issues as their subjects. However, these subjects frequently lead to additional confrontations with her father's legacy. For instance, in *Les Silences ou la vie d'une femme* (1976), Chaix sets out to focus on her mother's life. She is sometimes stymied by her mother's refusal to discuss anything related to the Second World War. Alice's silence calls attention to what she seeks to avoid discussing – Albert and his wartime collaboration – and implies shame. In *L'Âge du tendre* (1979), Chaix intends to reflect on the struggles of her entry into adolescence. Yet her coming-of-age story cannot exclude Albert, since his liberation from prison throws the feminine universe in which she has grown up into turmoil. Similarly, *Juliette, chemin des cerisiers* (1985), Chaix's narrative recounting the life and opinions of a servant who worked for Albert's family for thirty-five years, must inevitably account for Albert's collaboration and its impact on the family. Even Chaix's daily journal covering her experiences between 1980 and 1982 – *Un 21 avril à New York* (1986) – cannot avoid Albert, if only in a passing allusion. The lingering impact of Albert's collaboration is evident in Chaix's sensitivity to reports of contemporary anti-Semitism in France. Plus, on one occasion, her children force her to confront Albert's collaboration by asking her about it.

Despite such continued returns to the past, Chaix's books attest to an evolution in Chaix's relationship with her father's legacy. Progress is evident, for example, in Chaix's selection of topics. Her focus shifts from Albert's controversial past to the past experiences of other family members and, eventually, to her own life and current experiences. Evolution marks not only Chaix's choice of subject, but also her identity. By the time Chaix publishes *Un 21 avril*, her books have introduced several new facets of her identity, including those of mother and published author. In addition, they have showcased Chaix's increasing awareness of the differences between her younger and adult selves. Finally, evolution is signalled by the appearance and development of explicit reflection on the role of generations in the narration of the past.

These developments come to fruition in Chaix's most recent work, *L'Été du sureau*, published in 2005. In fact, the opening pages of the book take Chaix's evolution as their subject. Central to these pages is the 1990 death of Alain Oulman, Chaix's friend and editor at Calmann-Lévy, and the subsequent fifteen-year hiatus in her published work. Significantly, the key to understanding Chaix's intense reaction to the death is an incident that attests to both Chaix's evolution and the ensuing societal resistance. Chaix's relationship with Oulman began after the reading committee at Seuil rejected her manuscript for *Le Fils de Marthe* on the grounds that 'Marie Chaix n'est capable d'écrire que de l'autobiographie.'[4] Not only does such an assertion restrict Chaix's identity to 'the author of lived experience', but it limits her, in a certain sense, to being 'the author who is the child of a World War Two collaborator', since Chaix's previous publications with Seuil had touched on her father and his controversial legacy. Moreover, the committee's claim ignores Chaix's appropriation of her father's voices and memories in *Les Lauriers*, as well

---

[4] Marie Chaix, *L'Été du sureau* (Paris: Seuil, 2005), p. 12.

as the non-autobiographical sections of Chaix's subsequent works. In light of this, Chaix's reaction to the death of her editor at Calmann-Lévy is understandable. Oulman had seen past the constrained categorization of Chaix and helped to prove Seuil mistaken by publishing a revised version of *Le Fils de Marthe*. Thus, his death marked the loss of both a friend and the embodiment of the possibility of being more than an 'enfant de collabo'.

Not only do the opening pages of *L'Été du sureau* take Chaix's evolution as their subject, they also perform it. Worrying about her readers' reaction to her prolonged silence, Marie wonders, 'Comment expliquer à des gens qui m'ont lue et ont souvent tout lu de moi, un livre appelant le suivant, pourquoi "ça" s'est arrêté?' (ES, pp. 9–10). The nature of the public–private interplay Chaix is confronting has clearly changed. Here, it revolves around aspects of Chaix which are independent of her father and Second World War collaboration. She must negotiate the tension between two facets of her identity: grieving friend and nationally recognized author. Her private life has had an impact on her public one, which prompts musings on how to explain the inherent connection between the two and the resulting literary silence.

The initial exclusion of Albert from the public–private equation, evident in Chaix's reflections on how to explain her silence to her readers, is consistent with the rest of *L'Été du sureau*. The public–private interplay revolving around Chaix's status as the child of a collaborator seems settled. She does not dispute the fact that 'Beugras, le nom du père, recelait la honte', nor does she shy away from identifying her father as 'mon père collabo' (ES, p. 39). Moreover, the cursory treatment of her father's wartime deeds suggests that Marie is no longer trying to fill gaps in her knowledge, nor is she as troubled by her father's past as she once was. The inquiry into her father appears closed, the questions answered. In fact, certain aspects of *L'Été du sureau* suggest that the tension engendered by status as a child of a collaborator is not merely settled, but is now moot. The inclusion of summaries of previous books, along with footnotes identifying the titles of those books, indicates that Chaix believes her audience now includes a generation of readers unfamiliar with her earlier works and with the charges against her father. She even goes so far as to state that, as early as 1974, 'nul ne se souvenait de lui, à part les quelques compagnons d'armes survivants' (ES, p. 40).

Evidence suggests that Chaix is progressively coming to terms with the past. Her discovery of her daughter Émilie's decision to divorce her husband is instrumental to this process. Reacting as if her daughter were

abandoning her, not her husband, Marie wallows in her misery. She
stubbornly ignores friends' reminders that she herself had divorced years
before. However, when her other daughter, Léonore, voices lingering
anger about Chaix's divorce, Chaix is forced to abandon her role as
victim and to confront the repercussions of her divorce in her daughters'
lives. Although she accepts responsibility for shattering the family and
acknowledges her daughters' anguish, Chaix does not condemn herself.
Instead, she invokes the notions of improvisation and invention. If any
guidelines for life exist, they are hope and good faith. Chaix claims to
have acted with 'la meilleure foi du monde' (ES, p. 90). Her life is not
necessarily 'glorieux', but it is the result of her best efforts (ES, p. 90).
In the end, she makes peace with herself: 'Si je me retourne aujourd'hui
sur mon paysage familial, je peux le regarder sans prendre la fuite, avec
quelques regrets bien sûr mais pas de honte' (ES, p. 90). She has judged
herself as a parent who made a decision that caused her children to suffer,
and she has found a way to come to terms with her own legacy.

In referring to her 'paysage familial', Chaix alludes to the family landscape in which she is a parent, for her realization is motivated by her
reflections on her divorce. However, Chaix's thoughts have interesting
implications for her relationship to her other 'paysage familial', in which
she is the daughter, not the parent. Albert's decision to prioritize politics
over his family effectively shattered the family, but he firmly believed
that his political activities were performed in good faith on behalf of
the futures of France and his children. One might surmise that he was
not ashamed of his 'paysage familial', for the same reasons Chaix is
not ashamed of hers. If Chaix can look back on her own decisions as
a parent without shame and find a way to face their consequences, can
she do the same for her father's decisions?

Although Chaix does not explicitly extrapolate from her own case to
her father's, she nonetheless reaches a similar verdict. Newfound insight
into her own decisions and legacy as a parent allows her to begin to
understand her own parents' decisions. She concludes that her mother
and father 'ont fait ce qu'ils ont pu', just as she had done her best as
a parent (ES, p. 105). Rather than rail against the past or her parents,
she decides to accept her parents' dual legacy of 'amour et séparation'
and to draw what lessons she can from their 'épreuves' and 'silences'
(ES, p. 90). In short, she pardons them: 'Je ne leur en veux plus' (ES,
p. 105).

Unlike similar pardons made in earlier texts, this one rings true.
Chaix's quest began in 1974 with Les Lauriers, in which she sought to

elucidate her father's decisions and to reflect on their impact on her own life and identity. Her struggle was mirrored in her use of turbulent techniques, such as transgression of lived experience and manipulation of ambiguity. Over time, her writing shifted away from these techniques, her focus moved away from her father and her identities began to multiply. By 2005, Chaix had moved from judging a parent to judging herself as a parent. An intensely private focus on herself offered up the greatest implications for a break with the past and with the sole identity of 'enfant de collabo'. Towards the end of *L'Été du sureau*, Chaix addresses her father's spirit, declaring: 'Je peux enfin laisser dormir sans douleur le souvenir de vous. Et partir' (ES, p. 174). Chaix has released her father, and now she is ready to release herself.

Chapter 20

'Un Passé qui ne passe pas': the memory of the Occupation in Patrick Modiano's *Accident nocturne* and *Dans le café de la jeunesse perdue*[1]

Alan Morris

That Patrick Modiano is fascinated by the 'dark years' of 1940–45 there can be absolutely no denying. In his first three novels, beginning with *La Place de l'étoile*,[2] the obsession – and the iconoclastic focus on collaboration rather than resistance – was plain for all to see. The author was patently driven by an exorcistic impulse centred on his father, Albert, a Jew linked to the black market and to established collaborators. After this initial intensity, Modiano's interest in the war, as expressed through his fiction, seemed to blow hot and cold. Virtually absent in a novel like *Villa triste*,[3] the early 1940s would suddenly return at least momentarily to the fore in subsequent works, such as *Remise de peine*,[4] which details Albert's wartime arrest and later release, possibly following the (perplexing) intervention of a member of the gang of French *gestapistes* run by Henri Lafont and Pierre Bonny – *la bande de la rue Lauriston*. At present, we seem to be in another quiet phase, with the subject featuring only episodically, on the face of it, in the author's most recent novels.[5] This is

[1] I gratefully record my thanks to the Carnegie Trust for the Universities of Scotland, without whose generous financial assistance this chapter would never have come to fruition.
[2] Paris: Gallimard, 1968.
[3] Paris: Gallimard, 1975.
[4] Paris: Seuil, 1988. Henceforth *RP*.
[5] The latest to date is *L'Horizon* (Paris: Gallimard, 2010).

not, however, actually the case, as evidenced in particular by *Accident nocturne*[6] and *Dans le café de la jeunesse perdue*.[7] Many of the characters' names, especially, hark back to the troublesome dark years, and give a hidden dimension to these two works. It is the aim of the present chapter to demonstrate this, and then to offer suggestions as to the significance of such a device.[8]

An excellent place to open the discussion is Modiano's *Dans le café de la jeunesse perdue*, which includes in its cast list Jeanette Gaul, Godinger and Mario Bay, Bernolle, Dr Vala and Maurice Raphaël. Although these six names will probably be lost on most readers, they have not been invented; each of them derives from a historical figure active during the Occupation. Jeanette Gaul was arrested for obtaining heroin from the infamous Dr Petiot in 1942;[9] Godinger and Mario Bay belonged to 'la Gestapo de l'avenue Foch' in Paris,[10] while Bernolle and Dr Vala both worked for the Bonny-Lafont gang,[11] as indeed did Maurice Raphaël.[12]

The Dr Vala of history also seems to have inspired the Dr Valat who turns up fleetingly in *Accident nocturne*,[13] and, once again, his is not the only name to evoke the Occupation here. Witness Solière. In December 1945, a man of precisely the same name was found murdered; he had been an important economic collaborator and a close friend

---

[6] Paris: Gallimard, 2003. Henceforth *AN*.

[7] Paris: Gallimard, 2007. Henceforth *DCJP*.

[8] Roger Godard has shown the importance of the Occupation in *Accident nocturne* (*Itinéraires du roman contemporain* (Paris: Colin, 2006), pp. 75–81), as has Dervila Cooke ('Violence and the Prison of the Past in Recent Works by Patrick Modiano: *Des Inconnues*, *La Petite Bijou*, "Éphéméride", and *Accident nocturne*', in David Gascoigne (ed.), *Violent Histories: Violence, Culture and Identity in France from Surrealism to the Néo-polar* (Oxford: Peter Lang, 2007), pp. 111–129). The present study will complement these two analyses.

[9] Her lover was a certain Jean-Marc van Bever. Tellingly, in Modiano's *Du plus loin de l'oubli* (Paris: Gallimard, 1996) a Gérard van Bever had already appeared.

[10] See, for example, 'Les Huit Accusés de la Gestapo de l'Avenue Foch sont condamnés à mort', *Le Figaro*, 20 May 1949, p. 2.

[11] Éric Guillon, *Abel Danos, dit 'le Mammouth': Entre Résistance et Gestapo* (Paris: Fayard, 2006), pp. 29 n. 3, 116–117, 129–130, 174. As Guillon shows (pp. 129–130), Bernolle was at one stage arrested by the policeman Blémant's men; Blémant is the name of another character in *Dans le café de la jeunesse perdue*.

[12] See Denis Cosnard's excellent *Réseau Modiano* website, http://pagesperso-orange.fr/reseau-modiano/raphael_maurice.htm (accessed 16 June 2010). Further evidence of this war-themed, onomastic game-playing is given by the appearance of a character called Mocellini (evocative of Mussolini).

[13] In a number of historical texts, the not-so-good doctor's name is similarly spelled with a *t*. See, for example, Philippe Aziz, *Tu trahiras sans vergogne* (Paris: Fayard, 1970), p. 40.

of Joinovici.[14] This link is significant. As early as *La Place de l'étoile*, Modiano had revealed his fascination for the man known as Joino, the ambiguous Jewish businessman who was one of the Germans' biggest suppliers during the war, and the same interest in this larger-scale father substitute had manifested itself – albeit less explicitly – in *Un cirque passe*,[15] thanks to the appearance of a character called Pierre Ansart. In real life, a Gaston Ansart was Joinovici's partner in a wartime *bureau d'achat*.[16] Interestingly, another of those involved was the ubiquitous Henri Lafont,[17] and the implicit presence of the French Gestapo in the 1992 text does not stop there. Guélin evokes the Guélin who apparently helped Pierre Bonny to get a job at the rue Lauriston.[18]

In addition to the orthographically unstable Dr Vala(t), another name to appear in both *Accident nocturne* and *Dans le café de la jeunesse perdue* is Accad, *prénom*: Georges, according to the first of these two novels, and the description of the character is revealing. It recalls that of the real-life Georges Accad at his post-war trial,[19] where he was accused not of being linked to the French Gestapo, which he was, but of being involved in three murders committed in May 1945. Two of the other names mentioned in the post-war press in connection with the killings are also worthy of mention: Léoni, who worked alongside Godinger and Mario Bay at the avenue Foch,[20] and Accad's lover, Jacqueline Beausergent. In *Dans le café de la jeunesse perdue*, a Leoni briefly puts in an appearance (*DCJP*, p. 58), and, more strikingly, in *Accident nocturne*, one of the key characters is not only called Jacqueline Beausergent, but visibly shares some distinguishing traits – such as blonde hair – with her earlier namesake from the papers. Not for nothing, then, ludically, does Modiano have his narrator say of

---

[14] 'Un témoin mystérieux apporte la preuve que l'agent d'affaire Solière était un collaborateur', *Front national*, 28 December 1945, p. 1; Henry Sergg, *Joinovici: l'empire souterrain du chiffonnier milliardaire* (Paris: Le Carrousel-FN, 1986), p. 122.

[15] Paris: Gallimard, 1992. Henceforth *UCP*.

[16] André Goldschmidt, *L'Affaire Joinovici* (Toulouse: Privat, 2002), p. 44.

[17] Cécile Desprairies, *Paris dans la Collaboration* (Paris: Seuil, 2009), p. 248.

[18] Jacques Bonny, *Mon père, l'inspecteur Bonny* (Paris: Laffont, 1975), pp. 206–207.

[19] See, for example, *DCJP*, pp. 83–84, and cf. 'Les Tueurs du "Bon Repos" devant leurs juges', *Libération*, 10 July 1948, pp. 1, 3; Robert Collin, 'Trois assassins rejettent sur deux morts un triple assassinat', *Combat*, 10 July 1948, pp. 1, 6; and Alex Ancel, 'Accad et Damiani appliquaient les méthodes de la Gestapo pour rançonner «leurs clients». La blonde Jacqueline leur indiquaient les «bons à faire»', *Le Parisien Libéré*, 10 July 1948, pp. 1–2.

[20] 'En cour de justice: Délateurs, Assassins, Tortionnaires', *Le Figaro*, 10 May 1949, pp. 1–2; 'Tribunaux', *Le Figaro*, 28 June 1949, p. 2.

the metadiegetic fiction that was one of his dreams: 'Seul le nom: JACQUELINE BEAUSERGENT était réel' (*AN*, p. 57); the incident acts as a teasing *mise en abyme*.

Thus, Modiano's two novels, *Accident nocturne* and *Dans le café de la jeunesse perdue*, where the role of the Occupation ostensibly seems to be diminished, actually contain a plethora of character names linked to the war, which suggests that the novelist is using the ploy deliberately. So the question now arises as to why this should be, and, as ever with this particular author, a variety of explanations can be discerned.

Most prosaically, the device is linked to Modiano's basic literary procedure – his reliance on the real to spark his imagination – and it also helps to consolidate the omnipresent tension between the true and the false in his work. The full significance of what Modiano is doing, however, can only emerge once the detail of his characters' actions has been considered, so let us return to *Accident nocturne* and look a little more closely at Jacqueline Beausergent. It is fair to say that Jacqueline makes a big impact in the novel – literally. She is the driver of a 'Fiat couleur vert d'eau' that hits the narrator at the start of the text, and hence she generates the ensuing narrative, which principally takes the form of a quest to find her. Initially, the accident is seen as a damaging experience, associated with pain and loss: the victim needs to be treated in hospital, with, tellingly, one shoe missing, and the physical hurt persists to the end (*AN*, p. 146). But some things do get better. The misplaced footwear is returned and the protagonist's life improves (*AN*, pp. 20, 104, 112), despite – or perhaps thanks to – an upsurge in memories from his childhood, triggered because they relate to a similar accident he suffered.

Even from this very brief summary, it may be obvious that the accident can be seen as symbolic, and much could be said here about the evocation of the death of Modiano's brother, Rudy.[21] But I shall concentrate instead on a key implication of calling the driver of the vehicle Jacqueline Beausergent, namely that the Fiat thereby becomes a token for the Occupation (to which there is a direct link via the *conductrice*) and the accident a sign of the discomfort that the period can still cause today, or the way that the memory of it can painfully impinge upon the present. This interpretation is perhaps all the more appealing in that one of the

---

[21] The vehicle involved is 'vert d'eau', which mirrors the 'vert très pâle' that was apparently Rudy's preferred option for his dodgem car (*RP*, p. 86). Hence, by association, the pain resulting from the narrator's being knocked down, and which releases memories of similar suffering from his childhood, could be said to represent the trauma that the novelist suffered as a result of his brother's death.

murders to which the real Jacqueline was an accomplice was that of a Jew (like Modiano's father). The other two victims were brothers called Peugeot. Little wonder, then, that the narrator is hit by a *car*! This contention that, in *Accident nocturne*, the horrors of the dark years metaphorically survive into the present is supported by the fact that Modiano had already used the same device in earlier novels. For example, in *Un cirque passe*, the aforementioned Guélin is a menacing figure who explicitly evokes the threats of the war (*UCP*, pp. 143, 148), while Ansart is behind the Gestapo-style 'arrest' of a man (*UCP*, pp. 96–101).

But there is more to the matter than this, for from the start of *Accident nocturne*, the metaphoric pain deriving from the Occupation is tied to details which evoke the novelist's father. To give but one illustration: as a result of the accident, the narrator is taken to hospital with Jacqueline in a police van, an event which echoes a similar trip that the author made with Albert, alluded to briefly later (*AN*, p. 76), and explicitly noted in other texts.[22] More significantly, it is eventually revealed that the car which hits the narrator is owned by Solière (*AN*, p. 111). Now, while confirming that the suffering can be seen to emanate from the Occupation – Solière's own onomastic connections to the period echoing Jacqueline's – this fact gains added meaning from the type of man the car-owner is. He is using an alias (*AN*, p. 145); he has offices in Paris (*AN*, p. 140); he is often absent on business (*AN*, pp. 140, 142, 147); and he is a man about whom not enough is known (*AN*, p. 147). This information is persuasive. Solière is obviously a reflection of the narrator's and the author's own fathers. Indeed, he is even explicitly felt to be 'de la même espèce que mon père' (*AN*, p. 144). The implicit search for Solière – as the owner of the Fiat – is, then, ultimately a transposition of Modiano's search for Albert, and particularly his painful search for the Albert of the Occupation.

What is more, the novel explains precisely what the narrator's father did during the war: he is claimed to have worked for the 'bureau Otto' (*AN*, p. 60), that is to say the infamous black market organization set up by the Germans. Can it therefore be a coincidence that he disappears 'dans le brouillard, du côté de Montrouge' (*AN*, p. 116), where collaborators were executed (*AN*, pp. 45, 82)? Certainly not. Nor can it be coincidental that, shortly after the accident, Solière advises the narrator to forget what happened, and gets him to sign a document admitting that he was at fault (*AN*, pp. 24, 93). Revealingly, this

---

[22] See, for example, Patrick Modiano, *Dora Bruder* (Paris: Gallimard, 1997), p. 71.

document is termed a 'compte rendu', which resonates with the need to *rendre des comptes* that characterizes the whole œuvre. Hence, once again in his fiction, Modiano can be seen to be evoking not only the *pain* (symbolized by the accident and its consequences), but also the sense of *guilt* he feels as a result of Albert's activities in occupied France: the activities of a Jew who worked alongside Germans and collaborators.

If this sense of guilt and remorse is long established in the life and the œuvre of Patrick Modiano, then so too is the other element of *Accident nocturne* that goes hand in hand with it: the Freudian images and overtones. The text relies heavily on *rêverie*, and seems laden with hidden meanings to be interpreted; each of the titles of Bouvière's three books comments indirectly on the main narrative, and one of them is called *Les Souvenirs-écran* (*AN*, p. 68); and then there is the obsessive quest to find Jacqueline Beausergent. As the novel progresses, Jacqueline increasingly emerges as a maternal figure. But she is not merely maternal. The narrator's pursuit of her seems to be that of a lover, and the very end of the text finds the two of them in a lift, possibly going up to make love. Perhaps this is only to be expected, given that one of the aliases the narrator adopted once was Georges Accad (*AN*, p. 54), the name of the real-life lover of the Jacqueline Beausergent of history. Expected or not, the inference to be made appears to be that, as ever, Modiano's literary 'dream' is marked by oedipal desires, namely the wish to kill the father-figure and sexually possess the mother-figure.[23]

Now let us move on to *Dans le café de la jeunesse perdue*, and to someone who has not so far been mentioned: Bowing. That this character is a writer of some sort is entirely fitting, for the novel itself, even by Modiano's standards, is strikingly narcissistic. Be that as it may, of more immediate relevance is the fact that Bowing once more has a name that harks back to the Occupation. Like the aforementioned Bernolle, Dr Vala and Maurice Raphaël, the real Bowing was linked to the Bonny-Lafont gang, featuring in its notorious North African Brigade, a paramilitary excursion that the novelist in turn evokes by the attribution of the sobriquet 'le Capitaine' to his creation.[24] 'J'ignorais que "la bande de la rue Lauriston" me hanterait si longtemps', Modiano had observed in 1988 (*RP*, p. 88). Twenty or so years later, little has apparently changed.

---

[23] Cf. Cooke, 'Violence', p. 127.
[24] The Bowing of history was not actually a Captain, but one of the 'sous-officiers' (Guillon, *Abel Danos*, p. 183).

A second notable aspect of the fictional Bowing is his commitment to recording the comings and goings of the group which frequented the same café as he did,[25] in an attempt to 'sauver de l'oubli les papillons qui tournent quelques instants autour d'une lampe' (*DCJP*, p. 19). This reported intention, comprising a typically *modianesque* image, is just one of the many literary traits and concerns he shares with his creator, and thereby gives an excellent indication of at least part of his role in the text – he is a reflection of the actual author of the novel. Furthermore, there is an undoubted emotional logic in the fact that Modiano is assimilating himself, however partially, to a man whose name evokes the French Gestapo – he is once again putting himself in the shoes of his father, embracing the troubling side of the paternal legacy.[26]

Bowing's status as a scribe can additionally lead to an alternative reading. As the character eventually disappears, having let Caisley, the private detective, consult his notes, before he bequeathed them to the first narrator of the four, we could view Bowing's jottings (*DCJP*, p. 19) as a metaphor for the narrative of the real-life group with which his historical namesake was involved, the Bonny-Lafont gang: the *bande*'s members have departed the scene, leaving behind only traces of their existence – names, itineraries, and so on – an unfinished jigsaw requiring imagination to complete the picture. And this fragmented story, it could be argued, is currently only partially accessible, available principally to those well versed in the arts of digging and detection, such as Caisley, *le privé*, obviously, the narrator-legatee (who is a student at the École supérieure des Mines), and ultimately, of course, Modiano himself.

In this way, the fictional Bowing and his incomplete records are doubly significant. They embody the intertwining of personal and collective narratives for Modiano,[27] the intermingling, via the Bonny-Lafont gang, of Albert's story and that of the French Gestapo in general. By attempting to fill in at least some of the gaps in these two narratives, through the famous project to 'me créer un passé et une mémoire

---

[25] Modiano gives a clue as to the hidden origin of Bowing when he has Dr Vala say to him: 'Votre cahier, on dirait un registre de police. . . . C'est comme si nous avions tous été pris dans une rafle' (*DCJP*, p. 26).

[26] The novel also actually includes the question, 'Suis-je responsable de mon père . . . ?' (*DCJP*, p. 117). More broadly, apropos of this imaginary self-construction as a collaborator, cf. the narrator of *Accident nocturne*'s brief assumption of the alias 'Georges Accad', and his obsession with Jacqueline Beausergent.

[27] Cf. Cooke, 'Violence', p. 123.

avec le passé et la mémoire des autres',[28] and by recognizing the burden of guilt that he has inherited, Modiano shows that, even today, he is paradoxically attracted to, and afflicted by, what Marianne Hirsch has called postmemory.

The sources that Modiano exploits as he forges this postmemory of the war are worthy of comment. Although he has diligently quizzed relatives and friends, he has also plainly sifted through the press of the time, gleaning names from the micro-narratives there. Or more specifically, he has trawled through the post-Liberation *faits divers*.[29] An awareness of this painstaking research throws extra light on Modiano's writing. On the one hand, the information culled from the 'news in brief' columns consolidates the detective strand in the author's texts, not simply because it provides 'clues' to be interpreted, but because, once interpreted, these *indices* relate predominantly to crimes and to criminals. On the other hand, the snippets used reveal much about the national view of the Occupation. As David Walker has demonstrated, the *faits divers* are a place of marginalization, a reserve for keeping disturbing items 'at a safe remove from the centre of society'.[30] This is obviously why so many collaborators and their atrocities featured there in the press of the late 1940s. By appropriating the names (and often backgrounds) of these *réprouvés*, Modiano, in his own quiet way, brings the social outcasts into the literary mainstream, and in that sense de-marginalizes them. Moreover, by concentrating on the 'small fry', he shows that collaboration was much more extensive than many would like to believe.

Thus, for Modiano, the novel is still a site for dealing with the memory of the Occupation and its abiding problems. Many other contemporary French writers, of course, adopt a similar stance, and have followed in the author of *La Place de l'étoile*'s wake, making him a sort of unwitting flag-bearer for his generation. This leading role has long been recognized. In his seminal work, *Le Syndrome de Vichy*, Henry Rousso pinpoints Modiano's emergence in 1968 as a key event in the quest for the lost narrative of the Occupation that was to take

---

[28] Emmanuel Berl, *'Interrogatoire par Patrick Modiano' suivi de 'Il fait beau, allons au cimetière'* (Paris: Gallimard, 1976), p. 9.

[29] Cf. Modiano's own comments on his personal library, which consists in part of 'un mélange de titres sur l'Occupation, sur le spectacle, sur Paris, sur les faits divers qui me sont indispensables pour mes romans' (Pascale Frey, 'Cinq écrivains et leurs bibliothèques', *Elle Décoration*, April 2008, pp. 177–182 (p. 178)).

[30] *Outrage and Insight: Modern French Writers and the 'Fait Divers'* (Oxford and Washington, DC: Berg, 1995), p. 2.

off massively in the following decade.[31] After the heady days of the
mode rétro, the reassessment died down somewhat, but never really
went away, as Rousso also acknowledges by dubbing the period from
the 1970s to the present a time of ongoing obsession with the early
1940s. In fact, even today, in the domain of the committed *roman noir*,
Didier Daeninckx and others are still virulently attacking neo-fascists
and Holocaust deniers, whose outlook and inspiration go back to the
dark years.[32] In this context of enduring anti-Semitism and the national
failure to put the Occupation to bed, Modiano, in *Accident nocturne*
and *Dans le café de la jeunesse perdue*, can again be seen as *representative*, a national 'barometer' indicating the state of France's relationship
with its wartime past and how it is remembered. By introducing the
names of past collaborators – in other words those who were associated
with the deportation and killing of Jews – he seems to be suggesting,
like Daeninckx and others but in typically more understated fashion,
that the shadow of the Holocaust and France's role in it continues to
loom large.

Modiano may simultaneously be doing something more besides. 'Le
fait divers est le premier monument érigé à la mémoire des victimes',
Daeninckx has asserted.[33] There are no real victims named in *Accident
nocturne* or *Dans le café de la jeunesse perdue* (unlike *Dora Bruder*) but
the author may well have had specific ones in mind for commemoration
– the nameless Jews who perished in the death camps.[34] For Modiano,
then, plundering the post-Liberation *faits divers* for names and inspiration is an attempt to infuse his texts with an extra layer of meaning, with
the meaning-full.

To conclude, the study of *Accident nocturne* and *Dans le café de la
jeunesse perdue* has now shown that, where the Occupation is concerned,
Patrick Modiano remains fascinated by two interlocking narratives: that

[31] *Le Syndrome de Vichy*, pp. 141–146.

[32] See, for example, Alan Morris, 'From Social Outcasts to Stars of the Mainstream:
The Combatants of the Collaboration in Postwar France', *Journal of War and Culture Studies*,
II:2 (2009), 167–179 (pp. 174–177).

[33] *Petit éloge des faits divers* (Paris: Gallimard, 2008), p. 13.

[34] That Modiano is trying to give his work the appearance of a *fait divers*, at least
in part, is illustrated by two key elements of *Accident nocturne*: the narrator's being hit
by the Fiat and his leitmotival memory of the dog that died when he was a child (*AN*,
pp. 10, 16, 86, 120, 122, 140). See Daeninckx, *Petit éloge*, p. 13 and Walker, *Outrage and
Insight*, p. 3 on the 'chiens écrasés' and 'fait divers'. Modiano has long since metaphorically
linked canines to Jews (see, for example, Cooke, 'Violence', pp. 118–119, 120).

of his father, the culpable yet victimized Jew, whose guilt-generating wartime activities encourage an oedipal response, and that of the *années noires* themselves, with their omissions and their lack of complete accessibility, and for which the story of Albert serves as a metaphor. These narratives of personal and collective inheritance demonstrate, I would suggest, that Modiano continues to serve as a gauge of France's view of its past during the Second World War. For as is confirmed by other key indicators (the analyses of Rousso; the novels of Daeninckx and others), the dark years are still posing problems, both individually and nationally, in the present. The Occupation has not, as yet, been completely laid to rest. It is still, as Conan and Rousso argued, and as Modiano knows only too well, 'un passé qui ne passe pas.'[35]

---

[35] Éric Conan and Henry Rousso, *Vichy, un passé qui ne passe pas* (Paris: Fayard, 1994).

Conclusion

As many contributors to this book have argued, narratives written about the Second World War form one of the vectors of cultural and genera-tional memory analysed by historians like Henry Rousso. Whatever their particular merits and differences, collectively such works contribute to a process of historical reflection about the destinies of individuals and nations. Given the massively humiliating and disruptive nature of France's defeat and subsequent Occupation by the Germans, it seems quite legitimate to see such cultural phenomena as helping to reshape and restore national identity and the myths which support it. Intention-ally or otherwise, fictional narratives are vehicles for ideologies and shifting belief systems, apart from the pedagogic and experiential or testimonial functions which authors of war stories often stress more explicitly. For some commentators, our continuing preoccupation with the war seems obsessive, symptomatic of an acute malaise or a moral deficit. For instance, writing about 'Theories of Trauma', Lyndsey Stone-bridge asserts that 'both Benjamin and Freud would have read the sheer volume of World War Two images and narratives as evidence, not of historical communication or the working through of the past, but of a profound kind of imaginative and psychical failure'.[1]

Although it is certainly true that a great deal of cultural material about war is tendentious, repetitive and predictable, Stonebridge misses the basic point that, while war may be bad, an entirely destructive phe-nomenon for most of those who suffer its consequences, writing about it (or experiencing it vicariously) may be good and is certainly an entirely different activity. The benefits brought by creative re-enactment may be ideological, psychological or aesthetic: for instance, offering counter-cultural

---

[1] In Marina Mackay (ed.), *The Cambridge Companion to the Literature of World War II* (Cambridge: Cambridge University Press, 2009), p. 203.

interpretations that subvert official myths; communicating the experience of individuals and groups rarely studied by historians; finding new forms of expression for experiences that seem indescribable. From a broader anthropological perspective, stories precede the establishment of written literature as a social institution, in that they have a primary existential function. As Pascal Bruckner puts it, they protect us from death: 'Tant que nous pouvons mettre le monde en récits, même pour narrer nos pires malheurs, nous sommes vivants'.[2] Situating narratives at the core of human identity allows a more fruitful explanation for our urge to construct and consume them than dismissing them as sterile fantasizing.

If narrative as a mode of thought or perception helps locate the self in an external world which it seeks to make comprehensible and coherent, it is perhaps unsurprising that most fictional narratives similarly create denotative clarity in time or space by clearly separating external and mental reality, establishing logical sequences of events and causality, and organizing technical and stylistic features in a self-effacing way that supports characters' interactions and readers' ability to engage intellectually and affectively with the story. These are the characteristics of a classic well-made drama, novel or film.[3] The hierarchy assumed by many academic critics (who focus almost exclusively on demanding literary works that challenge conventional narrative practices) has the unfortunate effect of peremptorily excluding the vast majority of novels, as if they were trivial entertainment unworthy of detailed attention. Readability is however a necessary virtue for authors whose aims are essentially to re-create and document historical experience, rather than engaging in aesthetic and philosophical innovation. While Dominique Viart and Bruno Vercier exclude 'la littérature consentante' from their ambitious and informative survey of contemporary French writing, more helpfully they concede that some popular authors have successfully pursued themes and problems raised by more demanding writers, using the conventions of the thriller for example to develop their 'volonté d'interroger et d'interpréter le réel'.[4]

---

[2] Pascal Bruckner, *La Tyrannie de la pénitence* (Paris: Grasset, 2006), p. 183.

[3] For a particularly lucid, detailed analysis of their narrative conventions, see David Bordwell's *Narration in the Fiction Film* (Madison: University of Wisconsin Press, 1985).

[4] Dominique Viart and Bruno Vercier, *La Littérature française au présent*, 2nd edition (Paris: Bordas, 2008), pp. 10, 368.

However, the assumption that work that is aesthetically innovative thereby heightens the reader's psychological and historical awareness still needs to be challenged. It may rather negate the conception of history as an intelligible process. As Catharine Savage Brosman suggests, Claude Simon's *La Route des Flandres* 'conveys the breakdown of meaning in midcentury Europe and the impossibility for the individual to control or see a pattern in events', but in a style so complex that 'it creates its own sort of elitist reader, against a background of a war that eroded such differences'.[5] Jean Kaempfer argues in *Poétique du récit de guerre* that since the modern (i.e. post-Napoleonic) war narrative evokes the extremes of experience in a dehumanized universe, it has abandoned the rational perspective of classical accounts that treat war as an affair of state conducted by great men inscribed in the march of history (such as Julius Caesar's, or perhaps General de Gaulle's, memoirs). Most twentieth-century literary war stories tend to be 'relations autistes de l'horreur', rebutting patriotic platitudes and glorifying myths, in order to establish a more authentic version of horrific events as endured by low-level combatants.[6] But while war may become unintelligible or a largely negative experience, the texts cited by Kaempfer (e.g. by Stendhal, Tolstoy and Barbusse) themselves remain entirely intelligible and form part of a perfectly rational, cultural critique of warfare.

Broaching previously taboo subjects has also become acceptable in works aimed at large audiences since the 1970s, no doubt partly because second-generation writers are no longer fictionalizing traumatic personal experience, and partly because more permissive attitudes and commercial imperatives make representing extreme violence and suffering more acceptable. To what extent has any French fiction published in the last three decades changed attitudes and knowledge about the Occupation years, in the way many writers (and some film-makers) between the 1940s and 1970s clearly did? Fiction writers who have no direct experience or memory of the war generally compensate for this deficit by research undertaken in historical sources (drawing on history books, personal interviews with veterans and survivors, and other forms of oral and written testimony, including fiction). This sort of research is in fact a generic marker of most historical fiction (often made explicit in prefaces, acknowledgements, bibliographies, which serve to stress the

---

[5] Catharine Savage Brosman, *Visions of War in France: Fiction, Art, Ideology* (Baton Rouge: Louisiana State University Press, 1999), pp. 80, 198.

[6] Jean Kaempfer, *Poétique du récit de guerre* (Paris: Corti, 1998), p. 10.

authenticity of the story). The main problem such writers face is inte-
grating this authenticating factual material into an invented narrative,
merging historical figures and events coherently and plausibly with
imaginary characters. Another is avoiding the impression that they are
simply recycling tales and narrative tropes already used more directly
and persuasively by earlier writers.

The boundary between pastiche and plagiarism can become a matter,
not just of critical reception, but of litigation, as the case of Régine
Deforges shows. The phenomenal success of Régine Deforges's multi-
volume *Bicyclette bleue* family saga (which by the publication of the sixth
volume had sold eight million copies in its various editions)[7] is perhaps
primarily due to her ability to adapt previous writers' plot and character
configurations while updating the tone and ethos for a post-1970s
audience more aware of the moral complexities of the Occupation.
Deforges was in fact originally commissioned by the publisher Ramsay
to 'remake' Margaret Mitchell's *Gone with the Wind*, but nonetheless
won a court case in Paris charging her with plagiarism brought by the
Mitchell estate in 1993. As Jacques M. Laroche has noted, Deforges owes
rather more to Cécil Saint-Laurent's *Clotilde Jolivet* saga, first published
in the late 1950s and re-issued in a revised version in 1985 after
Deforges's success.[8]

Most recent Occupation fiction that belongs to the family saga
or romance category tends to be blandly predictable (or reassuringly
familiar, depending on one's tastes). It is often packaged and marketed
so as to make it easily recognizable, for example in the choice of cover
illustrations and titles; originality is not a requirement. Thus Michel
Jeury's *Le Printemps viendra du ciel* (1995), though primarily about
a young woman's Resistance activity in 1944, has a cover photograph
showing a red-headed girl in a blue dress riding a bicycle past a line
of cars during the 1940 exodus (cited from the 1999 Pocket edition;
the reference to *La Bicyclette bleue* could hardly be more shameless).
Catherine Servan-Schreiber's *Louise et Juliette* (Lattès, 2009) depicts
two sisters torn apart by their respective husbands' choice of resistance
and collaboration; the cover shows two chic bourgeois ladies with their
gas-mask boxes. That both are shown indistinguishably from the rear,
with all background having been deleted, unintentionally but accurately

---

[7] Olivier Le Naire, 'Le Scandale et la gloire', *L'Express*, 6 June 1996, p. 130.

[8] Jacques M. Laroche, 'A Success Story in the French Popular Literature of the 1980s:
La Bicyclette bleue', *The French Review*, 60:4 (1987), 502–510.

reflects the novel's failure to present much interesting psychological or historical detail.

The same could not be said of Jonathan Littell's hallucinatory blockbuster *Les Bienveillantes* (2006), which might be described as an anti-family saga that delights in destroying and perverting the affective bonds celebrated by more conventional authors (in that when its vile protagonist is not involved in full-scale genocide, he occupies himself by murdering his mother, his stepfather, his gay lover and the friend who has saved his life, as well as fathering twins with his twin sister). That a novel running to nearly 1000 pages, written in French by an American about a deranged Nazi war criminal, should have been published uncut by Gallimard, awarded two prestigious French prizes (the grand prix de l'Académie française and the Goncourt), and achieved international critical and commercial success, must surely count as one of the oddest mysteries of contemporary publishing. Is it worth taking seriously, as a work that reveals something new or interesting about the mentality of an impenitent Nazi killer, or is this a more cunning form of pastiche, a hoax intended to entice and expose the reverential earnestness and lack of moral and literary judgement with which too many critics approach any work that purports to be about the Holocaust? Littell's lack of restraint (his prolixity, his failure to offer a balanced perspective, his distressing and protracted descriptions of mass killings, his blending of naturalistic documentary with episodes that are fantastical or grotesquely comical, his use and abuse of other writers' work) can either arouse visceral rejection or the suspicion that perhaps this is a revolutionary reworking of the established conventions used to write war novels.

Guillaume Adler (whose grandparents perished in Auschwitz) did not join the reverential chorus. In a well-honed essay published in *Les Inrockuptibles*, he expressed 'le sentiment de m'être fait escroquer intellectuellement' by 'une bouillie narrative', suggesting that Littell has enjoyed unexpected commercial success and esteem because 'Il joue parfaitement avec nos refoulements collectifs'.[9] Nevertheless, given this self-replicating chain of critical responses, one ends up having to take the phenomenon of *Les Bienveillantes* seriously, even if its shortcomings seem manifest, whether the book is judged as entertainment, testimony or highbrow fiction. Introducing *The Cambridge Companion to the Literature of World War II*, Marina Mackay suggests that 'the most important claim literature

---

[9] Guillaume Adler, 'La Mise en divertissement du mal', *Les Inrockuptibles*, 12 December 2006, p. 21.

can make on our historical imaginations is to show how things felt at the time', and to give voice to experiences that appear 'both literally and figuratively unspeakable'.[10] In his recent novel about the assassination of Reinhard Heydrich, *HHhH* (2009), Laurent Binet remarks in a caustic aside that Littell's Max Aue is not a convincing historical reconstruction, but a figure for our age: 'nihiliste postmoderne, pour faire court . . . *Les Bienveillantes*, c'est «Houellebecq chez les nazis», tout simplement'.[11] However ethically dubious, the project (and the controversies that it has aroused) affirms the enduring vitality and ambition of the literary imagination and the continuing cultural re-adjustments to the historical catastrophes that have shaped contemporary France.

---

[10] Pages 3–4.
[11] Quoted from Livre de poche edition, 2011, pp. 326–327.

Index